ZEN AND THE ART OF ART
FOUNDATIONS

Jacqueline Hill

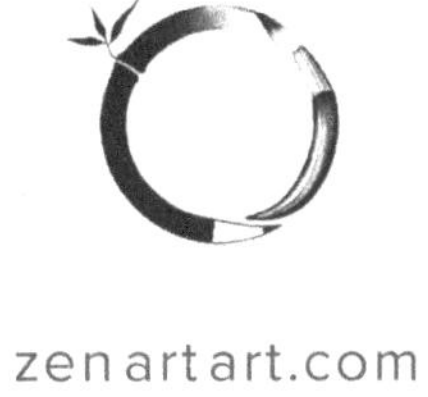

zenartart.com

Cover Image by Jacqueline Hill — original painting © 2019
Interior Images by Jacqueline Hill — © 2019
Cover Design and Interior Design by Art at Heart — © 2019

ISBN: 978-0-6487007-0-8 (paperback)
ISBN: 978-0-6487007-1-5 (ebook)

Published by Art at Heart Press
artatheart.com.au

Zen and the Art of Art
zenartart.com

The Master smiled.
'The power of your mind is mightier than
the hand that wields your brush,' he said.

To Phil

With his feet on the ground,
he lets me fly
and catches me when I fall.

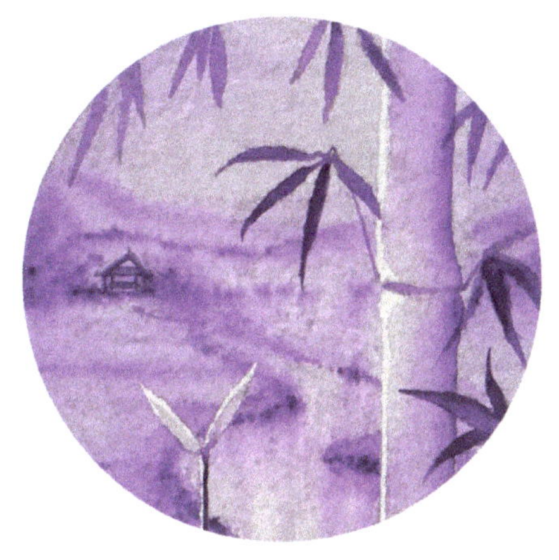

CONTENTS

He who loves practice without theory
is like the sailor who boards a ship
without a rudder and compass
and never knows where he may cast.

Leonardo da Vinci

ZEN AND ART

Jojo's eyes widened. She looked up at the simply carved wooden building rising from the leafy bamboo forest. This must be the art dojo[1], she thought.

Off to the side she saw a clearing under the canopy of tall bamboo foliage. In the clearing, dappled with shadows, were some large stones that looked like comfortable seating. Beyond the forest a huge mountain rose through a fine mist. An ancient monastery clung to the side of the mountain.

This was the place she had heard about. The place she had come such a long way to find.

She took a deep breath. She was glad to leave behind all her appointments, her computers and mobile phone for the time she was here. In this beautiful place in nature, far from the busy cities, she could focus on her art.

She heard a soft creak and turned back to the dojo building. Standing in the open door was a man who looked as old as the mountains. He was wearing soft grey robes.

'Welcome,' said The Master.

About this Book

This series of books distils all the teachings I have created, given and refined over the last decade of teaching art to complete beginners.

You have in your hands the *Foundations* book, which is the core information of every class that I teach. This information works for every medium and every technique, from drawing through to painting and mixed media.

This book is the foundation of the entire *Zen and the Art of Art* book series[2]. I recommend that you read this book before any of the Learn to Draw or Learn to Paint books in the series.

Why Zen and Art?

Over the years I have blundered my way through, in the school of hard knocks, trying to learn this fascinating science of drawing and painting.

While I've attended some short workshops with artists I admire (some great teachers, some awful), I've also had to fight my own inner demons along the way.

I've found working on my mindset to be one of the most powerful pathways to success. I'm constantly amazed at how much the practice of *art* reflects, imitates, is affected by, manifests and represents *life* and *mind*.

My teachings have a strong flavour of Zen and mindfulness, and I'm sure that's why we achieve such success with our students. We do as much work with the mind as with the hand on the pencil or brush.

Hundreds of beginners have attended structured Learn to Draw and Learn to Paint courses in my studio and on my international art retreats. I taught these complete beginner adults using the same method written down in this book for you. This teaching method, refined over the years, ensures each student really understands the *whys* and the *hows* of painting and drawing.

It's an easy set of guidelines that anyone can understand and learn. I'm amazed (and so are they) at the fabulous art they produce. Their success comes from having a methodical pattern to follow and unlocking the blocks in their minds.

The Power of the Mind

I know a woman who was an Olympic target rifle shooter and broke records at both national and international levels. She enhanced her technique by studying *Zen and the Art of Archery* and *Zen and the Art of Motorcycle Maintenance*, along with autogenic meditation. The sport of target rifle shooting is around 10% physical and 90% mindset. This woman is my mother, Yvonne Hill.

For many years I was a member of an Ironman Triathlon training squad. I learned from a very experienced coach how to train for, race and healthily survive competing in these 10 – 14 hour endurance events. My body endured 226km of ocean swimming, cycling and marathon running in a single day (without even a lunch stop). We called it 'a long day at the office'. After completing two Ironman Triathlon events, I'm sure it's true that the race is 20% physical and 80% mental.

It is difficult to ignore the power of the human mind.

Art Reflects Life: Your Art Mind

When creating art, sometimes your art can reflect your life.

While teaching beginner classes, I am surprised how much students' personal issues and lives show up while they are painting.

- People who are timid and nervous in real life will be timid and nervous when trying to draw or paint.

- People who are bold and brave will be more open to taking a risk with a brush in their hand.

- People who have low self-esteem will mentally beat themselves up, which really hinders their learning.

- People who are determined to succeed in many areas of their life will do every exercise and every homework task; they will overtake many other students, solely because they've practised and practised.

We play with mind exercises in class that help students overcome the barriers in their minds. I'll share many of them with you in these pages.

When something shows up as an issue or a block in the process of creating art, try asking:

How is this like my life?

You may be surprised at what the answer shows you.

Zen Mind in Art

I have found that I need to work with people's minds in the classroom as much as with their techniques and skills. So my classes focus on the mindset approach and students have had amazing success as a result.

There are two mindsets to be aware of. In the *Zen and the Art of Art* series I'll call them Modern Mind and Zen Mind. Your understanding and awareness of these two minds, as they apply to your art learning, is crucial. It will unfold as we cover each lesson in these books.

Jojo had all the time in the world to play with her art in the beautiful dojo. Woven mats cushioned her bare feet. Her tunic felt soft and comfortable. The walls of the dojo were unadorned but one opened out to a dark wood balcony that overlooked a clearing in the bamboo forest. She could see across to the monastery on the side of the misty mountain. The Master sat silently, hands tucked in his sleeves. Everything was just as she'd hoped. Well, almost everything.

She tossed her brush down with a sigh.

'What is it?' asked The Master.

'There are so many choices with painting that I get overwhelmed,' she said. 'Why can't painting be a step by step thing like everything else in the world? Why is it such a big secret?'

She looked at her blank paper and frowned. 'I wish I had a nice, neat plan to use while I'm being all creative. To help when I'm starting. And to help when I get stuck.'

The Master smiled. 'There is a plan,' he said.

Jojo looked up at him, eyes wide. 'Really?' she asked. 'I've never seen it! What's in it? What do I do? What's the secret?'

The Master held up his hand. 'Practise patience,' he said. 'And patiently practise.'

She frowned.

'With your eyes wide open,' added The Master.

Jojo looked at her discarded brush. 'Patience is one thing I don't have a lot of,' she mused. 'But I really want to learn.' She looked back at him. 'Will you tell me the whole plan now? Right now? Please? Sensei?'

'Patience, Little Grasshopper,' said The Master. 'You first need to understand your Modern Mind, which wants to know everything and do everything in a rush. Then you'll need to awaken your Zen Mind, which is patient and timeless.'

The Master

In my journey I would have loved an experienced and highly skilled artist in my studio to answer all my questions. I would have learnt the skills I needed in one-tenth the time, without all the frustration.

In the 1970s there was a TV show called *Kung Fu*, starring David Carradine. His old Master was called Sensei, and the young student was called Grasshopper.

The Master you will meet in these books is my imaginary Sensei. He's the person I wish I'd had close by for all those years where I stumbled and fell with my art. In these books you will also meet Jojo, his Little Grasshopper.

You can imagine Jojo is the young version of me (or maybe you): a little green Grasshopper starting out in drawing and painting.

I tried at first to keep the two roles gender-free, but it became too difficult to avoid referring to 'he' or 'she'. Please forgive the genders I have assigned; they could easily have been a female master and male student.

I hope The Master can help you in your journey, through these books.

Play Time — The Doing

In the movie *The Karate Kid*, Mr Miyagi advises the boy to repeat a 'wax on, wax off' exercise hundreds of times.

You will achieve success in your art by getting the miles in the brush (or pencil), just like the Karate Kid.

I have included exercises in this book for you to enjoy. They are called Play Time for a reason. Don't think of them as tests, or exams. There is no judgment here. They are a chance for you to experience and play. Keep a fun mindset while doing them!

If you are too excited and need to read the book right through first, make sure you allow for a slower, second reading and take the time to enjoy the Play Time sessions. You will be amazed at how much better your understanding becomes.

The Master says, 'Remember, it is in the doing that the mastery comes.'

Panic Stations

'When I'm learning all this new stuff I sometimes feel really panicky,' said Jojo, adjusting the straw basket in her arms. The vegetables inside shifted. 'Like I'm never going to get it. Sometimes I just want to run away.' Jojo dropped her eyes to the fresh beans she'd just picked from the kitchen garden.

The Master smiled kindly. 'While you are learning new skills, feelings of panic or confusion can come over you. It means the brain is knitting up new pathways for your new skills.' He placed a handful of ripe red berries in the basket. 'Once you get through these feelings and you have learnt the skills, it will feel a lot easier. Just remember: the only way over *a feeling is* through *it.'*

'So I just go with it?' asked Jojo.

'Just go with it,' echoed The Master. 'The way to get over fear or confusion is to move through *it to the other side.'*

Jojo still looked sceptical.

The Master explained further. 'If you stay in the one place, you will stand still. While you are learning a new skill, you can feel as if you were in the middle of a crisis,' he said. 'Keep going. This feeling will pass as you gain skills and get through the other side.'

'Ok,' said Jojo. 'I'll remember that next time.'

Before We Start — Safety in the Studio

Dangers in the Studio

Be aware of the dangers in the studio. Keep yourself physically safe.

Sometimes when we are in Zen Mind, we are not as logical as we need to be to keep ourselves safe. Make sure you have a set of rules to live by and arrange your studio so that it is safe.

Treat yourself to the best paints you can afford. This will give the most encouraging results for a beginner. If you use cheap and nasty paints you will get dull, lifeless paintings. Often it's not you, it's the paints! Give yourself the best chance of success by buying the professional paints instead of the children's or students' range.

But take care. The professional range of colours may include toxic pigments such as cadmium, chromium and cobalt. Don't ingest these in any way. Read an artists' safety book[3] to really freak yourself out about how dangerous some pigments are if they get inside your system.

Some rules to live by include:

- Always keep food and drink on a separate table from art making. Mistaking turps[4] or solvents for water is far too easy when they are in the same area. I could tell you a horror story that happened to an artist I know. But let's avoid horror stories.

- Always label bottles of liquid very clearly. The very toxic Turps, Solvents, Methylated Spirits, White Spirits and Acetone all look just like clear water. If you decant any of these into smaller bottles, label them clearly so there's no confusion. Not just for you, but for others who come into your studio. I even label my water spray bottles with a big H_2O label to be sure.

- Don't vapourise, sniff, lick, eat or smoke paints!

- Don't ever hold brush handles in your mouth.

- Never, ever, reshape brushes by putting them in your mouth, even after thoroughly washing. I can't believe I have to tell you this, but I do know a teacher who actually tells all her students to do this!
- Keep any hairdryers well away from buckets of water or tubs of turps. Keep turps away from electrical outlets or naked flames.
- Never smoke or drink alcohol in the studio.
- If you have pets or young children, keep toxic things safely up high or locked away.
- Keep three red things in the studio:
    1. a fire blanket
    2. a fire extinguisher
    3. a First Aid Kit

In the Resources section at the end of this book, you can find a printable Studio Etiquette chart[3] along with lots of other lovely charts. Paste it up on your studio wall or somewhere near where you make art.

Emotional Safety

It's not just about your physical safety. You need to keep your heart safe, too.

Keeping Your Heart Safe

When you are learning, especially in art, you are often in your little Inner Child state. You must protect and nurture this tender little soul.

Choose a teacher who is gentle, non-judgmental and loving in their approach of teaching you and your little Inner Child. Find someone who allows you to explore your own creativity and style.

Critics and Critiques

I'm not a big fan of doing painting 'critiques' at the end of each class session. It can be a frightening experience for a complete beginner who is already out of their comfort zone. Having an insensitive teacher announce all the flaws of a painting in front of everyone hurts your Inner Child.

If forced to review student paintings, I would prefer to do a painting 'praises' session. Sharing all the great things that each beginner has achieved encourages them to be bold and grow.

Your Inner Voice

It's not just the teacher that you need to be kind. *You* must also be kind and gentle to your own little Inner Child.

Avoid saying things like:

- I'm hopeless at this!
- I can't draw to save myself!

- I have no idea what I'm doing!
- I just can't do it right!

If you hear thoughts like this (or, even more powerful, words spoken out loud), replace them with thoughts and words that are the *opposite*. It will feel a lot better!

Try instead:

- I'm learning, I'm learning!
- I'm getting this — it may be slowly, but I'm getting this!
- I can do this!
- I think I can. I know I can! (be 'The Little Engine That Could'[5])

Say them out loud. Shout them from the rooftops!

CHAPTER 1
THREE EMPERORS

Here is the place;
here the way unfolds.

Dogen Zenji

CHAPTER 1 CONTENTS

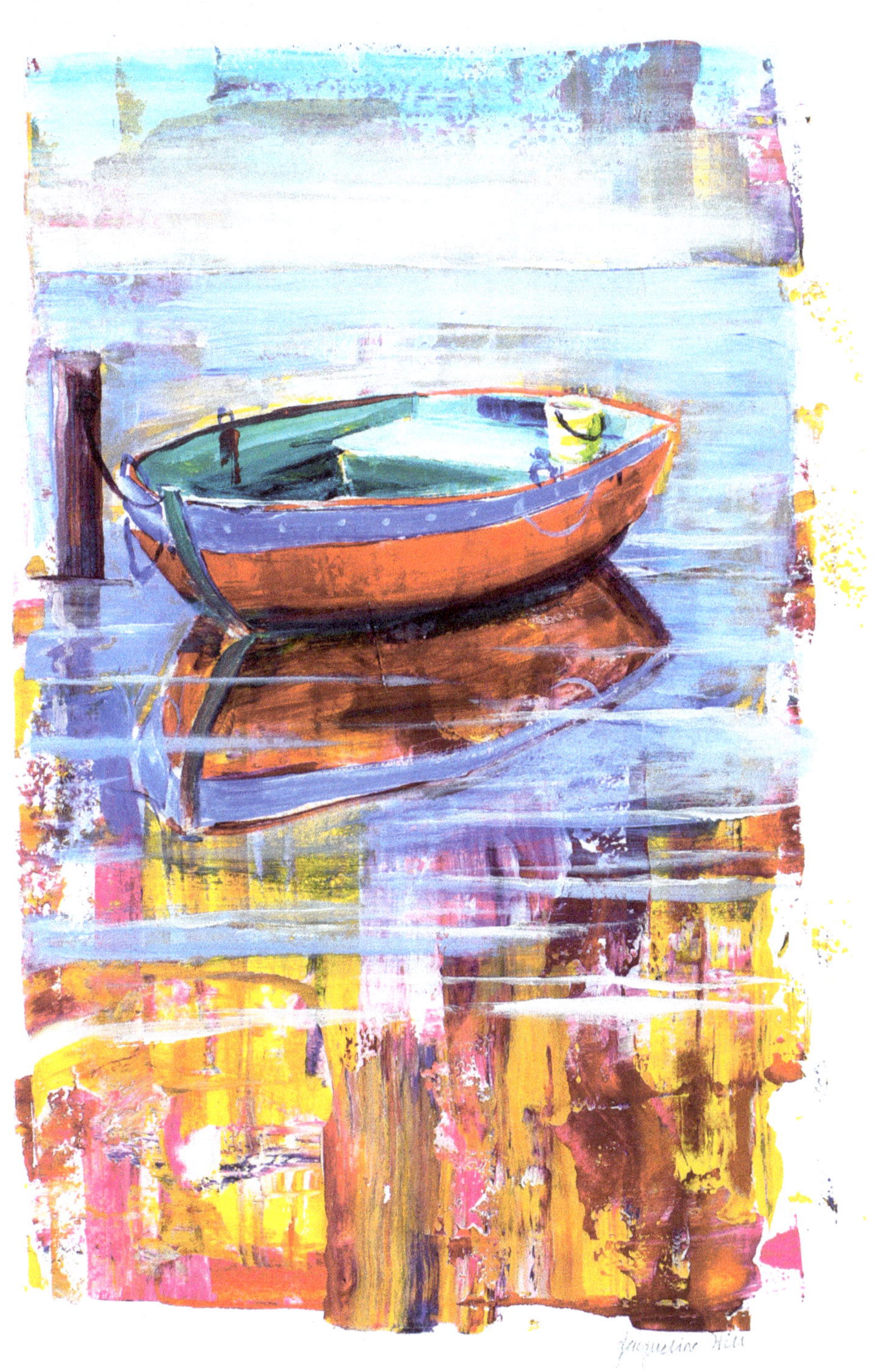

1-1 'Red, Moored' Mixed Media on Paper 29 x 42cm (11.5 x 16.5")

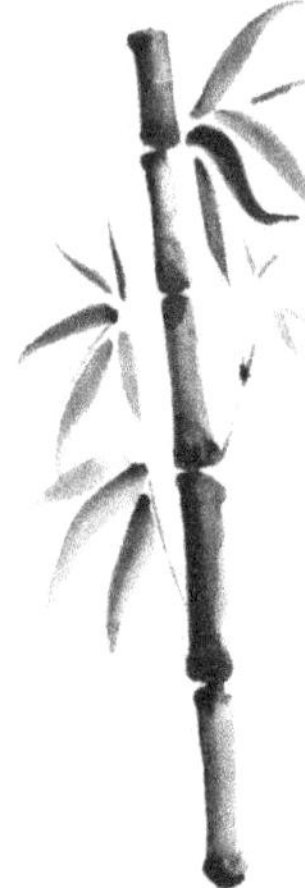

Jojo put her brush down. 'I need a plan or at least a guideline about how to proceed with my paintings,' she said.

The Master lifted a steaming bowl of vegetable soup to his lips.

'When I first started painting, I had no idea where to begin,' she said. 'Now I just begin by squeezing out the lovely paint colours and adding them straight to the canvas. Sometimes I start with a quick drawing, but I like focusing on the colours.

'But somewhere in the middle, things go wrong and it doesn't look like what I want. I can't even put my finger on what's wrong. If I knew what was wrong, maybe I could fix it!'

The Master smiled knowingly and rested his bowl on the low wooden table.

'I try adding brighter colour,' she continued, 'but it never works.'

The Master nodded. 'Patience is what you need to learn,' he said. 'And a knowledge of the rightful order of things. The elements you think are most important may not be so.'

Many beginner students come to me with no idea where on earth to start a painting. Others have trouble with finishing paintings. They know the painting is not quite right but can't find the problem, let alone know what to do about it.

In this chapter you'll learn how to solve many problems most beginner artists have. Even some artists who have been painting for years don't know all of these secrets.

Often I hear beginners say:

- I've painted a painting, but I feel like it just doesn't have the magic. There's no punch in it.

- Things I've painted or drawn don't look real. Some of them are a bit wonky.

- My painting looks flat and boring.

- I get halfway through painting and it has something wrong with it, but I don't know what.

- I think I've found the spot in the painting where something is wrong, but I don't know what to do about it.

- I don't know if my artwork is finished yet — how do I know when I've solved all the problems with it?

The secret of the Three Emperors will solve all these problems forever.

This was one of the most crucial ideas I uncovered, and it changed my painting career forever — for the better.

When I started, I had no idea about these three elements. No-one told me any of this!

After a few years of playing around, learning through trial and error, I started to understand that each element was *really important* and that it was crucial to tackle them in the right order. I started to use them as a mental checklist. Now I find it so much easier; it's almost second nature to create a painting that works.

In this chapter, you will master the following ninja artist tricks:

- ✓ Knowing exactly what the first step of any new painting or drawing is.
- ✓ Understanding what to check at each stage of a painting. With a simple checklist, you can immediately uncover any problems.
- ✓ Being aware of the three most important elements in your painting.

By having these arrows in your bow, you'll be able to get real pizzazz in your paintings. You'll create artworks that have depth, distance and atmosphere. And the objects you paint will look far more realistic — regardless of whether you are drawing, painting photorealism or painting with bold, loose brushstrokes.

Ready to begin?

Let's look at an easy plan for starting a new painting. This strategy will help you know:

- ✓ How to start your painting
- ✓ How to keep working through, solving problems
- ✓ When to stop and sign it

The 3 Easy Steps to Paint a Painting

The Master stood on the wooden balcony, watching clouds roll past the mountains.

'So, Sensei, what is the plan?' asked Jojo.

'It's simple,' said The Master. 'Watch out for these three things — Shape, Tone and Colour.'

'Well that sounds easy,' said Jojo, leaning on the balcony rail.

'Ah, yes,' said The Master. 'But you need to understand each of them very well so that you can separate them.'

'Oh,' said Jojo thoughtfully.

She followed The Master down the steps and into the clearing.

'Then you need to get all three working well and in the right order,' said The Master. 'Have you heard the story of The Three Emperors?'

'No...' said Jojo. They settled comfortably on the stone seats.

The Master began.

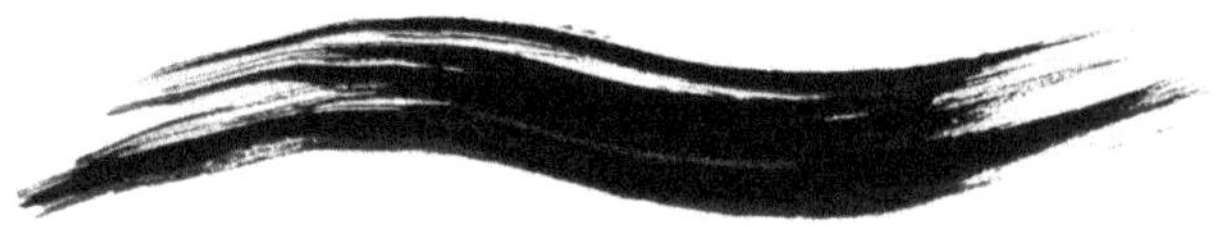

The Three Emperors

In the dark distant past of the East there lived three emperors.

The first Emperor, Iro, was the Lord of Colour and Hue. His empire was filled with all the shimmering colours of the rainbow. It was a beautiful magical place, enchanting and exciting.

Iro shouted to all, 'I am the most powerful emperor of all because I own beauty. It is obvious. Travellers choose to come here first, to see the colours that make them so happy. The travellers always remember my lands and tell others.

'My supreme lands of colour and beauty capture their eyes first, and stay the longest in their minds, so I must be the most powerful!'

In a neighbouring land ruled the Emperor of all Lightness and Dark. Emperor Notan's lands had no colour at all. They were simply shades of light and dark with beautiful areas of contrast. His armies were masters of brightness and shadow. The tones ranged from the lightest of bright light all the way down to the blackness of nothingness, and everything in between.

'You may have shimmering colours,' said Notan. 'But how can the colours mean anything without dark and light? Without tone, there is no depth. Your lands are flat and without meaning. With my contrasting shades of light and dark, the land has form and has three dimensions. I would rather have form and meaning than just a harlequin of superficial colour.'

The third Emperor, Zukei, was the quiet ruler of the lesser-known land of Shape and Line. There was no colour or tone in his lands. He was the Lord of all two-dimensional form. He knew his armies were really the most powerful of all — they were rarely noticed but their subtle work was absolutely crucial. They had the power to build worlds.

'Both your beautiful empires do have very attractive features,' said Zukei. 'However, without a plan for what shapes the three-dimensional forms will take, they may end up lopsided and distorted. Your mountains would be tipping over, and your trees ugly and unattractive.

'Would a carpenter start building his house without a plan?' he asked. 'Whatever shade or colour of paint goes on the walls, the guidelines for the shapes and positions of all the pieces are crucial to the success of the final house, are they not?'

Father Sun pushed in to stop the arguing. 'You are all important!' he said.

Then Mother Moon looked at all the men shouting and spoke firmly. 'Why not work together with each of your strengths? Could you not get your house in order — by building your house in the rightful order?'

The three emperors grumbled at first but agreed to try it the way Mother Moon suggested. To combine their lands into one, they knew Zukei the Lord of Shape needed to start.

Zukei and his quiet, thoughtful people laid out the shapes for the lands first. They carefully placed lines and details to create a beautiful arrangement. While Zukei worked, Notan and Iro waited, stamping their feet with impatience.

When Zukei was finished and happy with his design, it was Emperor Notan's turn. The Lord of Tone's armies of Light and Dark spread the shading across the lands to bring depth and form and distance. The lands he built looked so much better when he followed the design that Zukei had laid out. The trees formed full round foliage and cast beautiful shadows, and the mountains rose high and far into the distance.

Finally, the very impatient Emperor Iro brought his armies in to paint colour all over. Zukei and Notan watched, making sure that Iro didn't lose the shape and tone that they had crafted. By making use of the perfectly imperfect shapes and the deep dimensional tones, the colours made everything sing with joy.

The combined lands came to life, with colour, depth and forms all in delightful harmony.

Father Sun shone down over the design. Mother Moon smiled.

The lands were beautiful indeed.

And they became very real.

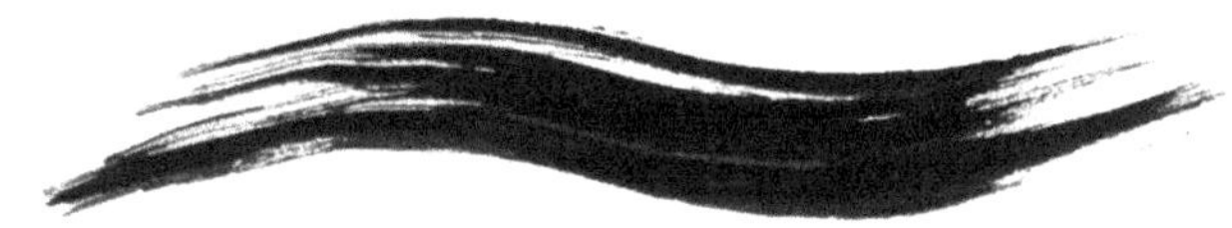

How to Paint a Painting in 3 Easy Steps

Jojo looked at the sky through the leafy bamboo canopy above the clearing. 'Ok, I think I get it,' she said. 'So it's just those three things? Shape, Tone and Colour?'

'Yes,' said The Master. 'Three simple steps. First Shape, then Tone, then Colour. And remember,' he continued:

'Shape is more important than Tone.

Tone is more important than Colour.'

Jojo frowned. 'I'm surprised that colour is the least important.'

'Many new to art making are surprised to learn that,' he said.

Starting with a Plan

'As a beginner, your painting plan should be simple and never vary,' The Master said. 'Shapes first. Then Tone. Then Colour.'

'It sounds like a pretty rigid plan,' said Jojo. 'Won't that kill my freedom to create?'

'First build your skill foundation,' answered The Master. 'You need to learn the rules before you can wisely break them. Are not the most beautiful cities started with a design plan?'

The Plan

Think of building a house.

The floorplans showing the design and layout (shape) are more important than the style of bricks (tone). And the bricks are more important than the colour you paint on the walls.

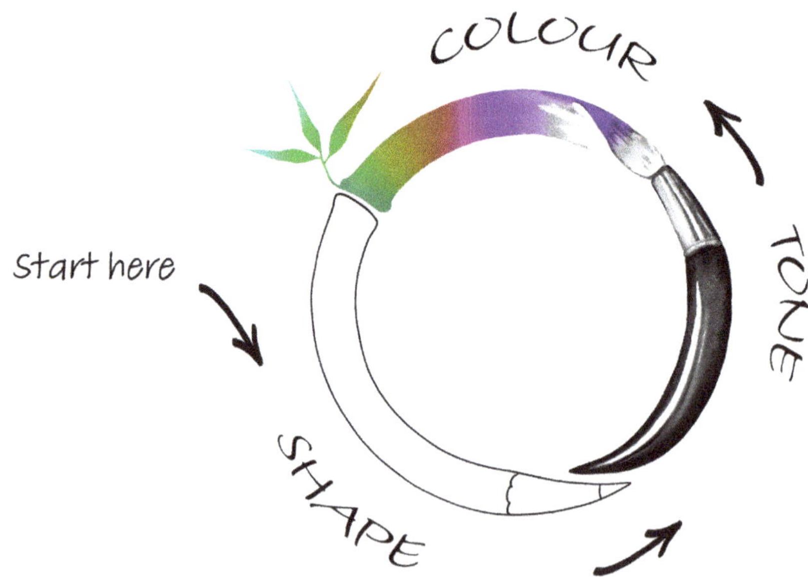

First Get the Shapes Right

First, get the shapes right in your painting: the line drawing. Get the proportions right. Draw and paint what you see, not what you remember. Get the composition right.

You should spend most of your time on getting the shapes right. Too many beginners rush through this stage to get to the fun colour stage.

Spend all the time you can on getting the shapes right, then the tone and colour stages are easy.

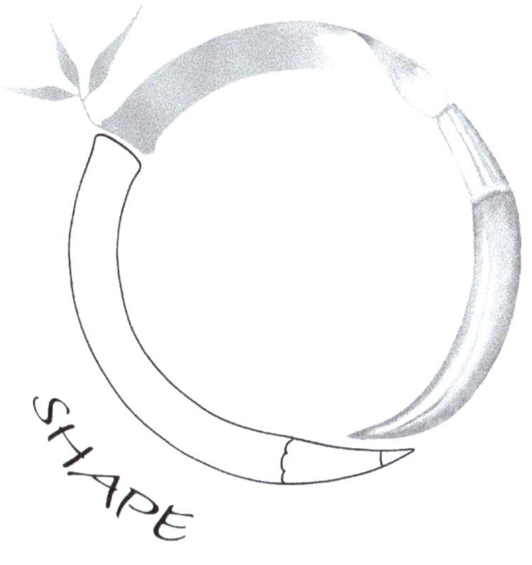

Second Get the Tone Right

Look for the darks and the lights and the mid-tones. While adding tone to your drawing or painting, make sure the shapes do not get distorted.

Before finishing the tone stage, check back over the shapes to make sure they are still good. Fix them right away if they're not!

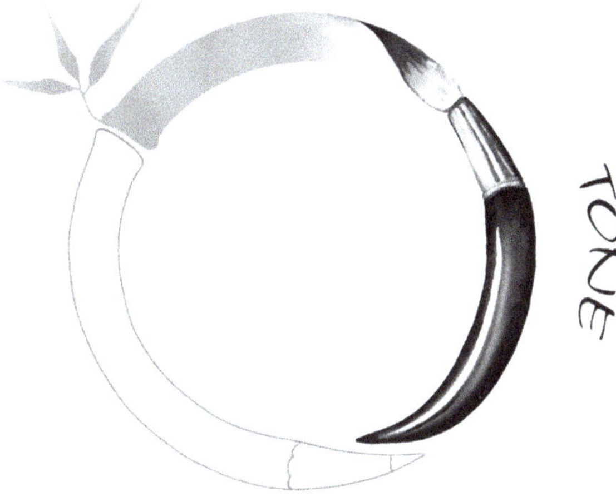

Third Add the Colour

Colour is the least important. If you have the shape and tone right, then it is usually a matter of colouring in. All the hard work is done.

When adding colour, check back over your work to make sure the tone and the shapes have not gone askew anywhere. Fix any problem spots as soon as you find them.

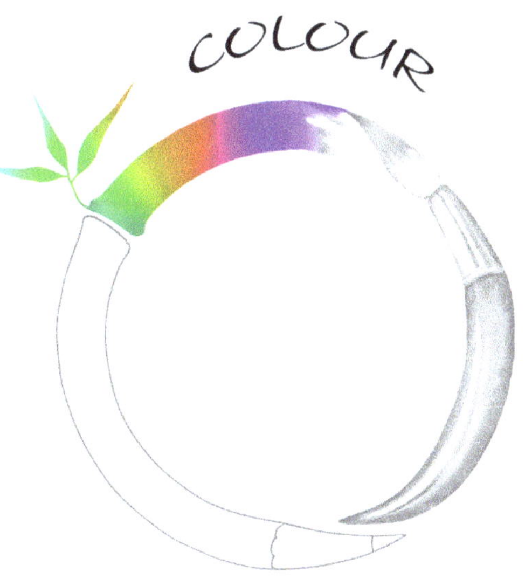

But How Does It Work in Different Mediums?

This process applies whether you are drawing, painting, making mosaics, quilting, anything.

To apply these three stages in different mediums, try some of the Play Time activities at the end of this chapter. You will find how this process works with drawing, watercolour, acrylics and oil.

All About Shape

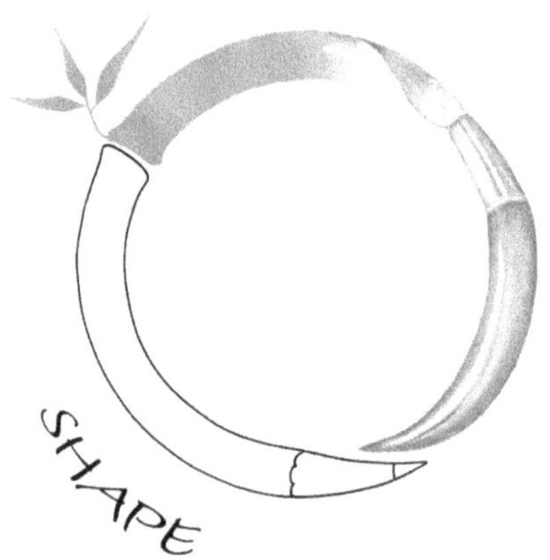

Shape is your underlying drawing that forms the basis of your painting.

It includes composition and the shapes of individual objects. You need to get both of these right.

Why it is Important

Jojo sat in The Master's studio again, this time with a pencil in her hand. 'Why are drawing and shape so important?' she asked.

'Because under every good painting is a good drawing,' said The Master. 'If your drawing has flaws, it will show right through to the tone and colour stages and into the final painting. Nothing you do at the tone or colour stages will fix bad shapes, apart from fixing the shapes themselves. You may as well get it right in the first place.'

'That makes sense,' said Jojo. 'I am so impatient; this is going to be a challenge.'

She looked at her sketch paper and tilted her head. 'What if I want to paint abstracts?'

The Master nodded. 'To push the boundaries of your art,' he said, 'you must first understand the underlying skills. If a student skips learning to draw, it will always show in their final paintings. No matter how abstract their subjects become.'

What it Means to Get Shapes Right

- Getting the proportions right so that the shapes look real.

- Drawing so that things look 'right' (ie they don't look 'wrong' to you or the viewer). Bad shapes can become an unwanted focal point (the most important area that you want your viewer's eye to rest on). This may distract from the focal point you want.

- Drawing things so that the viewer can recognise them. For example, when you've painted a capsicum, you don't want them to say, 'What a nice tomato' or 'It's lovely! What is it?'

- Drawing things that are three-dimensional on a two-dimensional base (eg on paper or canvas) without distorting them.

- Shutting down the Modern Mind and its memories of things you are drawing. Instead, opening up your eyes to really see what is in front of you and moving into the Zen Mind space.

- Getting the composition right. For more on this topic, see Chapter 3 Kissing Frogs.

- Creating a pleasing design — whether you are going for a peaceful feeling or a jarring, edgy feeling. This starts with the underlying lines.

- In a portrait, getting a 'likeness' of the person so that your artwork *looks like* the person. This is done by building measurements and proportions very accurately[6].

How to Get it Right

Become aware of Modern Mind and the tricks it plays on you. Learn to truly see with your eyes and get that down. More tricks on how to disengage your Modern Mind later in Chapter 4 Reality Check.

All About Tone

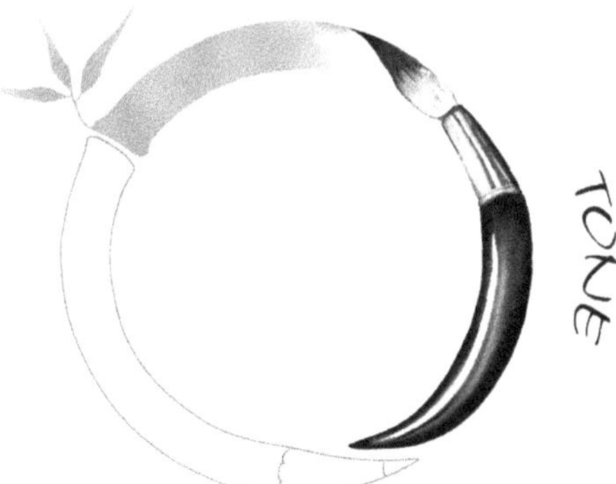

Nearly every beginner painter I come across doesn't pay enough attention to tone in their paintings. It's rare for a new student to come into class even *knowing* what the word tone means, when applied to painting. It's nothing unusual — I didn't know when I was a beginner.

A breakthrough in my art happened when I finally understood tone and how it relates to shape and colour, as well as what order of importance they all had.

- To get punch in your paintings, pay attention to tone.
- To get depth in your paintings, pay attention to tone.
- To control the entire mood and design of a painting, pay attention to tone.

What is Tone?

Tone is also called value in art.

Tone is the lightness or the darkness of an area of an image you are looking at. To discern tone, you need to ignore colour completely.

To ignore colour, you need to imagine what you are looking at is in black and white, like a greyscale image.

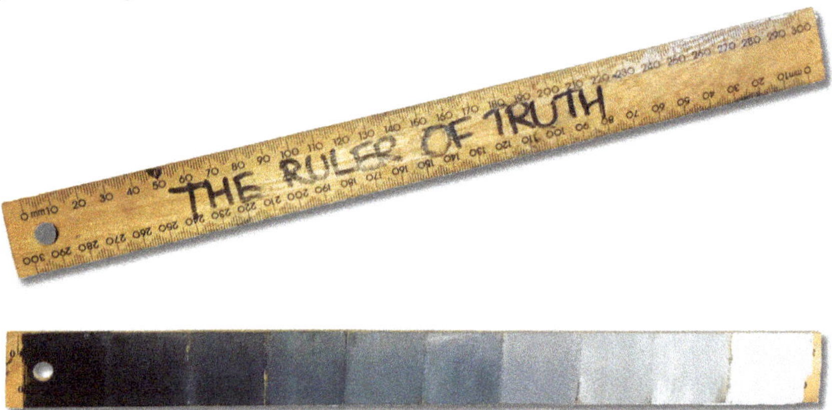

The Tonal Scale & the Ruler of Truth

I keep a Tonal Ruler like this one in my studio at all times. I call it my Ruler of Truth. It helps me to remember how important tone is, and it's also a useful tool for judging tone.

It tells me what the real tone is when I am looking at a colour.

I also carry it with me when I go outdoors to do *plein air*[7] painting.

Creating a Tonal Ruler is more challenging than you may expect. But it is a great exercise to teach your eyes and your brain how to recognise tone. We do this exercise in some of my Learn to Paint classes.

For detailed instructions on how to create your own Tonal Ruler[8], see the Resources section at the end of the book.

4 Ways to Judge Tone

Here are four ways to judge tone:

1. Squint. Judging the tone of a subject is difficult when we get distracted with the lovely colour. Close your eyes slowly until they are almost shut. Look through your eyelashes until you can only just see what you are looking at. And the colour should disappear.

The goal is to see no colour — to focus on the blurry grey and black and white of the tonal levels.

2. Photocopy. If you are working from a photo, the old-fashioned solution is to use a photocopier and get a black and white (mono) print of the image. The modern way is to use a photo editing app to switch it to a black and white image. If you only have a hard copy of the photo, just photograph the photo with your phone or camera. Instant tonal view of the image, wherever you are!

3. The Ruler of Truth. If you have painted your own Tonal Ruler[8], then you can hold it against the image and match each tone. I like to add squinting into this equation. Let's say you're looking at a distant mountain and you want to find the tone of the mountain. Hold the Tonal Ruler up against it. Squint and move the ruler up and down until you find the box that most closely matches the tone.

4. Red Filter. This is a little piece of thick transparent red plastic that you can look at an image through. The strong colour knocks out all the other colours so you see a monotone image. It's a very red image, but you can definitely see the tone. I found my red filter in a kit for quilters that included a colour wheel.

My favourite way is the one that doesn't need any tools. I love just using my eyes to squint, because they are a tool I can't misplace in my studio. They're always with me!

All About Colour

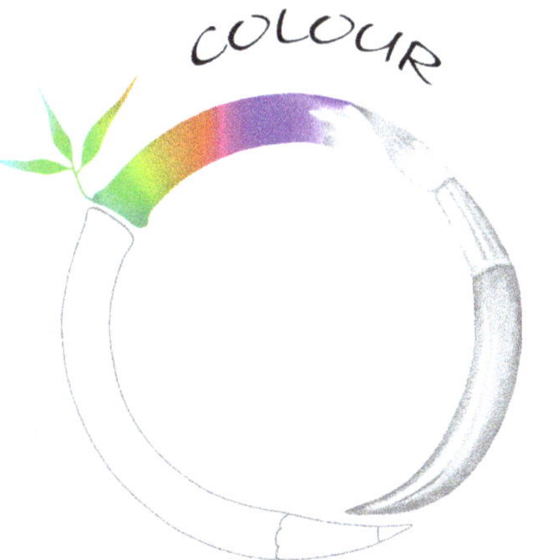

Colour is the easiest emperor to conquer!

Colour can have a huge impact on the final artwork, as long as your shapes and tones are right. It can evoke strong emotions in the viewer.

It can be the thing that people say they love the most about your painting... but if your shapes or tones are not right, the colour may not be able to sing.

We will deal with the details of colour in later chapters.

Tone is More Important Than Colour

Understanding tone is crucial to your paintings.

This concept that I have applied for years was encapsulated precisely by an Australian artist friend of mine[9]. Now, with his permission, it's something I quote to all my students.

He said:

Tone is more important than colour.
Once you get the tone right,
it doesn't matter what colour you use.

This is so true. It's very exciting to have this sort of freedom with colour in your paintings. Look at some examples.

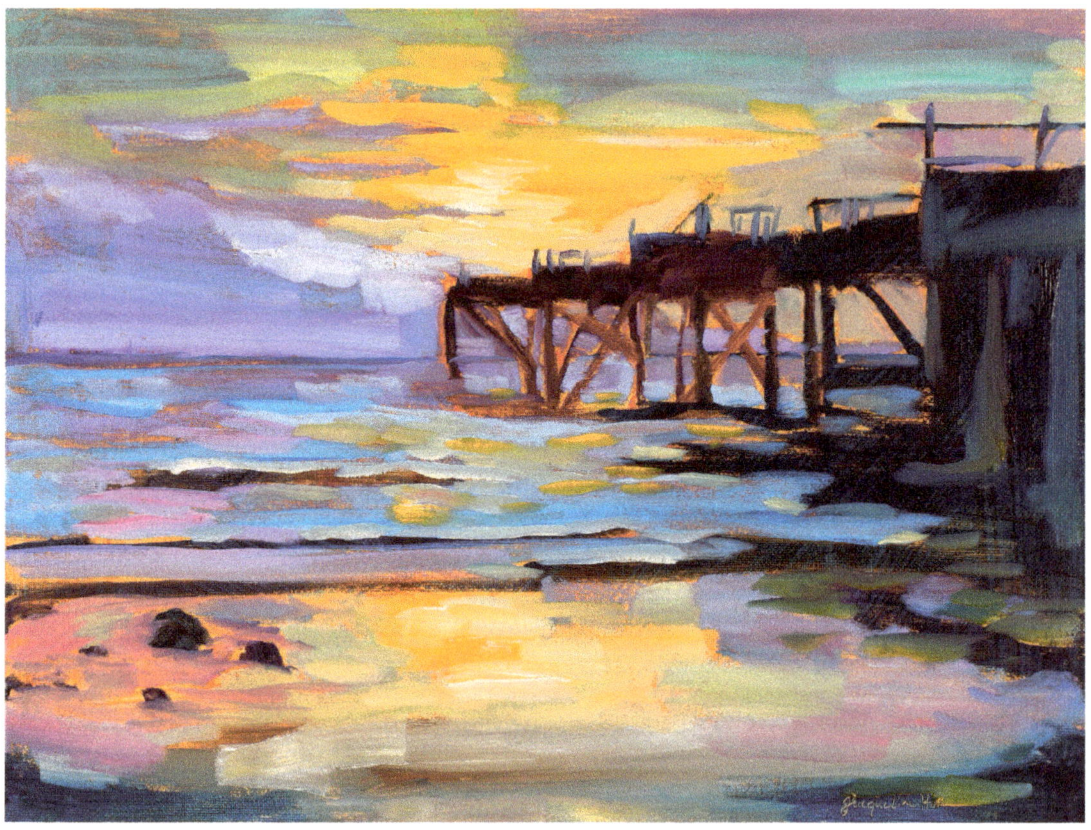

1-2 'Jetty in Gold' Oil on Canvas 40 x 30cm (16 x 12")
Daily Artwork No 365 for 2018.

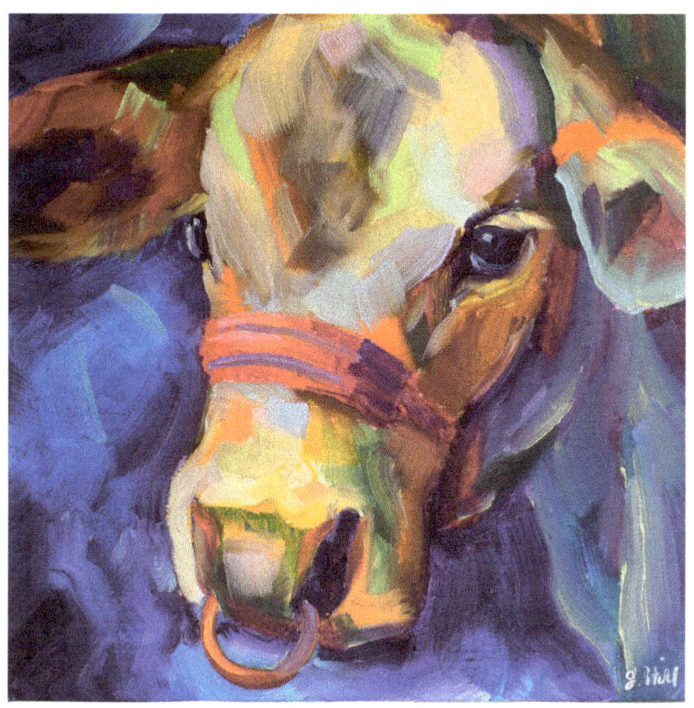

1-3 'No Bull' Oil on Wood Panel 15 x 15cm (6 x 6")
Daily Painting No 152 for 2015. Private Collection, Taringa, Queensland, Australia

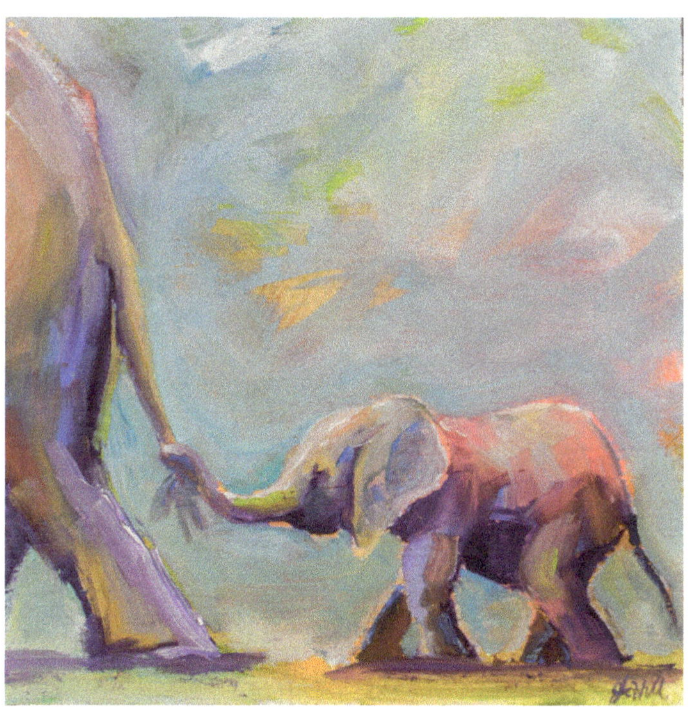

1-4 'Road Train' (Baby Elephant) Oil on Wood Panel 15 x 15cm (6 x 6")
Daily Painting No 320 for 2015. Wilson Collection, Currumbin, Gold Coast, Australia

Tone & Key

It all sounds very musical doesn't it?

Low Key

A *low-key* painting or drawing is one with a lot of dark tones and minimal highlights. A painting like this can seem moody, dark, sad or set at night. These paintings are often dramatic.

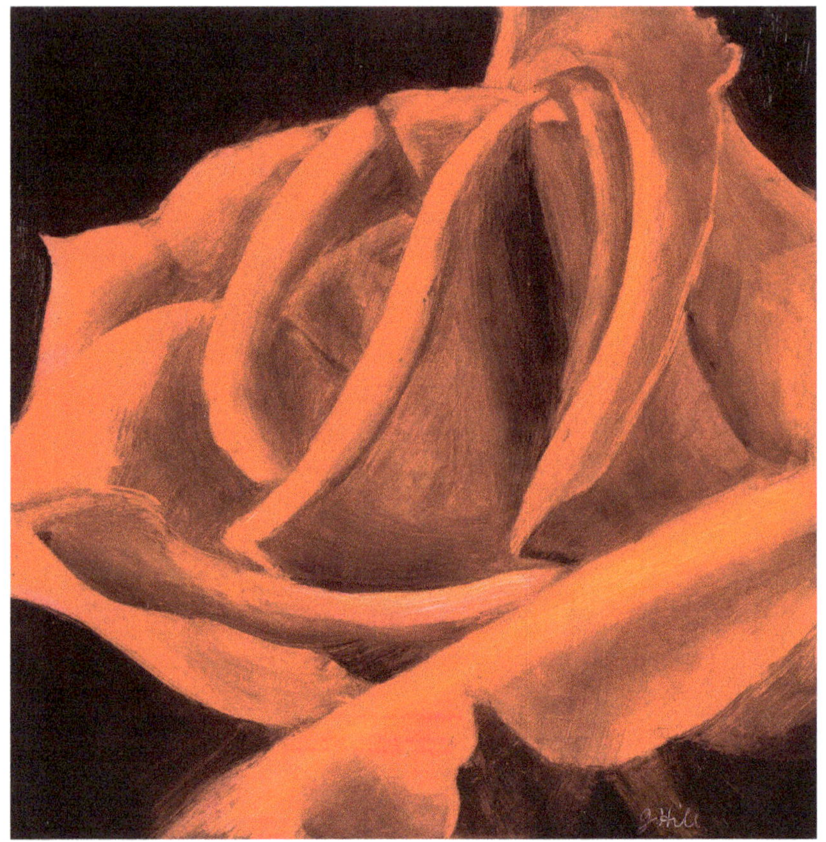

1-5 'Drama Queen' (Red Rose) Oil on Wood Panel 30 x 30cm (12 x 12")

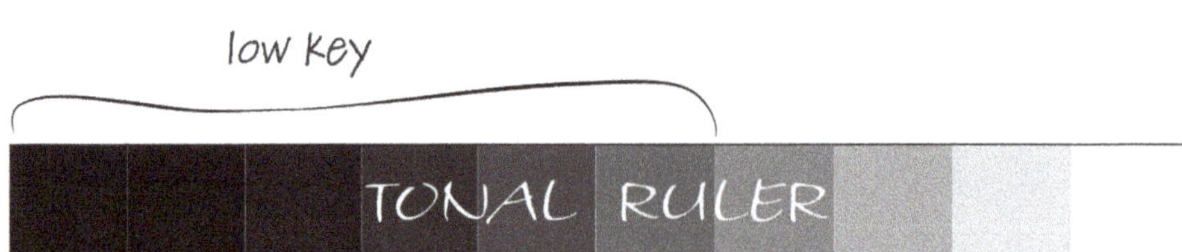

High Key

A *high-key* artwork is one that is filled with the mid to high tones and minimal dark tones.

A painting like this can seem filled with light. It is often joyful or ethereal. It depicts scenes of light, such as sunlight, spilling and reflecting everywhere and frightening all the shadows away.

One or two dark tone marks, however small, create a foil for the rest of the work. Without the comparison, the rest wouldn't seem so light.

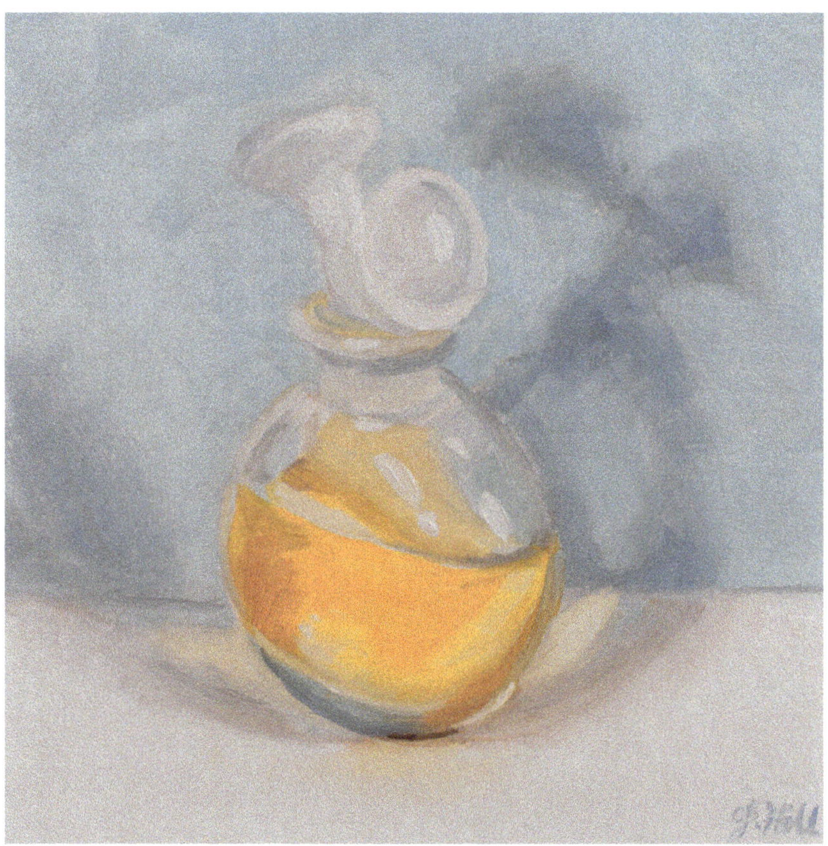

1-6 'Chloe' Oil on Wood Panel 15 x 15cm (6 x 6")
Daily Painting No 336 for 2015.

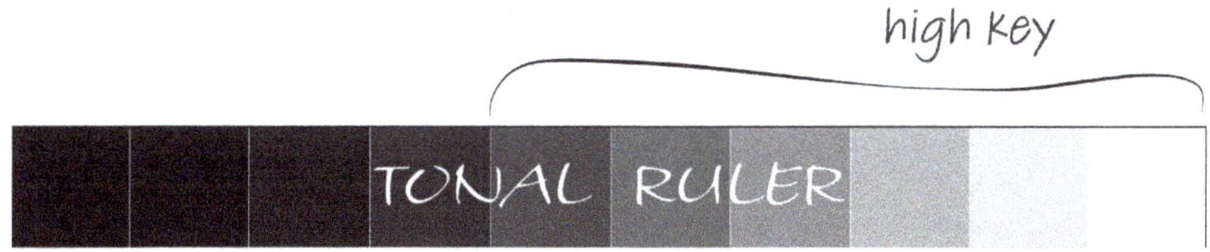

The Ting in the Crystal

After you have painted all those tones in your painting, it's time to add the final highlights.

If you are painting watercolour (from light to dark), it's when you put the tiny dark, sharp details in.

When I add those final tiny highlights on, I think it's like the 'ting' when you hit the edge of a crystal glass. The ting is the most beautiful singing sound.

That's how I hear the delight of the little tiny highlights at the end of the painting process. Everything comes together, and the final 'tings' just make it.

Can you see (or hear) the tings in the previous painting?

The Order and Importance

'So Shape is first,' said Jojo. 'Second is Tone. Then third is Colour?'

'You are beginning to understand,' said The Master. 'And remember, Shape is more important than Tone. And Tone is more important than Colour.'

Jojo looked at her pencils and paints. 'Is it the same for every medium?'

The Master tilted his head. 'When you apply the paint, the order may be a little different. But you must always consider these things in this order, even if the paint is not applied in this order.'

Play Time

To set up, select a shape to draw or paint. It should be a real thing (not a photograph) and it should be simple. Choose a roundish shape, such as a pear or a peach.

Make sure you have some contrast of light and shadow. You may need a lamp to shine on one side of your subject.

You can create fairly small works in these play paintings; all of them will fit on a single page of your sketchbook. Choose your favourite medium, or if you're a complete beginner, the easiest may be pencil.

Once you've finished this Play Time, take a look at finished examples on the Zen and the Art of Art website, at *www.zenartart.com/foundations*[10].

Resist the temptation to peek until you've done the experimenting yourself! The *doing* of this exercise will teach you so much more.

Pencil Play Time

1. Draw your shape, just with a line drawing. Do the same two times alongside so you have three line drawings of the one object.

2. Look for the tones and shadows then shade[11] them in on the second drawing only. Try to avoid being distracted by the colour: just look for the light and dark, regardless of colour.

3. Add colour to the third drawing. Make sure to choose very dark and very light colours to reflect the darks and lights you found in the second one.

4. You should now have three images, showing *shape*, *tone* and *colour*.

Check out some finished examples online[10].

Watercolour Play Time

As watercolour is a transparent[13] medium, you traditionally paint from light to dark. This means first laying in the light washes, and then working through the mid-tones before finishing off with the darkest darks. (Always leave paper white for the lightest whites.)

1. Draw the outline in pencil, lightly. Draw it another two times alongside to get a set of three.

2. Look for the tones and shadows. Choose a single colour paint (a dark colour is best — try Dioxazine Purple if you have it). Create a tonal painting over the second drawing. Use plenty of water to dilute the colour for the paler shades. Try to avoid being distracted by the colour: just look for the light and dark, regardless of colour, and paint that.

3. Add colour to the third drawing. Make sure to choose very dark and very light colours to reflect the darks and lights you found in the second one.

4. You should now have three images, showing *shape*, *tone* and *colour*.

Take a look online at the finished examples[10].

Painting Play Time — Acrylic, Ink, Gouache or Oil

This exercise outlines the tonal underpainting method used often by the old masters.

In acrylics and oils, you traditionally paint from dark to light. This means painting in all the darkest darks, then working through the mid-tones before finishing off with the lightest lights.

You can use acrylic, ink or oil. For oil, use a turpsy underwash for the first layer. If you use gouache[12], try to not disturb the undercolour by overbrushing in the third painting.

Paint it on heavyweight sealed paper such as mixed media paper or use primed canvas.

1. Draw the outline, either in light pencil or as linework using a brush with thinned down paint, if you're confident. The paint medium you use should be fast drying. Draw it another two times alongside so you have three drawings.

2. Look for the tones and shadows in the object. Choose a single colour paint and mix different tones using either opaque white or a transparent medium. Choosing a dark colour is best — preferably a muted, non-staining colour such as a Neutral Tint or Dark Grey if you have it. Create a tonal painting of those tones over the second drawing. Try to avoid being distracted by the colour: just look for the light and dark, regardless of colour, and paint that.

3. Repeat this tonal painting on the third drawing. Make sure to use a fast-drying medium and ensure the painting is dry before going on to the next step.

4. Add colour to the third image once the tonal underpainting is dry. Paint colour right over the top.
   - If you use thin, transparent colour, this is the fastest and easiest way to add colour to a tonal underpainting.
   - If you use opaque paint, make sure to match the tone (the dark and light) of your colours to the dark and light notes you made underneath.

5. You should now have three images, showing *shape*, *tone* and *colour*.

Now take a look at the finished examples[10].

CHAPTER 2
EMPERORS UNITE

The truth knocks on the door and you say,
'Go away, I'm looking for the truth,'
and so it goes away. Puzzling.

Robert M. Pirsig,
Zen and the Art of
Motorcycle Maintenance

CHAPTER 2 CONTENTS

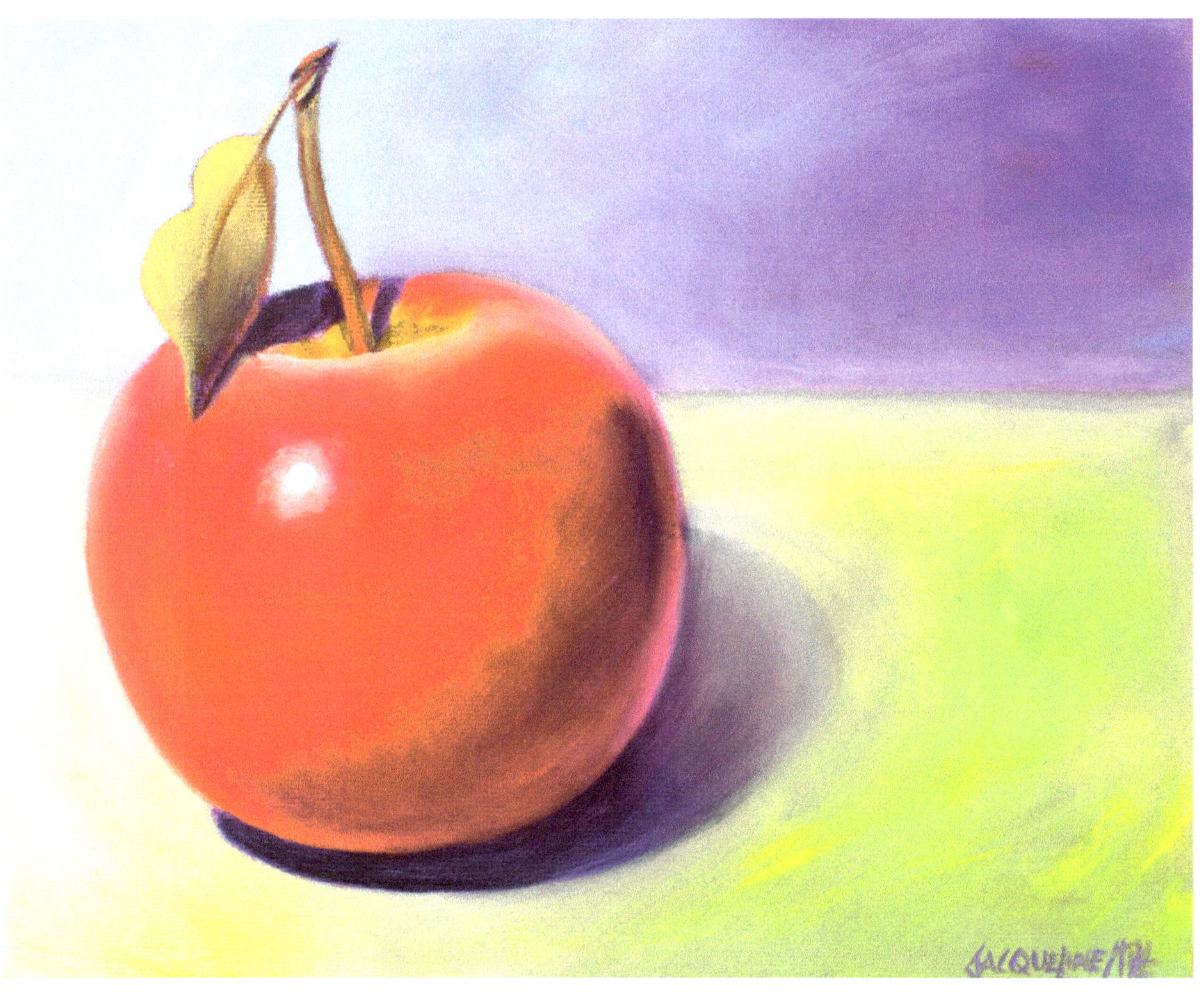

2-1 'Apple IV' Oil on Canvas Board 25 x 20cm (10 x 8'')
Igras Collection, Chuwar, Brisbane

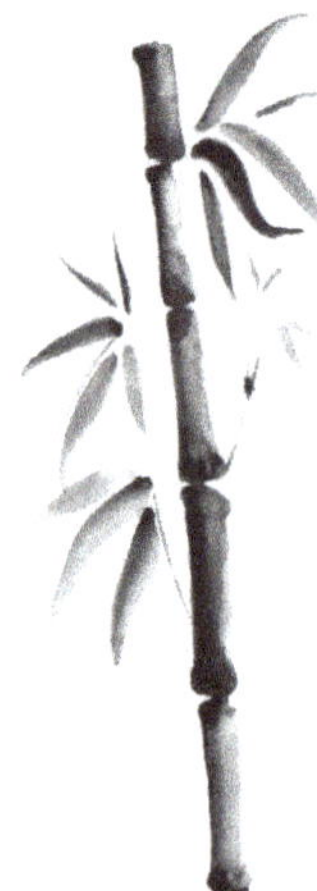

Jojo concentrated as her brush moved across the paper. A line of deep purple paint flowed behind. 'I got the shapes all correct,' she murmured. 'And then I started with tone. But now my shapes have gone out of whack.'

'Once the colour is in, you need to tweak the shapes and tones again too,' said The Master. 'As you work the painting, it is natural that some previous marks may go astray. At each stage, you need to check the previous stage is still correct. Go back and fix them. It won't take long. Be patient, Little Grasshopper.

'Keep your 1-2-3 checklist close by and make sure that the Shape, Tone and Colour are still ok when you come to finish your painting.'

'Just like tasting the soup before serving it up,' laughed Jojo.

The Master smiled. 'Just like tasting the soup,' he said.

Reviewing & Fixing As You Go

Always check the previous stages as you work your way through the three.

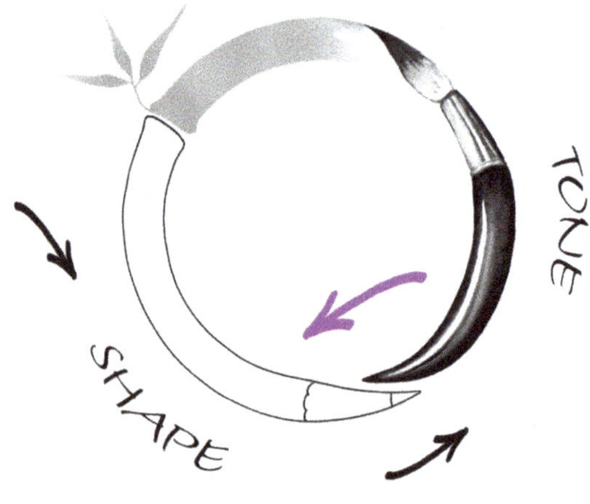

As you work on your tone, you may notice that your shapes become a bit distorted. You need to keep your eyes open to look for this and correct it as you see it.

Don't leave it alone!

Fix it right away.

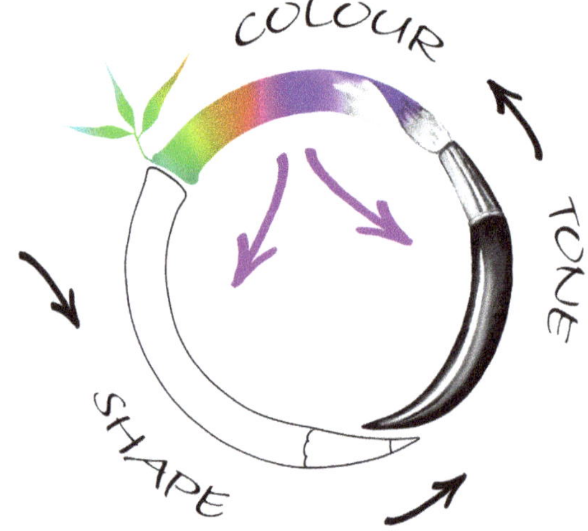

Then when you are working through colour, your shape and tone may become a bit distorted. So fix them right away.

It's not hard. They are only little tweaks. But you must be vigilant for these small problems and jump on them straight away.

You will get to the finish line much quicker and with much less stress than if you skip any of these vital steps.

All you have to remember is:

- While you are getting the tone in, check back over your shapes as well.

- While you are getting the colour in, check back over your shapes *and* tones.

Here's your final map of the whole process:

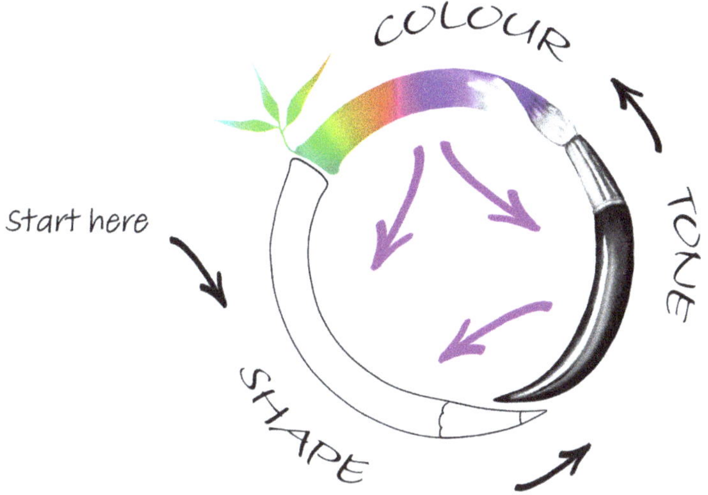

Painting in Different Mediums

'How does this work in the different painting mediums?' asked Jojo.
   'The best way to understand is to do,' said The Master. 'The mastery is in the doing.'

You can practise the 1-2-3 method in the Play Time at the end of this chapter. All the steps are laid out clearly for each painting medium.

If you have ever painted in oils and acrylic, you may already see how these three steps apply to those paints. I teach my beginner students to lay down a tonal under-painting, get it dry, then lay colour over the top. It's amazing how punchy the results are compared to not doing the tonal work first.

But watercolour is transparent[13], so you can't do it this way.

Medium	Painting Order
Acrylics Oils Inks Gouache Pastel	Dark to Light
Watercolour Graphite	Light to Dark

- With opaque paints, always paint from *dark to light.* This means painting in all the darkest darks first, then working through the mid-tones. Finish off with the lightest lights in the painting.
- With transparent watercolours, always lay down the palest washes first. Then gradually work through to finish off with the darkest details on the last layer.

Because of this, you have to be really aware of tone to know what order you'll paint in — *before* you begin!

The Tonal Plan

For watercolour, I recommend creating a small painting sketch as a tonal version of the final watercolour you are about to create. It really gets your mind clear about the tone in your painting before you begin. Use this little tonal sketch as a plan to follow while you paint the large painting.

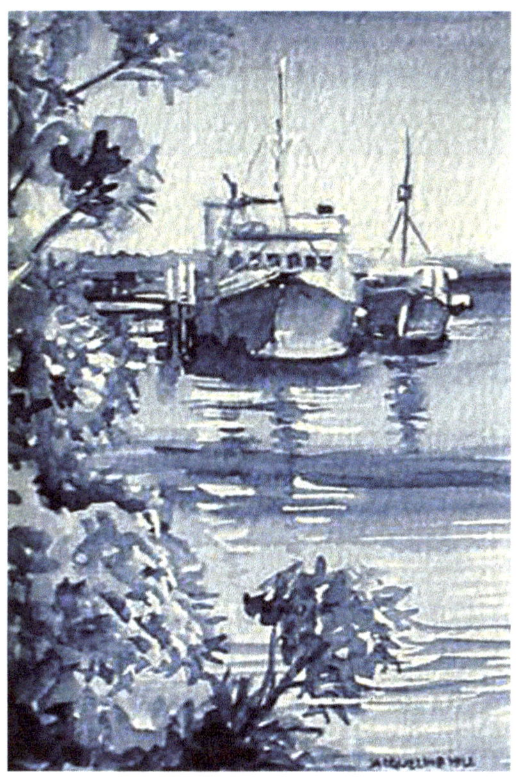

2-2 'Blue Boats' Watercolour on Paper 15 x 21cm (6 x 8")
Private Collection, Brisbane

The other advantage of doing a little tonal painting is that you can work out any composition problems.

It's a trick I often use with oil and acrylic paintings as well. I create a little business-card size (3 x 2" or 90 x 55mm) sketch in charcoal to get the composition and tones worked out before I start. You can also use a black Chinagraph pencil.

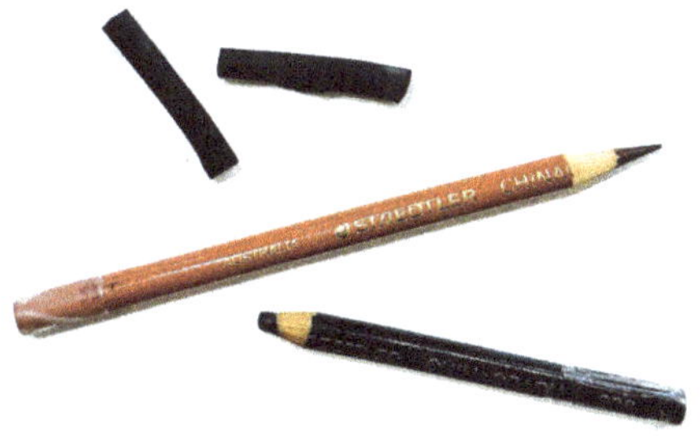

Because these sketches are small (about 90 x 55mm or 3 x 2"), they only take a few seconds to create. If one isn't to your liking, you can just create another until you are happy with the plan.

Here's my charcoal sketch for a larger pastel painting of a tawny frogmouth. The pale line through it shows you that I planned to use a landscape composition but changed my mind during the sketch and made it vertical (portrait).

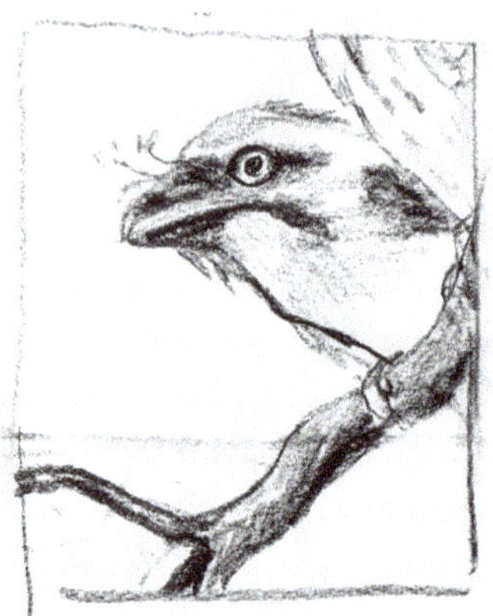

2-3 'On the Lookout' (Tonal Study) Charcoal on Paper 6 x 8cm (2 x 3")

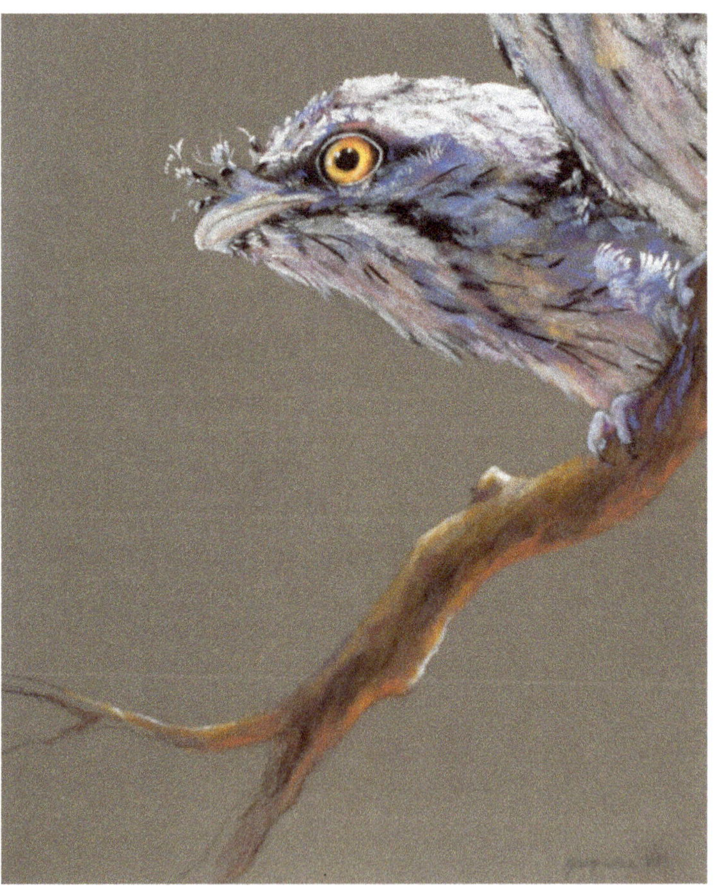

2-4 'On the Lookout' (Tawny Frogmouths) Pastel on Mi-Tex Card 21 x 29cm (8 x 11.5")
Private Collection, Berwick-upon-Tweed, Northumberland, United Kingdom

But Rules are Meant to be Broken

Jojo sighed as she swept the studio floor. 'That sounds like a lot of rules to follow when I just want to paint and have fun,' she said.

The Master gathered his brushes and cleaned them gently. 'When you start out, it is important to build a foundation of knowledge and skill,' he said. 'Then you can bend and twist the rules to find your own place in the world of art.

'Do you feel happy when your painting is not working? And are you having fun when you don't understand how to fix it?' he asked.

'No,' Jojo answered. 'It feels horrible.' She leaned on the straw broom. 'I think I would have more fun if I finished my paintings. And if I liked them.'

The Master placed his brushes into his cloth roll and tied the knot.

'Ok, I'll try starting with Shape. After that I'll think about Tone. Then I'll add Colour last, and see how my paintings turn out,' she said. 'And I have to practise patience!'

'And patiently practise,' nodded The Master.

You may be thinking that all these rules make it too structured when you are in creative painting mode. You may say, 'This is art, not science!'

You can set aside times to play with colour in your painting stages without worrying about this.

But once you learn this skill (through practice), it will affect all of your paintings: even in your creative playtime. You will create much better art.

When you've learnt the basic skills, you can break the rules. It's important to know *when* you are breaking rules and *why*.

The Story in Your Painting

What do I mean by story?

Story can mean anything you like. It could be a literal story —the cat reached up the tree to chase the bird, but the bird flew away.

Or the story can be something a bit more subtle.

In the *On the Lookout* painting, I wanted to portray my joy of seeing the tawny frogmouth lean forward and look closer at something. The original image was so beautifully backlit. I also wanted to express my delight at how the sun was hitting those little fluffy feathers on his beak and wing.

Play Time

1. Have you done the Play Time exercises in Chapter 1 Three Emperors yet? Did you find that your shapes or tones became a little distorted when you went on to the next stage in the plan? If you haven't already, go back and fix up any shapes or tones if you can.

2. Try drawing or painting a new simple shape, such as a piece of fruit, or any other simple shape that interests you. Try using the three step plan of the Three Emperors to build the shape and finish it. Does it look three dimensional now?

3. Try a slightly more complex shape, such as a flower or a teapot, and follow the plan to build the painting or drawing.

CHAPTER 3
KISSING FROGS

Deal with it before it happens.
Set things in order
before there is confusion.

Lao-Tzu

CHAPTER 3 CONTENTS

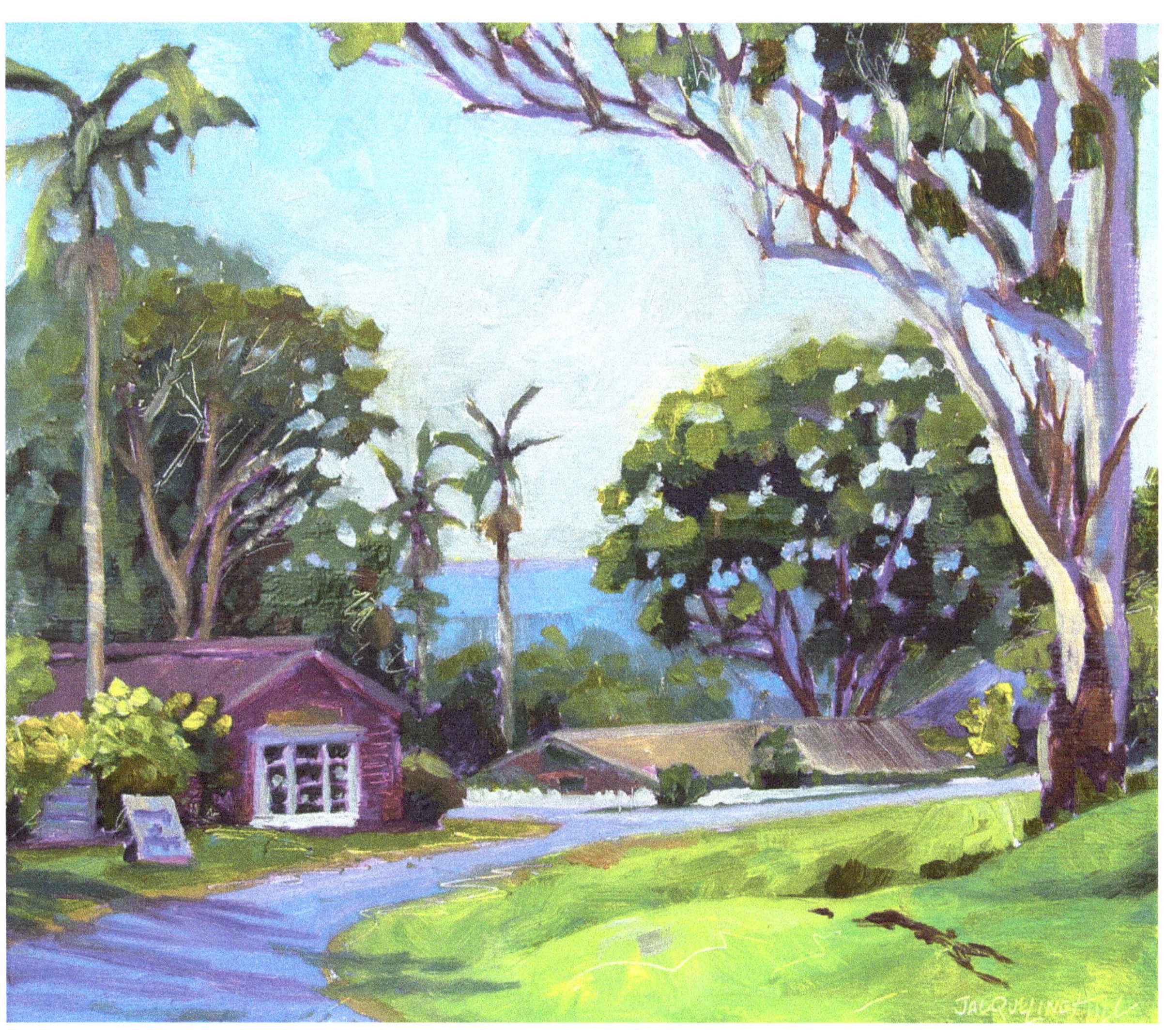

3-1 'Odds N Ends Store' (Mt Tamborine) Oil on Wood Panel 25 x 20cm (12 x 10")
Painted on location.

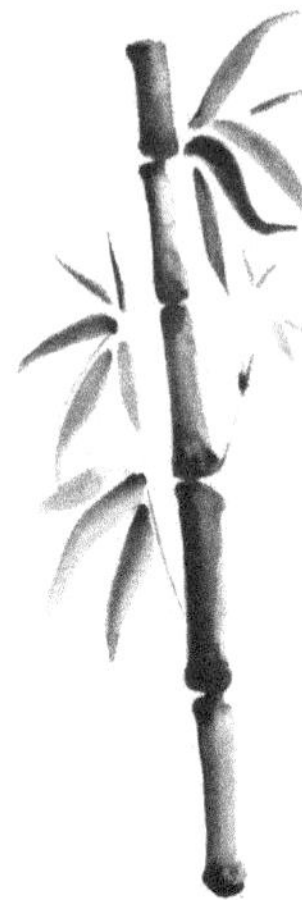

Jojo stood over her painting, biting her lip. 'I don't get it. I've got the shapes right, the tones right and lovely colours. But looking at the painting overall, something feels… off,' said Jojo. 'But I just can't put my finger on what it is.'

The Master said, 'I think you already know.'

Jojo looked at him, confused.

The Master continued, 'You said it yourself. The details are right, but it feels wrong when you look at the painting overall.'

Jojo crossed her arms. 'Do you mean something is wrong with the whole painting?' asked Jojo. 'That's depressing.'

'No,' said The Master. 'I don't mean everything is wrong. Just one little thing that affects the whole.'

Jojo stared at her work, tilting her head.

'Your composition,' he said.

What is Composition?

Composition is the arrangement of the objects in your painting. It's the placement of everything: your overall design of the shapes.

Flirting

I heard an artist say once:

> *Flirt with your reference material — don't marry it.*

This applies to whether you are painting from photographs, from life or from memory.

Painting a tree? You don't have to paint every leaf. You can choose to leave anything out of your painting that you think won't add to the final artwork.

Sometimes I use my photo reference for just the shapes and tones, and then I put whatever colour I want in. I love leaving things out that I know will *distract* from the final artwork, too.

If the fruit or flowers you are painting have bruises, or if the leaves have mildew or spots, you don't have to paint them that way. If you want to, you can paint the most luscious vibrant piece of delicious fruit the world has ever seen.

Building Worlds

When you create a painting, you are creating your own little world. You can play god on your little canvas and place things wherever you like!

Painting a farm scene? If the horses are standing in the wrong spot in the paddock, move them to where you want them! Take trees out, put imaginary trees in.

When you are an artist you can move mountains with just your brush and your imagination.

All About Basic Composition

Part of your work with the Shapes stage is assembling all the pieces of your painting into a harmonious arrangement.

When you get the composition wrong, it can really influence the viewer's love, indifference or hate of the artwork.

Composition can be approached in many different ways. But for now let's just look at how to avoid the most glaring mistakes I see beginners make.

Rule of Thirds

The Rule of Thirds applies to rectangular canvases (or paper), whether the rectangle is oriented horizontally (landscape) or vertically (portrait).

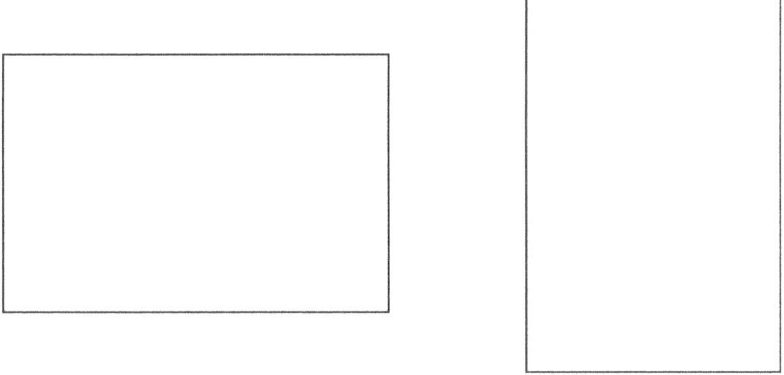

The Rule of Thirds says you must be aware of the vertical thirds lines, as well as the horizontal thirds lines:

So just imagine this grid overlaying your painting:

The aim is to have any strong lines, focal points or points of interest reside on these lines.

To understand how this works, let's look at photography as an example.

The Rule of Thirds in Photographs

Behind the lens of every good photographer's camera is an artist who composes the shot carefully before shooting.

When you take a photo of Aunt Mabel out on vacation, you might start lining up the photo with the horizon nicely halfway up and Aunt Mabel smack bang in the middle.

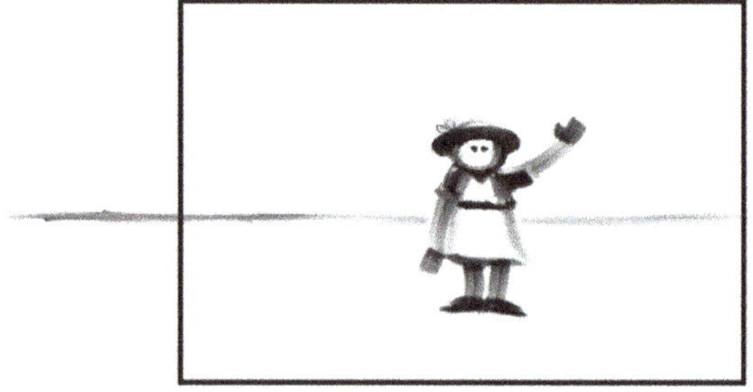

But this is the worst way to take an artistic photo! A painting using this composition would be terrible. If you entered this photo or painting into a competition it would most likely be knocked out in the first round.

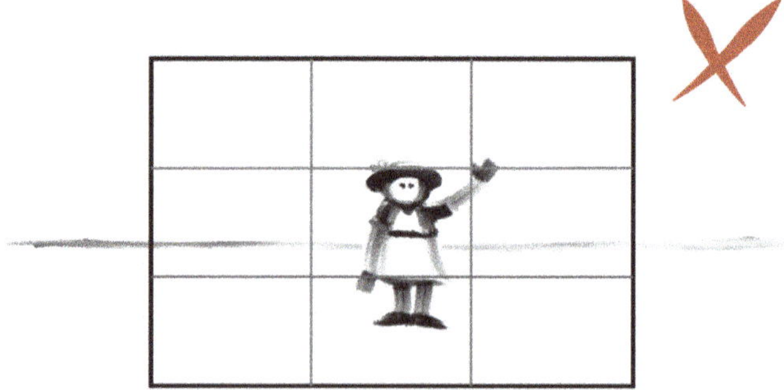

To use Rule of Thirds, you can start by lining up the photo with everything in the middle. But then you need to shift the camera either up or down, so the horizon is on one of the thirds lines.

This means you get either a lot of sky or a lot of land.

Before taking the shot, you would also shift your camera slightly to the side so that Aunt Mabel is standing on one of the thirds lines.

Then you'll take a much better photo:

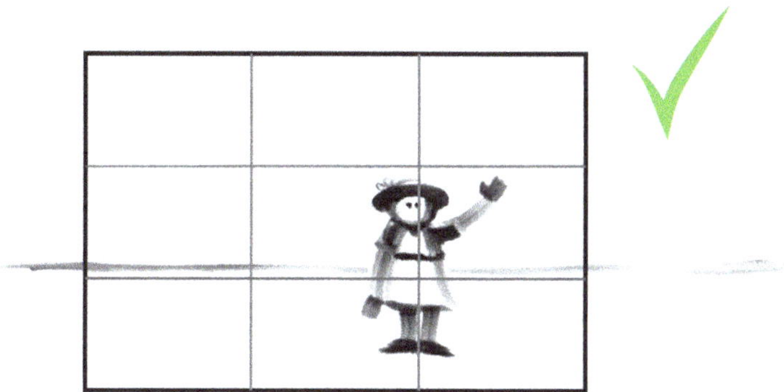

The Rule of Thirds in Paintings

Without this rule, you might be tempted to paint your favourite tree in the centre with a horizon along the middle. But now you know to push the main focal points and the strongest lines onto the thirds lines, horizontally and vertically.

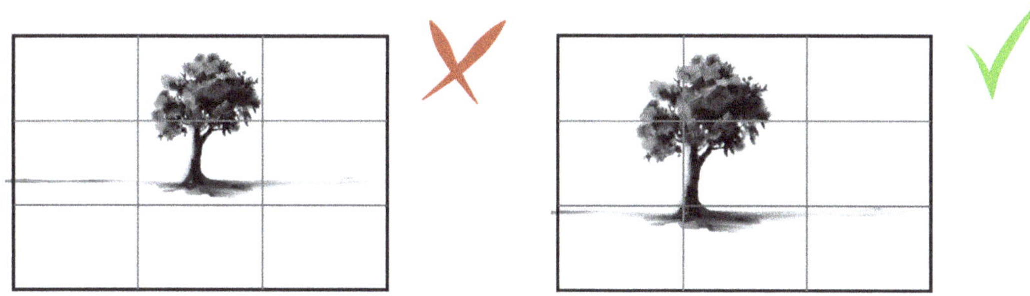

Some cameras show you a grid of the thirds lines when you look through the lens. This reminds you of the rule and helps you line your objects up when you're taking the photo.

Modern Mind likes everything neat and tidy, all divided up nice and even. So it will automatically trick you into putting objects right in the middle. But you must overrule the Modern Mind and think like an artist.

Paintings with strong vertical lines in the centre are quite uncomfortable to look at. A viewer may say, 'That painting is not my favourite, but I'm not really sure why.'

Make sure to add this to your checklist for creating a good painting. Put it up the top so you think of this right at the beginning when you are working out the composition. It's pretty hard to change it later on!

Does it Have to be Exact?

No.

You don't have to place things exactly on the thirds lines. It can be a quarter or ⅜ — it doesn't matter. Just remember to *not* stick things right in the middle when composing a rectangular painting.

What About Square Paintings?

Square or round paintings are a totally different kettle of fish. When composing these, it is *good* to put the point of focus in the centre.

With a leading line or pathway into the painting, the eye should follow in a spiral around to meet the focus in the centre.

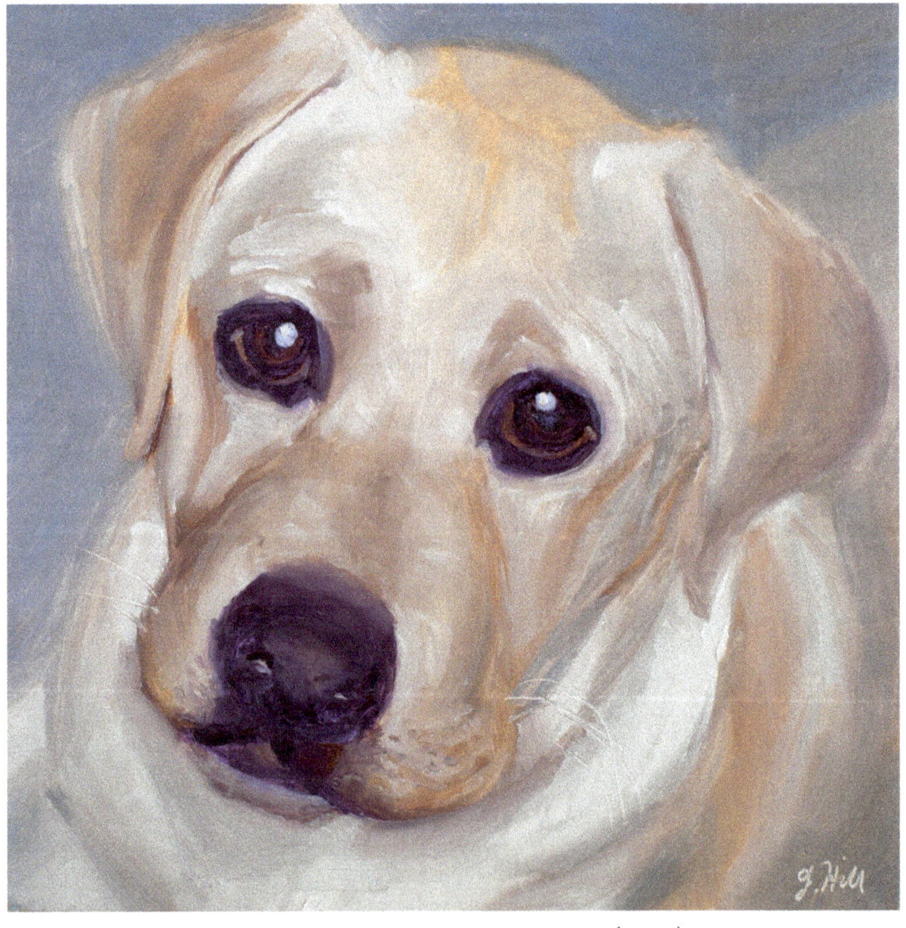

3-2 'Minty' Oil on Wood Panel 15 x 15cm (6 x 6")
Daily Painting No 71 for 2015. Hatt Collection, New Farm, Queensland, Australia

Focal Points & Points of Interest

A focal point is something the eye is drawn to in a painting. It can be:

- The brightest red flower in the vase

- The lightest highlight in a sea of darks and mid-tones

- The glint in the eye of a tiger face

- The strong sharp line where a dark area hits a light area

- A place in the painting where everything is in crisp focus if other areas are blurred out

- The only person in the painting (we are built to notice the human figure)

These focal points should be placed near the thirds lines. They can also be inside the centre box (the middle of the nine squares made by the thirds lines). It is better *not* to place these in the outside edges, ie outside the thirds lines.

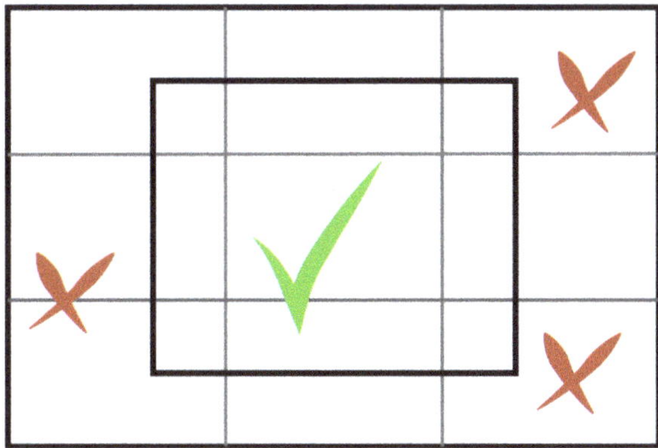

Kissing

Kissing is really good to do in real life.
But not so good in paintings, drawings and photographs.

What is Kissing?

The term *kissing* in art composition (and photography) refers to the edges of objects in your arrangement touching when they shouldn't.

Examples

Sometimes we have fun doing it on purpose. Taking a photo of your friend pretending to hold up the Leaning Tower of Pisa, for example.

But most of the time we don't want kissing in our photographs or paintings.

Let's look at an example.

Say you are photographing Aunt Mabel with the farmhouse and a tree in the distance. You need to be careful when she holds her arms out and says, 'One day all this will be yours.' Make sure that her fingertips don't touch the tree in the far distance.

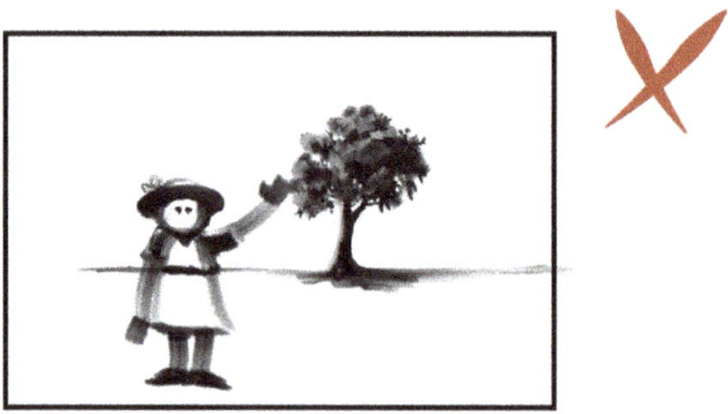

Can you see the waistband on her dress is also kissing the horizon?
Make sure your tree in the foreground doesn't kiss the house in the far distance.

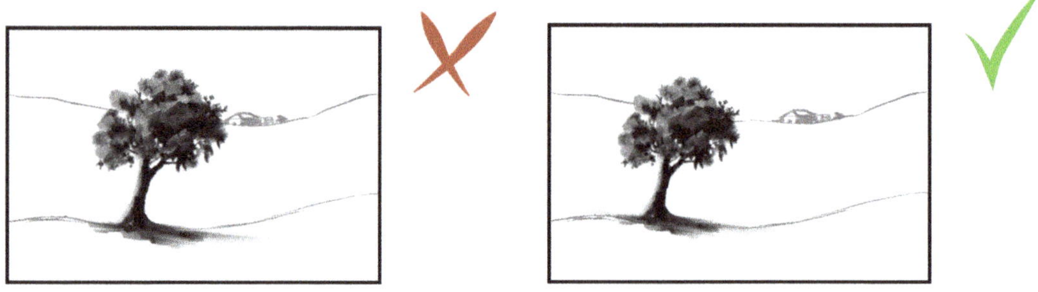

How to Fix a Kissing Problem

Change the composition (either the angle of your camera or the arrangement in your artwork) so that either:

- The front item crosses over the one behind, so it goes right past the edge
- The two items are moved apart so that they don't touch at all

Here are the two ways to fix the kissing problem — either cross over or stay away:

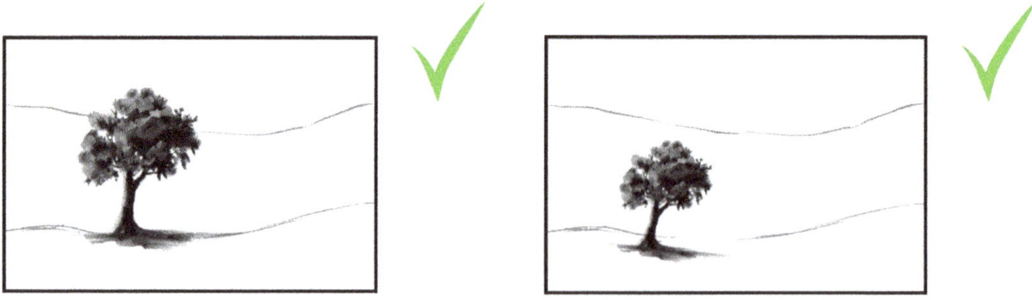

When an edge of one object touches the edge of another, the viewer is unsure where they are in relation to each other. This creates a point of confusion. The eye will rest on that spot as the brain tries to work out which object is in front of the other.

If you leave points of kissing in your paintings, you create focal points that you really don't want. The viewer's eye and brain will get all tangled up on that spot, trying to work it out. Avoid kissing in your paintings! But keep on kissing in real life.

Differences make dynamic paintings

Jojo carried a bucket of water to The Master, who stood near the clearing under a tree, scattering seeds to a wren family. She sat down nearby, smiling at the chirping birds, and started to wash her brushes.

'Sensei, how do I paint paintings that are really lively and dynamic?' she asked. 'I've seen some in the galleries that just literally stop me in my tracks. I find myself staring at them for ages. How do I paint like that?'

'You need to understand the Yin and Yang of painting,' The Master said.

'The yin yang symbol? The black and white one?' asked Jojo.

'Yes,' The Master nodded, dusting his hands of the seed. 'It has the strongest possible contrast between black and white. And yet a tiny amount of each is contained in the other.'

Jojo was quiet.

'This symbol will guide you to create dynamic paintings that also have balance,' he added. 'In this simplest of symbols lies a map to where you want to be.'

The secret to making paintings dynamic is to master *randomness* and *differences*.

If your painting is full of differences, then it will be balanced, interesting and often dynamic. Creating differences is easy to say but not so easy to do in paintings, especially as a beginner.

You will be battling Modern Mind to overrule all the times it wants you to do same, same, same. It will trick you as often as it can, and it will be a subtle underground saboteur. You need to be vigilant of Modern Mind.

Keeping your Zen Mind open will help. This way, you can see what is truly there in front of you, as you study a subject.

More on this in the next chapter, Reality Check.

Balance

In the yin yang symbol, the small inner circles echo the shade of the opposite, larger shape.

You can use this as a reminder for extending dynamic range in your painting. It can also remind you to keep balance in your painting by sprinkling the opposites among one another in small quantities.

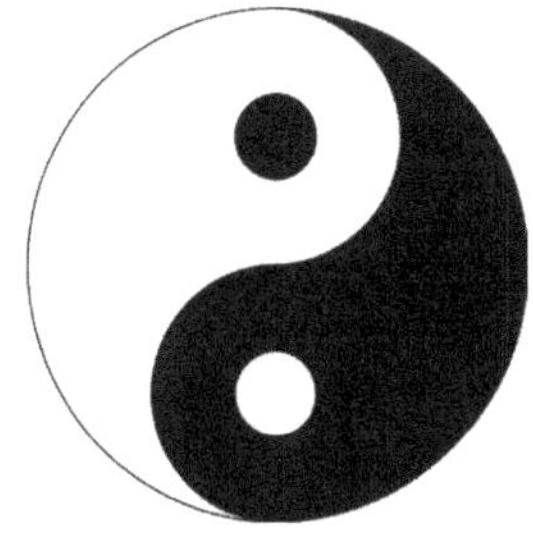

Example

Here's one example, in its most primitive form. If half of your painting has a strong red colour and the other half has a cool blue, you need to get each side to interact with one another (talk with one another). You can do this by introducing a small splash of red (or two) into the blue side, and a small splash of blue into the red.

Can you see how I've done this, with blue and orange, in this painting?

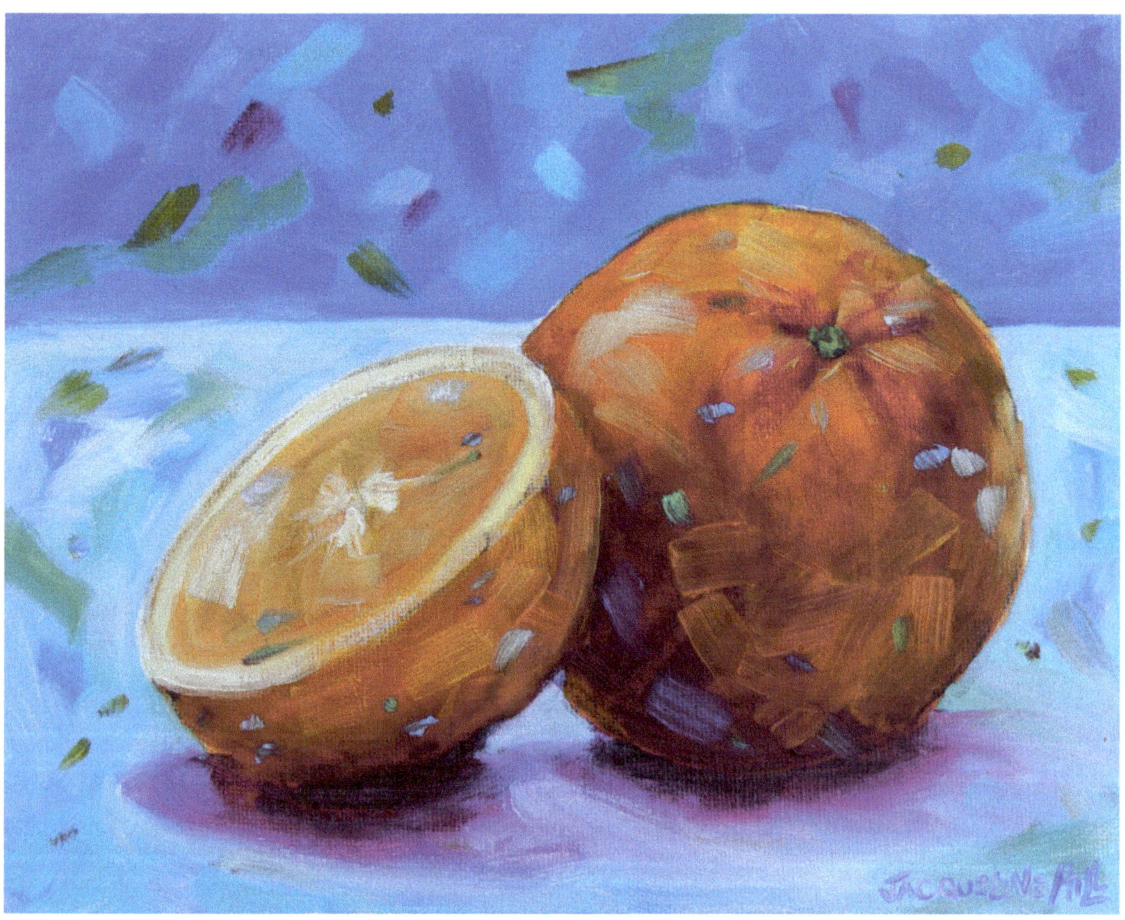

3-3 'A Song of Orange' Oil on Canvas 25 x 20cm (10 x 8")
Miall Collection, Toowong, Brisbane, Australia

Differences Make Magic

If you keep aware of differences in your artworks, and keep including them, you will make magic in your paintings. There are many ways to make differences, including line, form, tone and colour. Let's look at a few.

Randomness

Almost everything in nature is random. If you look at a group of trees, hardly any two are the same, and their clumps of foliage are all different. Mountains are all unique as is every pebble. Open your eyes to see the randomness all around you in nature.

Randomness happens with:

- Trees
- Foliage
- Rocks
- Pebbles
- Mountains
- Grass
- Flowers
- Plants
- Clouds... and more

Dark & Light

The tones in your painting should include the full range on your Tonal Ruler, from the darkest darks all the way through to the lightest highlights.

If you have lots of contrast in your paintings, they will be dynamic.

Beginners often stick too much to the mid-tones.

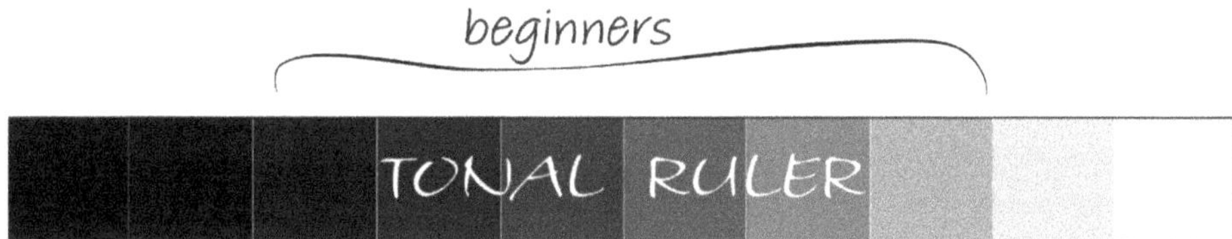

If you concentrate on getting strong darks in and popping light highlights, you will win.

Warm & Cool

Areas of warm and cool colours in your painting can be really lovely. More on this in Chapter 10 Heated Hues.

Hard & Soft

The term 'lost and found edges' refers to hard edges, which are clear, and soft edges, which are so blurred that the viewer cannot tell precisely where they are.

Having this variation in a painting makes a beautiful artwork. The viewer may gaze at it for a long while, as their brain tries to find the missing pieces.

Transparent & Opaque

Using both transparent and opaque areas in your painting can build a beautiful artwork.

More on transparency[13] in Chapter 12 Mixing Maestro.

When Can I Break These Rules?

Any time you like. But preferably after you've understood and used the rules of composition several times, so you really know them.

Lots of wonderful edgy modern paintings, as well as some rare old masters' paintings break the rules.

The tawny frogmouth painting, *On the Lookout*, at the end of the last chapter breaks a few rules. This was deliberate. I was aiming for a dynamic, interesting painting that was different from the norm.

The Rule of Thirds is broken to create a dynamic, unusual composition.

The viewer is lucky if they discover the second frogmouth, but it is not important to my story behind the painting.

In the *Rose in a Glass Vase* painting at the start of the next chapter, the neck of the vase is centred, seeming to break the Rule of Thirds. In fact the strongest elements of the painting are roughly on the thirds lines. The stem in the neck is an essential element to link the two strongest areas together, so they 'talk'.

Play Time

Paintings

Look over any artworks you may have already painted.

If possible, print small photos of each so you can scribble marks on them.

- Look for where the:
    - strong lines in the painting are — especially horizontal and vertical. If you've printed them out, draw the lines over the image.
    - focal points are. If you've printed them out, circle these focal points.
- Look for where they might break these rules:
    - Rule of Thirds
    - Kissing
    - Randomness and Differences

    Circle each of these if you've printed them out.

What would you do to fix any problems you may have found in these paintings?

Photographs

Look over the last set of travel photos you took.

- Check over them for where the:
    - strong lines are — especially horizontal and vertical
    - the focal points are
- Look for where they might break these rules:
    - Rule of Thirds
    - Kissing
    - Randomness and Differences

What would you do differently the next time you take travel photos? Or when you take photos of things to paint from?

Other Paintings

Do you visit art galleries often? Either small private galleries or the state or national galleries (art museums)? You should! They are places where your little inner artist gets inspired and encouraged by other artists. These places will swell your artist's heart and mind with joy.

The next time you are at a gallery or an art show, walk around and enjoy the artworks. Then walk around a second time and pretend you are a judge. See if you can spot the flaws in the paintings.

Be quiet about it, of course. We don't want to break any artist's heart!

If the artist is very experienced, have they broken any rules on purpose? Can you see the reason why they may have chosen to do this? Or does the artwork just annoy you because of it?

Either answer may be what they were trying to achieve.

CHAPTER 4
REALITY CHECK

Everything has beauty,
but not everyone sees it.

Confucius

CHAPTER 4 CONTENTS

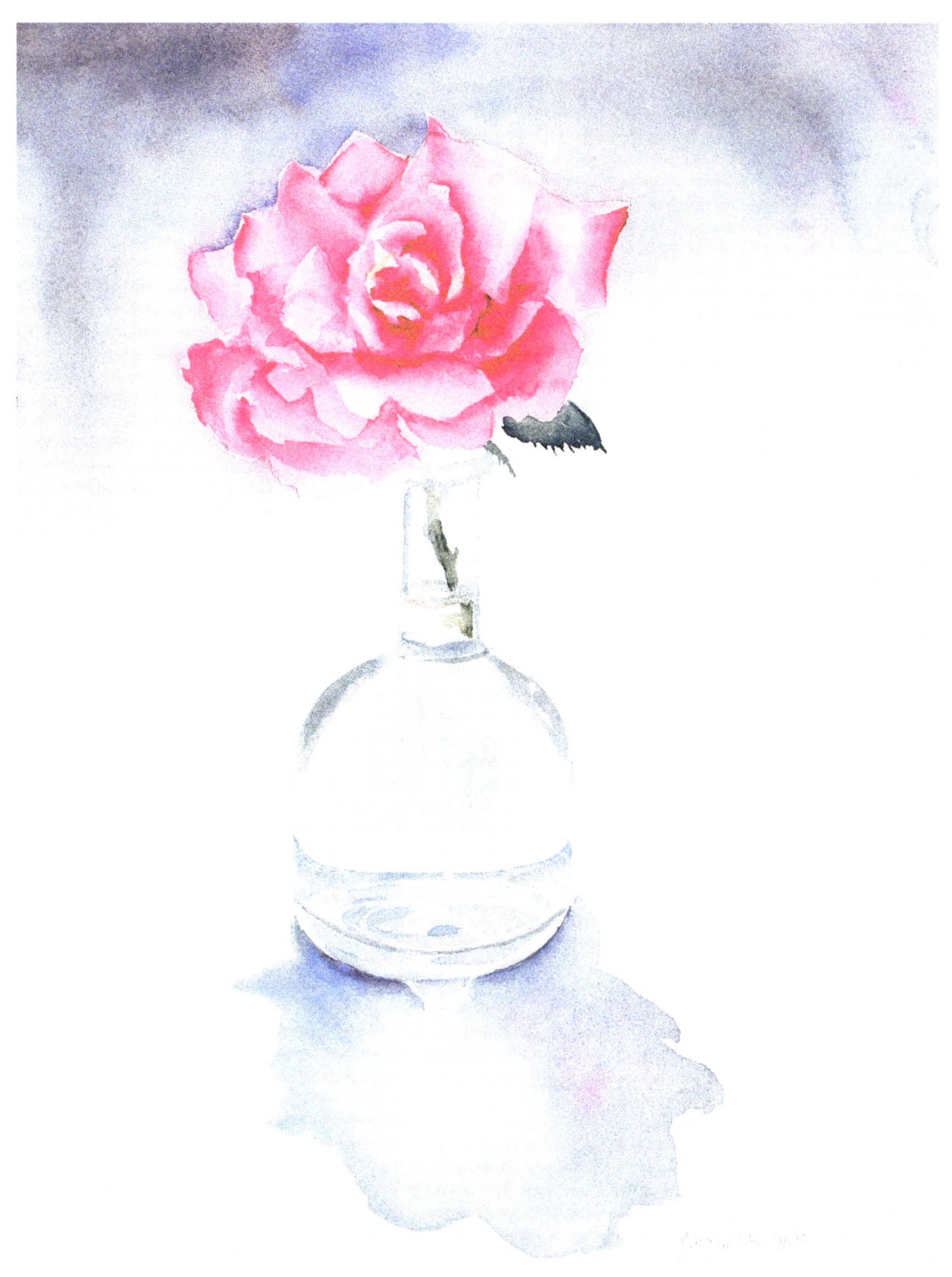

4-1 'Rose in a Glass Vase' Watercolour on Paper 29 x 42cm (11.5 x 16.5")

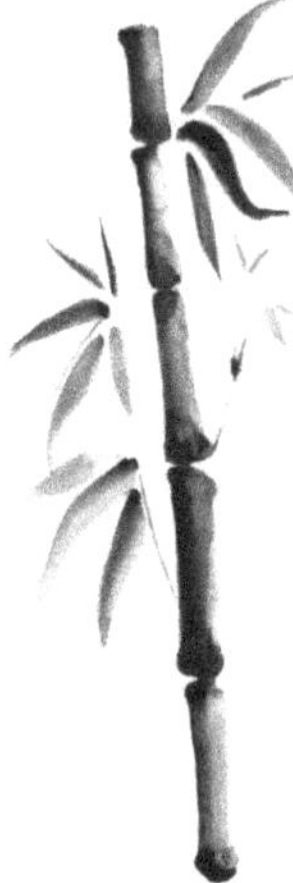

The Master handed Jojo a handmade clay cup. It was glazed with dark silver and a pretty swirl pattern encircled the middle. She gratefully warmed her chilly fingers around its curved sides. Steam curled through the early morning air as she blew on the tea.

'I know that Shape is the most important thing,' said Jojo. 'But I really have trouble with getting my drawings right. How do I become a better drawer?'

'That is a big question,' answered The Master, picking up a matching cup. 'The answer is simple to state, but often difficult for beginners to implement.

'Are you ready for a challenge?' he asked.

'Mmmmm, I suppose so?' said Jojo, sipping her tea.

'The simple answer,' said The Master, 'is to open your Zen Mind and see what's really there in front of you.

'The difficult thing,' he continued, 'is the battle you may have to overcome your Modern Mind.'

'What exactly is Modern Mind?' asked Jojo.

'Modern Mind is the friend of the time-poor modern citizen,' said The Master. 'And the enemy of the artist.'

Shape: The Battle Against Modern Mind

The first stage, getting the shapes right, is not the easiest thing to do. I often find it the most challenging and energy consuming. It also takes the most time.

The biggest hindrance to the Shape stage is our Modern Mind, which tries to help us out and save us time. Modern Mind is all about efficiency, rushing and 'time is money'. But as a result, it often gets everything wrong.

To create good art, we need to build the practice of being in Zen Mind. This is not as easy as you may think. Our Modern Mind muscle is very strong due to the time-oriented, busy culture we live in.

It's important to become aware of the Modern Mind and how it compares to the Zen Mind.

Modern Mind

Modern Mind contains a library of *Memories*. It's the area of your mind (conceptually at least) that looks after Library, Language and Logic.

Think of the Library as a big memory bank of reference material, full of information and memories that get us through every day of our lives. Modern Mind looks up words in the Language department for us so we can speak sentences and understand one another.

Modern Mind is very linear and time oriented — it's aware of time passing. It wants to help you save time by giving you shortcuts to get tasks done.

Zen Mind

Zen Mind is harder to describe. It's helpful to think of mindfulness. That is being totally present in the current moment of time. Free of emotions or memories or hopes and the future. Letting go of history or possessions or beliefs. Forgetting about other places and other times.

Let's talk about how it works in terms of your art and drawing.

Zen Mind is more concerned with *reality* at this moment in time. It allows you to see what is truly there in front of you, right here and now, without memories getting in the way.

It doesn't have time awareness. When you are in Zen Mind, time slips away without you noticing.

Getting in the Zone

Sometimes I am truly 'in the zone' of painting or drawing.

I feel like the artwork flows and works all by itself. When I step back, I am surprised not just by how many hours have gone by, but also how lovely the artwork is.

It feels like I am hardly even present. That the artwork flows through me without me really being there, except as a conduit.

I feel like it wasn't me who painted it.

Zen Mind is about getting out of your own way and letting the flow pass through you.

When I am in Zen Mind I am unaware of how much time passes. If I need to finish a painting session at a certain time, to be somewhere else, I must always set an alarm. If I don't, I will keep painting, blissfully unaware of the time.

When I am in Zen Mind I see shapes, tones and colours really clearly. However, I cannot retrieve the words I need.

Changing Your Mind

When I am at the easel (and in Zen Mind) I sometimes start to lose my words. If I need to speak, I feel like my brain is foggy and cannot find the words it needs.

While I'm in the studio painting, someone in my office may come and ask me a business or accounting question. I can usually answer these easily when I'm not painting. But if I'm in Zen Mind, they are very likely to get a befuddled look on my face followed by, 'I don't know...'

My office staff have come to know that when I am in my studio with a brush in my hand, it is the wrong time to ask me those questions, or anything to do with logic. I am totally in Zen Mind and they've learned to leave me to it. They save up the questions for a time when I am in Modern Mind.

As I walk from the studio into the office, I can almost feel the big cogs turning very slowly in my head, to shunt from one brain mode to the other. It can take 15 – 30 minutes before I have shifted to the other mode enough to start sounding sensible again!

The same thing happens when going in the other direction.

Some days I plan a painting session to work on commissions in the studio. I avoid going into the office and sitting at the computer first, even for 5 minutes. It puts me into the Modern Mind — the wrong Mind for painting. Going from computer to easel, I feel confused for the first half hour or hour.

When I first got started with painting, it took me a lot longer to switch modes. I worked out that I had to spend a whole day in either Zen Mind (in the studio) or Modern Mind (at the office computer). But these days I can switch Minds a lot more quickly. I hope you can too!

It all starts with awareness. Start to become aware of your own Modern Mind and Zen Mind.

Childhood Drawing

Mini Play Time!

1. Take out a piece of paper and a crayon or a pencil.

2. Imagine you are little again when you first worked out how to draw a house.

3. If I say to you, 'Quick, draw a house!' — what do you first think of doing? Is it a square with a triangle on top? Draw it!

4. When you were a child, did you add details to this house? What did they look like? Draw them in.

5. Did you draw a tree? A sun? People? Anything else? Add them all in.

This Play Time should be quick and easy — most people remember what they drew pretty easily as you may have drawn it many, many times.

Finish this Play Time before reading on.

My Childhood House Drawing

The house that I always drew as a child was a square and a triangle.

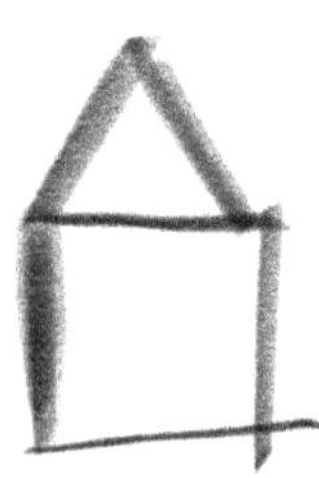

It always had a chimney. And smoke.

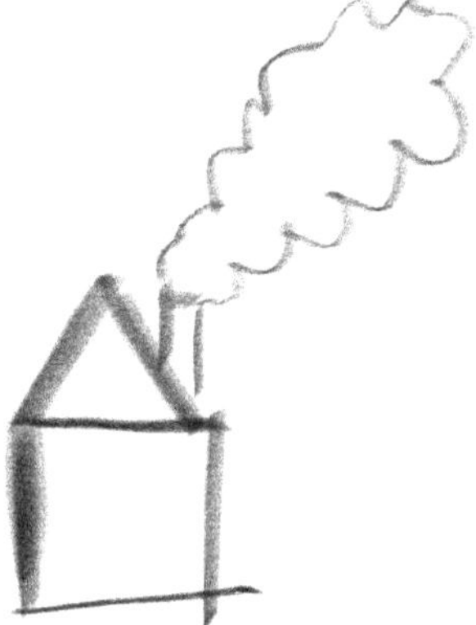

When I was little, I added one door plus two windows.

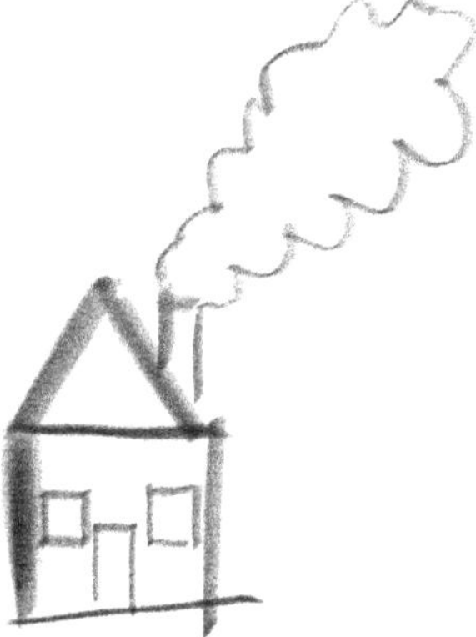

After a while I started to add curtains:

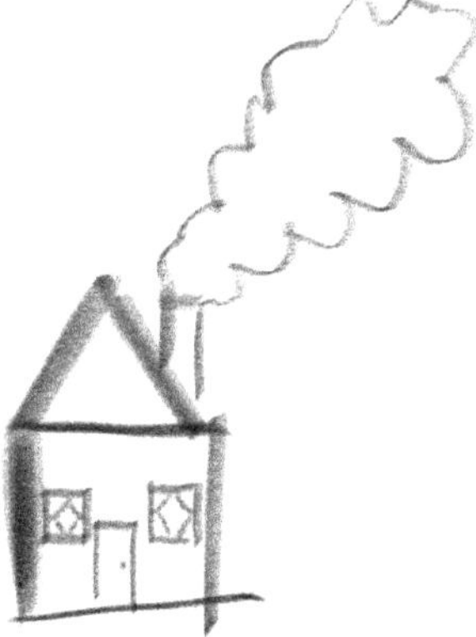

I always drew houses the same way. Did you?

Was the sun shining in the sky?

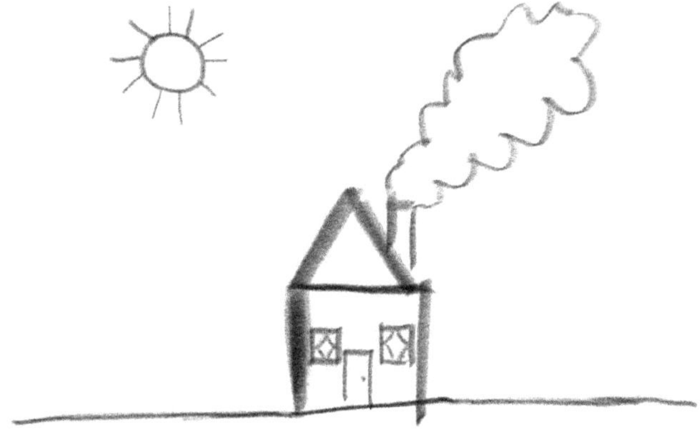

Was there a tree? Did it look like a lollipop?

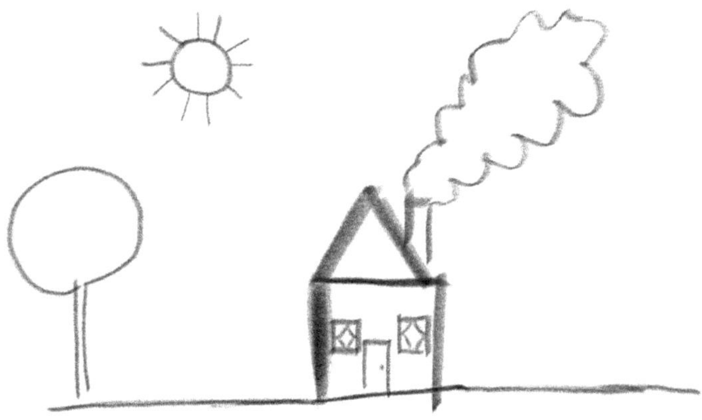

Did you draw people? What did they look like?

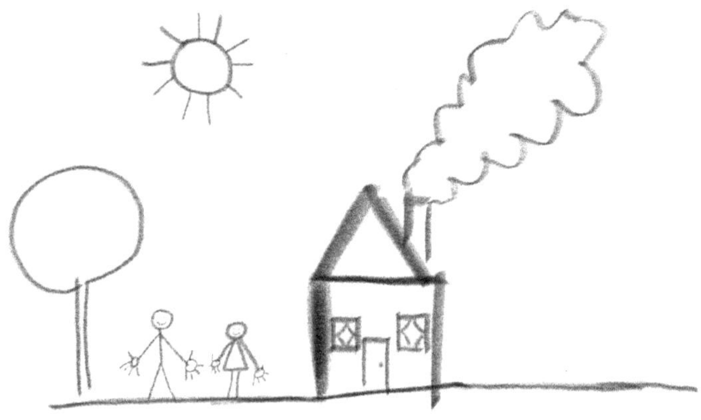

I used to add a pathway and a letterbox too.

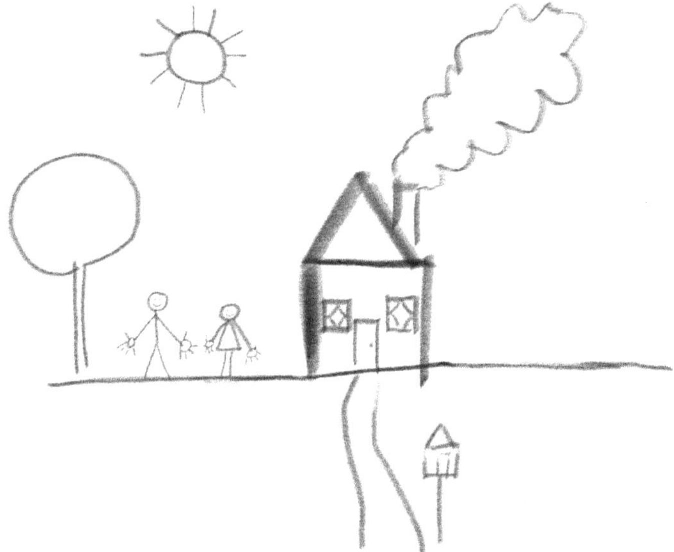

Compare your drawing to mine. Often it's amazing how similar they are. That's because of the common symbol language we all use to represent things. We all use the same word for 'house' and we all understand a *symbolic picture* for a house.

When we were much younger, we drew for fun and just expressed ourselves. No-one could tell what the things we drew were. We may have been frustrated when they couldn't interpret our visual language. They may have been frustrated too.

Then we got to a certain age of development. We realised that we could get an idea across to another person by using a universal symbol. A universal symbol is a bit like how words work, but with a drawing.

We all experienced the joy of someone understanding what we drew, so we repeated it again and again.

The problem with this is that the drawing has no relationship to reality — it is just a symbol.

Have you ever seen, in your life, a house that looked like the one you drew?

But everyone understands this symbol means a house.

Does the sun look like a yellow circle with lines coming out of it? Is the sun even yellow?

Do trees in nature ever look like a lollipop?

Memory Versus Eyes

Our Modern Mind, which is concerned with time and efficiency, responds quickly when you want to draw a tree.

Modern Mind says, 'Don't you worry your pretty little head about that. I have a super quick way for you to get through this task and get on with the next one. Time is money!

I've got a tree symbol in my archives so you can draw that one. Quick line for the trunk, circle on top, done! Quick! Draw it like this! Everyone will understand. Next!'

The only problem is that Modern Mind has served you up a representation of a tree: a lollipop, which looks nothing at all like the real tree.

Modern Mind is trying to save you time by giving you a symbol that everyone will interpret as a tree. But it's not the *real tree* that your eyes and your Zen Mind see!

We need to say, 'Thank you, Modern Mind, for your input, but go away. I am going to draw what I really see with my eyes, right here, right now, in the present.'

Logic Versus Eyes: Getting the Right Shapes

Mini Play Time

1. Put a mug in front of you on the table.

2. Draw it quickly on a piece of paper, or in your journal. (Don't read on until you've done this step).

3. Take a photo of the cup by lining up the camera right where your eyes were while you were drawing it.

4. Print out the photo and compare it to your drawing. It's important to have two flat, two-dimensional versions of the image to compare, so Modern Mind can be removed from the equation.

5. Check that the curve of the base in the photo matches the curve of the base you drew. Are the height and width the same proportions? Where is the handle of the cup? Is your drawing of the handle correct?

The most common thing beginners do when drawing any sort of cylindrical shape (a cup, a glass or a vase) is making the bottom shape too flat and horizontal.

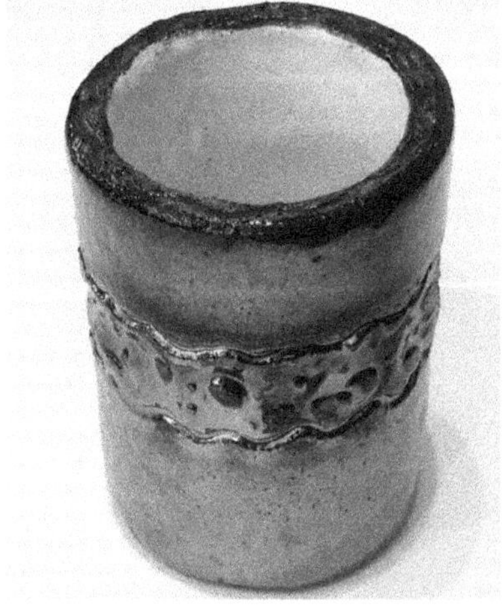
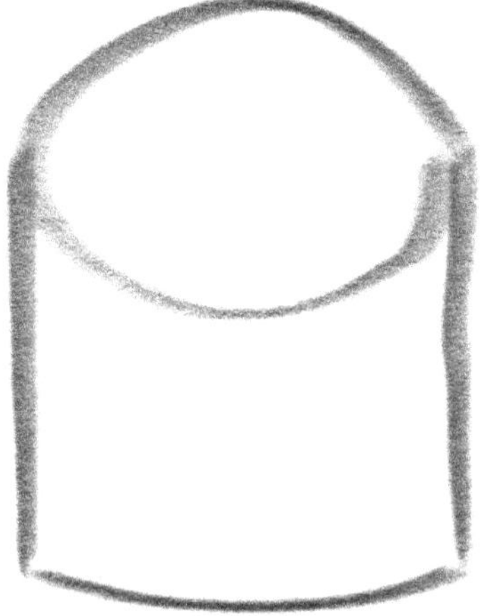

Modern Mind is getting in the way here as well.

How to Banish Modern Mind

Modern Mind uses logic to tell you what to draw.

For the base, it says, 'That base is sitting on a flat tabletop. So the base is flat. Don't draw it with a curve. How can it be curved when it's sitting on a flat tabletop?'

But if you measure the width and height of the curve, you will be surprised to see what the reality is.

Get into Zen Mind. Forget about memories and logic. Look very closely at the base of the cup.

Can you see the exact spot where the curve stops, where it meets the sides? I've marked the spot on the tabletop:

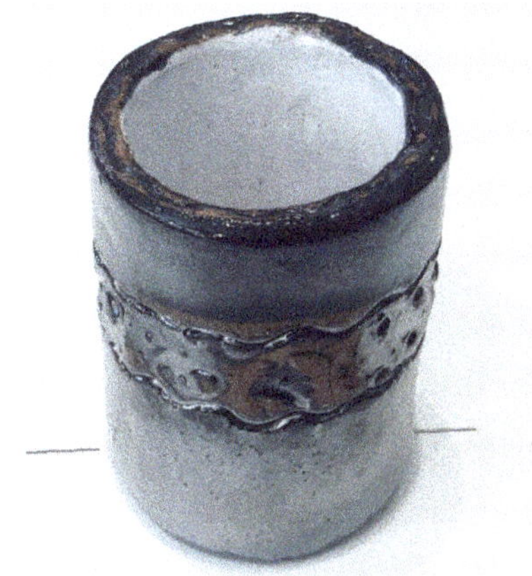

There's another way you can do this. Hold up your pencil horizontally in front of you and place it across the base where the bottom of the straight sides starts to go curvy.

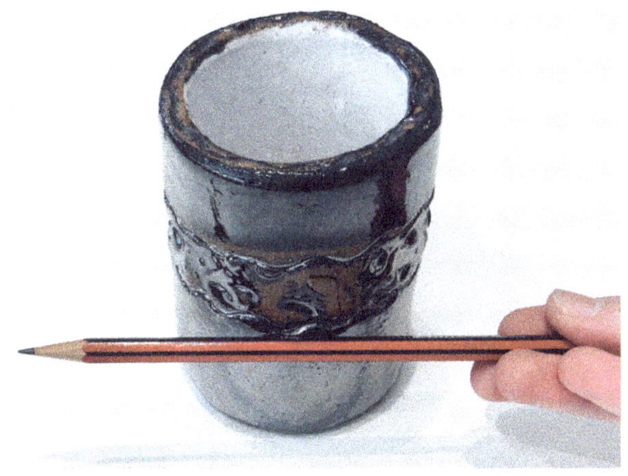

Look at how tall that curve is below the horizontal line made by your pencil. It may be a lot deeper a curve than you thought.

If you start to draw this deep curve on the paper, you may hear Modern Mind yell out, 'No, no, that's not right! The curve's not that deep!'

But you've got to say, 'Shut *up*, Modern Mind. You tell me nothing but lies. The measurements never lie.'

With any luck, Modern Mind will get so confused that it will run away and be quiet so you can get on and draw.

After you tell it that *the measurements never lie*, Modern Mind says, 'That's nuts, I don't understand, I'm outta here.'

Learning how to overrule Modern Mind while drawing a simple shape like this is essential to creating accurate drawings.

Drawing is All About Proportions

Your Modern Mind will tell you lies all day long.

It operates on memory and logic, aiming to help you cannon through tasks. You use it often in your busy life in this modern era where everything needs to be done fast and efficiently because we are all loaded down with too many things to do and not enough time to do them.

The way to shut down Modern Mind is to use measurements of proportions. If you get in the habit of measuring proportions, then Modern Mind will leave the room.

Measuring proportions is about finding halves, thirds, quarters in what you see.

Ask questions like:

- is this higher than that?

- is this wider than that?

- is this level with this or just below?

Look carefully at what you see in front of you, being mindful and bringing Zen Mind in. When you see what is really there, your drawings will improve.

Just remember, *the measurements never lie*.

More on this in the *Learn to Draw* book in the *Zen and the Art of Art* series[14].

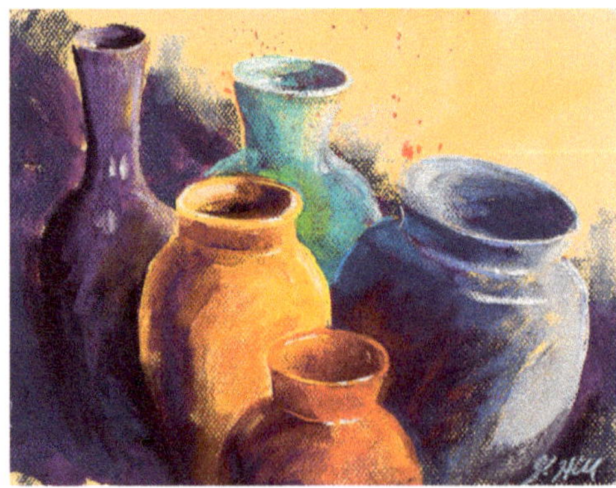

4-2 'Hot Pots IV' Pastel on Mi-Teintes Paper 42 x 29cm (16.5 x 11.5")

Play Time

Drawing a Glass with Your Zen Eyes

1. Set up a glass or tumbler on the table in front of you. Or draw the same mug from the Mini Play Time before but this time with your Zen Mind — eyes open and in the present here and now!

2. Draw it this time by using pencil measurements.

   a. Measure the height versus the width. Is it a third higher than it is wide? Is it the same? *Believe* the measurements and proportions: they do not lie.

   b. Measure how deep the curve is on the base. Draw it that way.

Having trouble understanding this technique? You are not alone.

So many people have trouble switching off Modern Mind. It's very understandable because we've been living all our lives in this fast-paced information era where time is so important. We're all time poor, so slowing down and taking time to see what's really there is not often honoured in our culture.

For more free drawing tips, see the website[14].

More Zen Mind Drawing

In all these Play Time exercises, take your time to see what's really there. Your eyes should be spending 80% of the time looking at the subject, and only 20% of the time looking at your paper. If it is about this amount, then you are more likely to be in Zen Mind.

In all drawings, use your pencil to measure up how wide and tall things are. Try to get the curve of things the way they actually are.

Keep trying to shut down Modern Mind as you go. Approach the following objects with the same steps as above.

1. Draw a mug, as shown above.

2. Draw a glass that's half-filled with water. Draw the water line.

3. Draw a saucer on the table in front of you.

If you were able to stay in Zen Mind for this Play Time, you may be surprised to see how much time went by. While we are in Zen Mind, we become unaware of time. It's a lovely floaty feeling when you get in 'the zone'. Once you've experienced it, you'll love it.

CHAPTER 5
WEAVING MARKS

*We have more possibilities available
in each moment than we realise.*

Thich Nhat Hanh

CHAPTER 5 CONTENTS

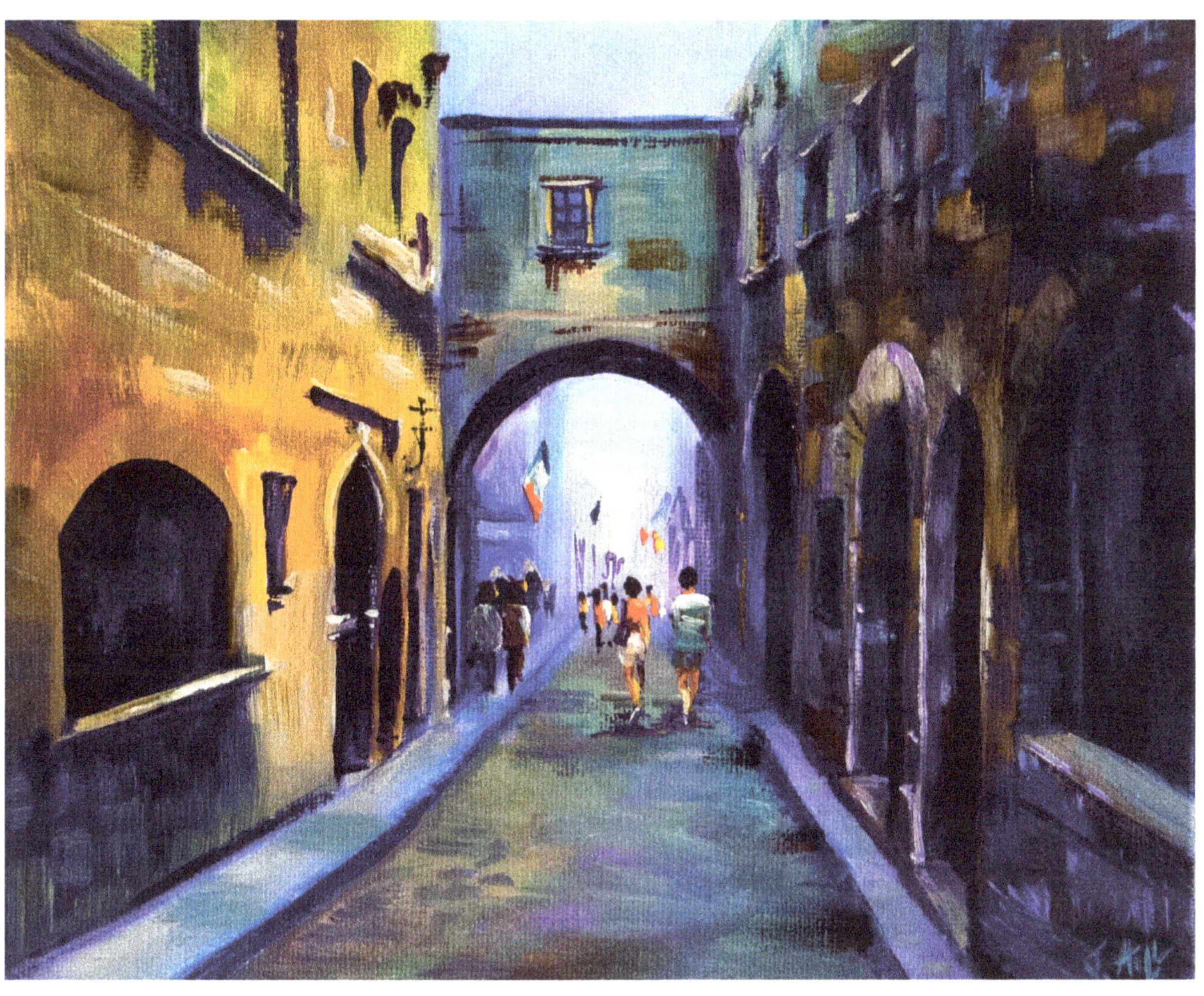

5-1 'Avenue of the Knights' (Rhodes, Greece) Oil on Canvas 25 x 20cm (10 x 8")
Chambers Collection, Eatons Hill, Queensland, Australia

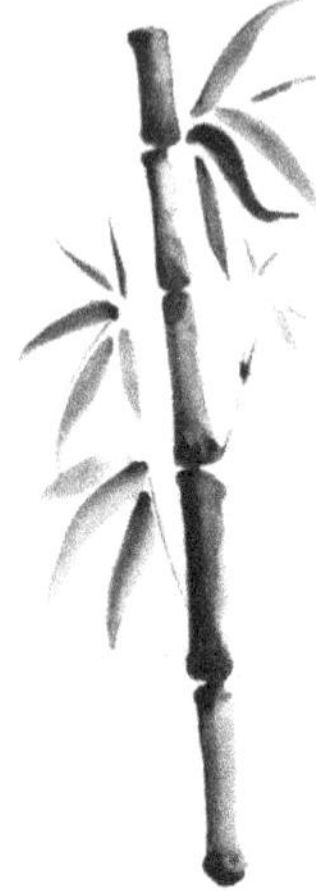

'With all my practice, I'm starting to paint better shapes.' Jojo sat in the studio and gazed over the balcony to the forest and mountains. 'But I have a terrible time painting trees! They look either like a child did them, or they look overworked. They don't look real at all.'

The Master waited.

'I love those beautiful trees painted by the impressionist masters and some of the modern masters. But I just can't get the same shapes, however hard I try,' she said.

The Master thought for a moment. 'Mastery of the trees comes from knowing the wood of your brush,' he said.

Jojo looked down at the brush in her hand.

'Miles in the brush,' smiled The Master.

'So it's about practice again,' said Jojo.

'Yes. But first, the learning,' said The Master.

'Ok. How do I start?'

'Before we learn the swordsmanship of the brush, let's start with the simpler mastery of the stick, or pencil,' said The Master.

Making Marks

When you get a brush or pencil or stick in your hand, you can make so many marks — more than you initially may think of. By mastering as many marks as you possibly can, you can create art in whatever style you want.

You will also be able to get away with buying and using fewer brushes. In some cases you may paint a full painting with only one brush!

By developing mastery of the brush (or pencil or stick) you can paint beautiful trees, foliage, randomness in nature, shadows, highlights, lines and shapes.

Mark making is one of the most important skills of a confident sketcher or painter.

With experience, you will end up preferring some marks over others. This will be an ingredient people will recognise as you develop your own *style*.

Pencil Magic

When you have a pencil in your hand, there are more ways to hold it than just in a writing grip. That grip only allows you to make a single type of mark, using the pointed tip.

Many beginners press too hard when using this grip.

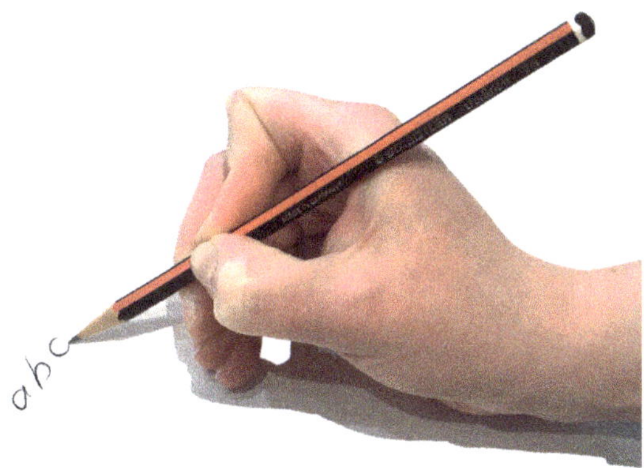

Try this different grip. Lay the pencil down on the table, pointing upwards, away from you:

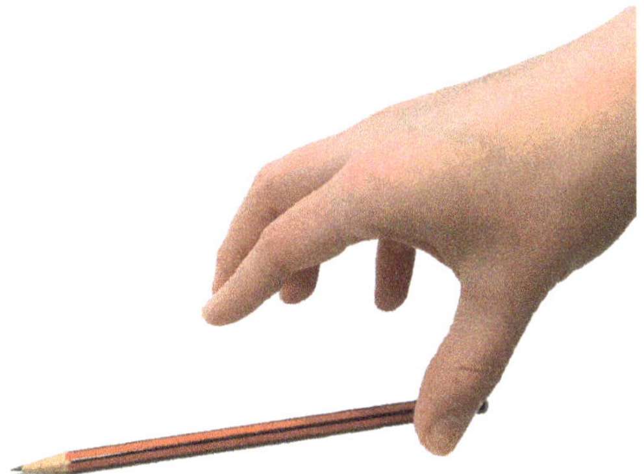

With your fingertips, pick up the pencil. Roll it between your fingertips. Does it feel like a much lighter grip?

Drawing this way is like using an overhand grip, where your hand is over the top of the pencil. (With the traditional writing grip, your hand is under the pencil.)

You can draw and shade easily using the side of the sharpened lead. And by varying the pressure and angle of the pencil, you can create all sorts of different marks.

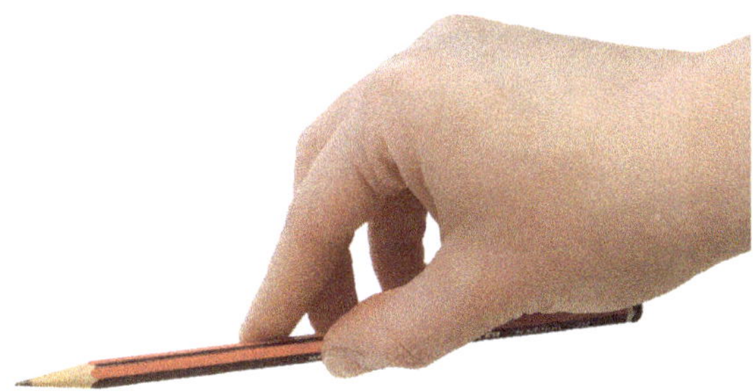

I call this the artists' grip.

You can vary your pressure on the paper more easily and you can freely tilt the angle. I find it instantly gets me to apply a much lighter pressure.

Try thinking of it this way. Imagine the pencil is very delicate, and if you grip too tightly it may snap in two. That may help you to get the feeling of holding it correctly.

When you get comfortable using the artists' grip, you can shift your hand towards the back of the pencil, giving you a longer implement to use.

Sometimes you will slip back to the writing grip. That's ok. Always try to draw and sketch softly, which means holding the pencil in a very light grip.

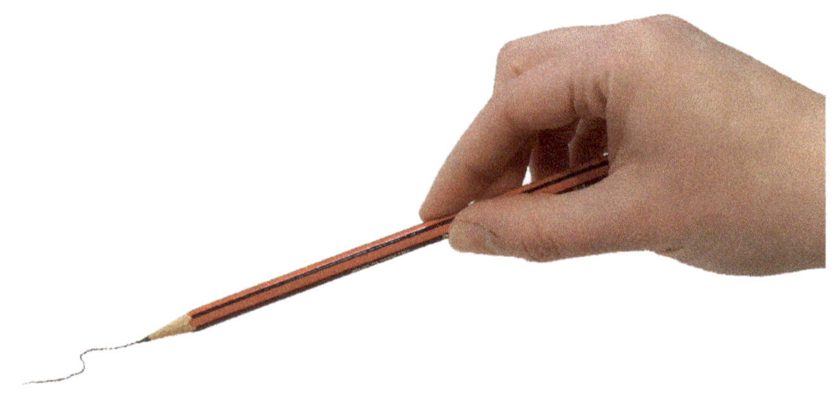

Start practising marks like these:

Change the pressure of your pencil and the angle that you tilt it on. See the huge difference in the marks you can create?

Your pencil can be held vertically up from the paper (perpendicular, or at right angles to the paper). This gives a sharp, pinpoint mark on the paper.

You can also tilt the pencil down so it's lying nearly horizontal. The side of the lead makes a wide mark that's more like shading.

Charcoal Magic

Charcoal is a lovely medium to play with, for mark making.

You don't just use the charcoal as a stick to make marks with the pointed end. (I call this using the charcoal as a pencil.)

You can make so many more marks by 'painting' with the charcoal!

Charcoal sticks are supposed to be broken into pieces. The length of the piece gives you the width of your 'brushstroke'.

Start by breaking off a piece that is around 1 – 2cm (½") long. Don't worry if it shatters a little; charcoal doesn't cost much! Just break it again. I grab really firmly on each side of the break point I want, then snap it quickly while still holding tight. This way I get less shattering and cleaner breaks.

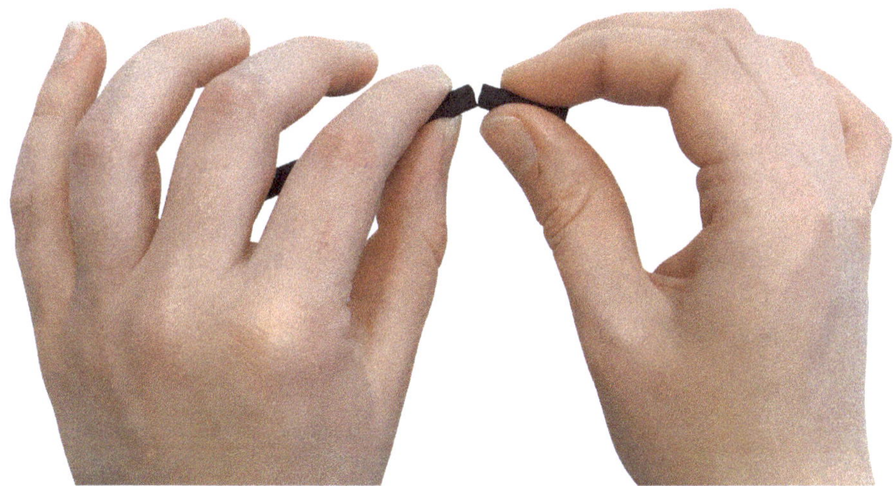

Now you have a shorter stick that has two very sharp ends (you can make sharp, dark marks with those). But you've also got this nice long barrel to 'paint' with.

Hold the stick in a pincer grip like this:

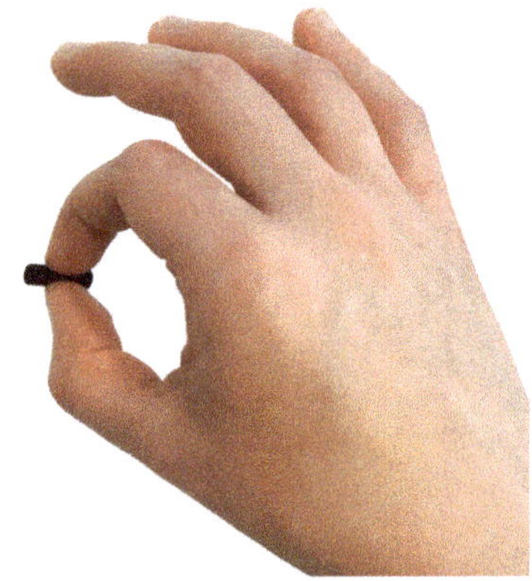

and paint with a downwards stroke while holding it this way:

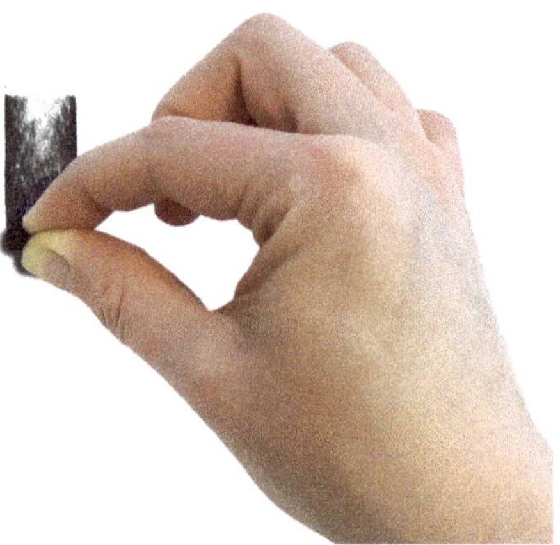

Can you see how the length of the stick piece gives you the width of your brushstroke? You can fill in an area with shading quickly, using the barrel side of the stick rather than the point:

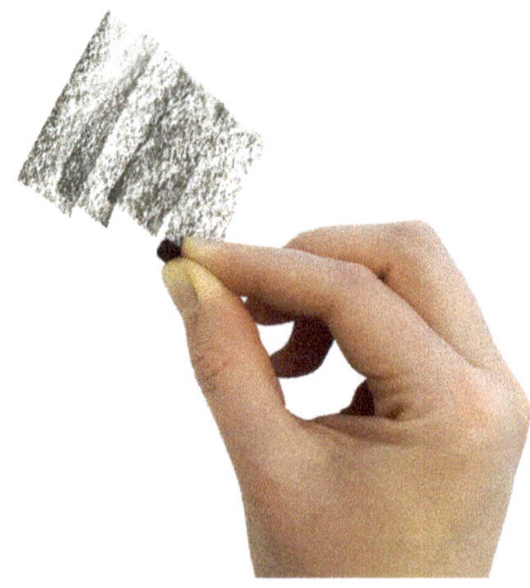

You can also make what I call a Sword Stroke mark by cutting it sideways along the barrel like this:

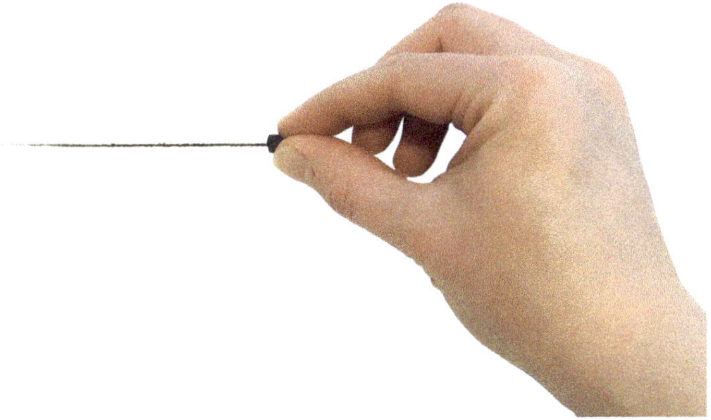

Then you can make a mark by tilting the charcoal up with more pressure on the tip but less on the barrel.

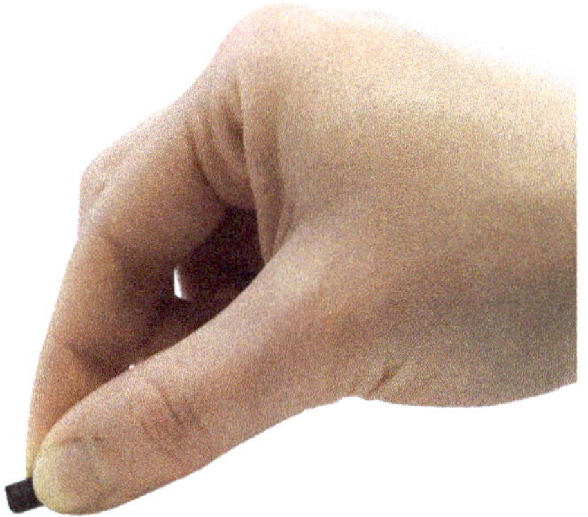

This gives you a beautiful gradient mark:

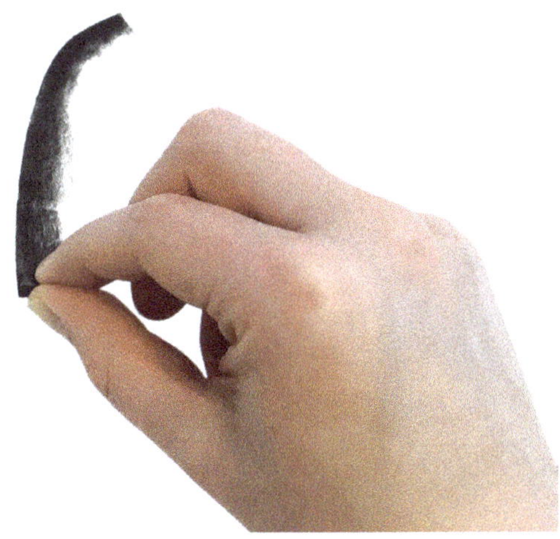

This mark is wonderful for putting shadows underneath objects. It gives you a hard edge and a soft edge:

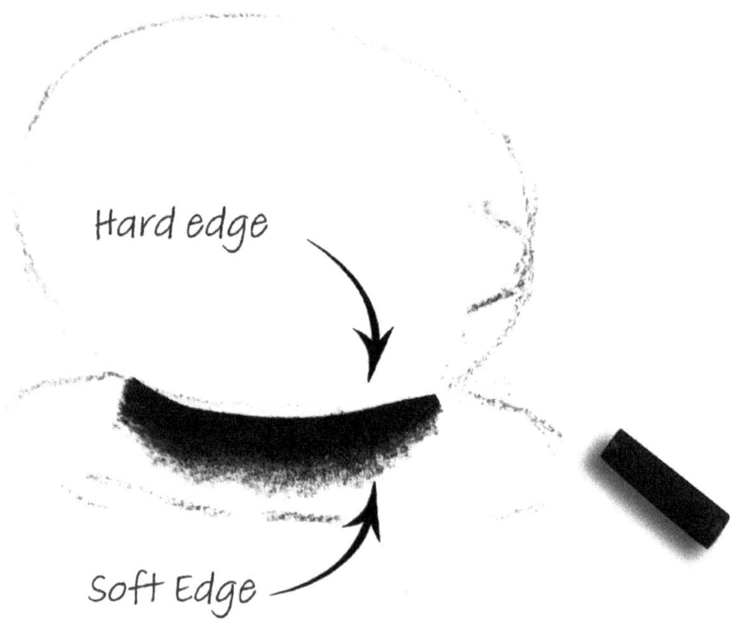

This soft and hard edge gives nice depth under this lemon. Here's my finished sketch:

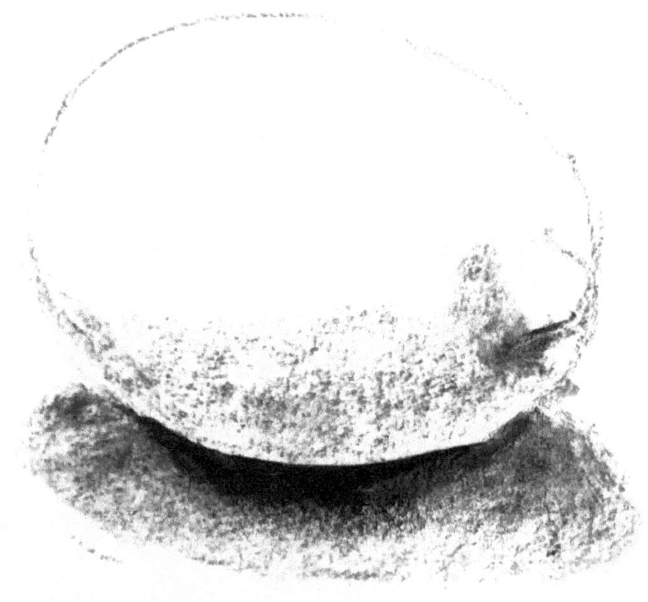

Even as you move the charcoal across the paper (or canvas) you can twist and turn, tilt and flatten as you go and create beautiful marks.

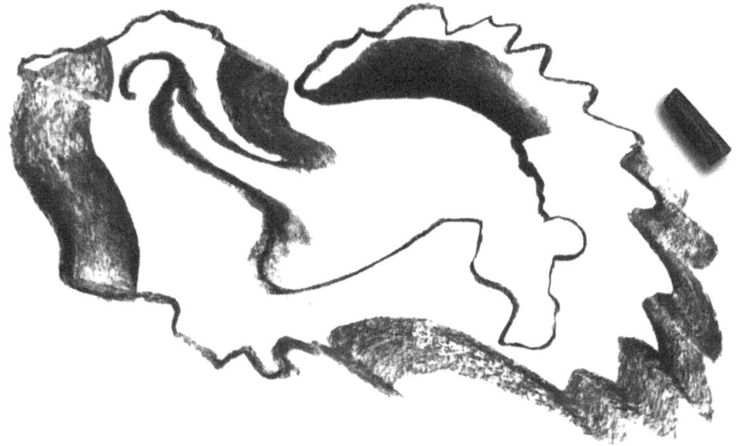

Another thing I love about charcoal is being able to lift it off the paper with an eraser. You can use either a white plastic eraser (cut these into fine sharp blades) or a kneadable eraser, rolled and pinched into as sharp a blade as you want[15].

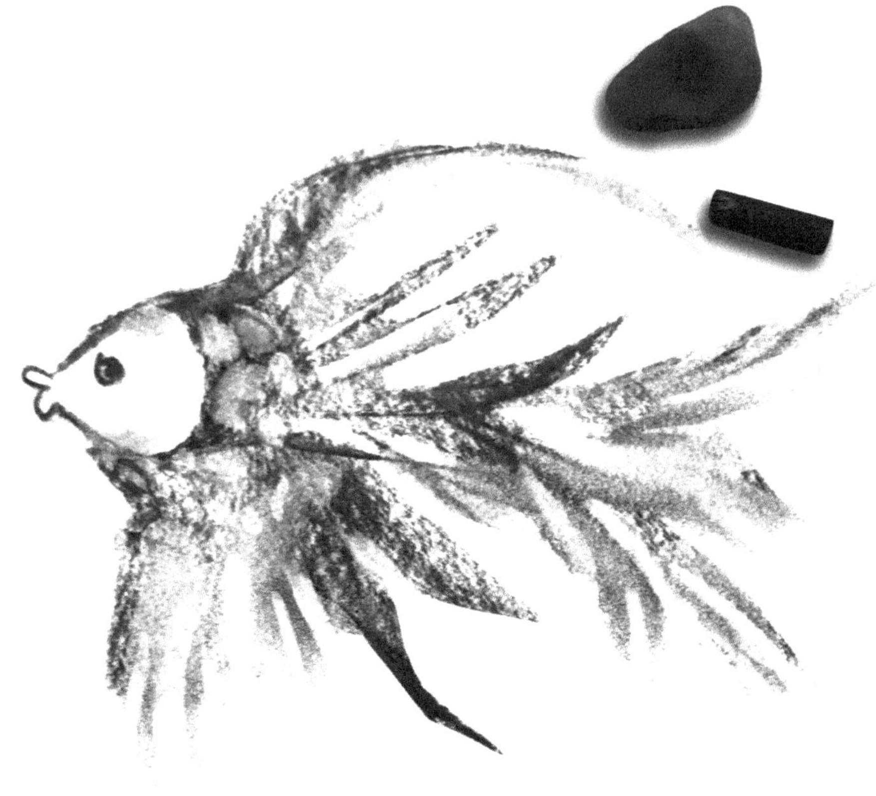

Pastel Magic

Pastel is just like charcoal, except with colour added. This is when we're talking about dry pastel or chalk pastel. Everything that applies in Charcoal Magic applies to pastel.

Those precious sticks look so lovely with their pretty labels when you bring them home from the art shop, don't they? But the first thing you should do with them is tear the label and break the stick, so you can use it to 'paint' brushstrokes in your painting.

For this reason I like to say pastel *painting* rather than pastel drawing. A great pastel painting can sometimes look a lot like an oil painting.

Oil pastel is similar, but it cannot be removed with an eraser.

Ink Pen Magic

If you use a fine liner pigment ink pen, you can practise making crosshatch marks for shading. Try one with about a 0.5 mm nib.

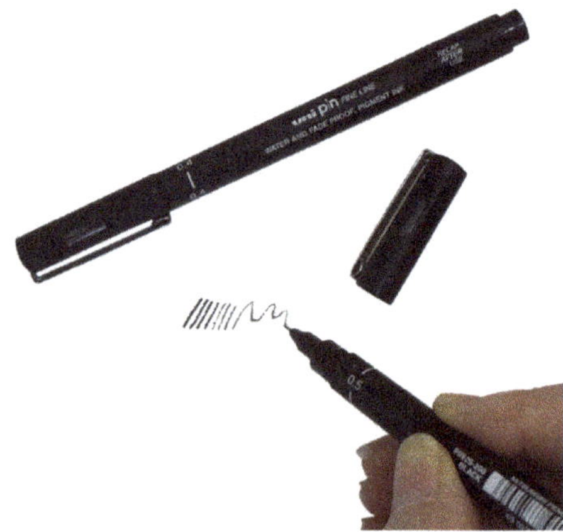

I love using an ink pen like this in my journal when I'm feeling brave. This is for the bold, because of course there's no chance of erasing anything!

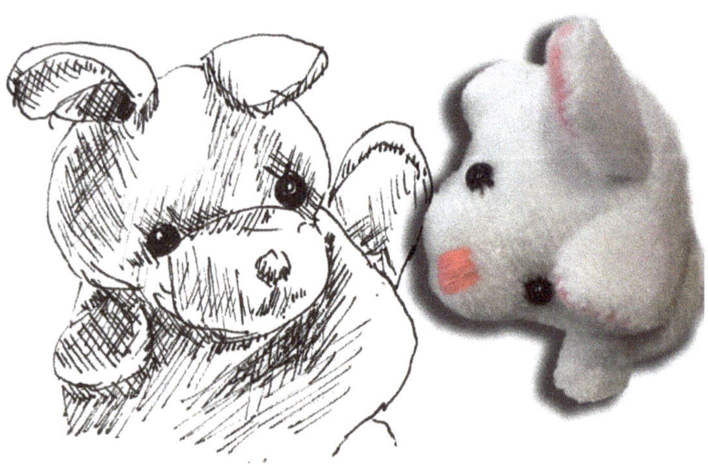

I like drawing with it just like I do with pencil — lightly at first, then with darker lines as I become more confident with the shapes.

A great way to learn crosshatching is to draw a shaded bar like the one below. Overlay each set of pen strokes in different directions so that the areas get darker and darker.

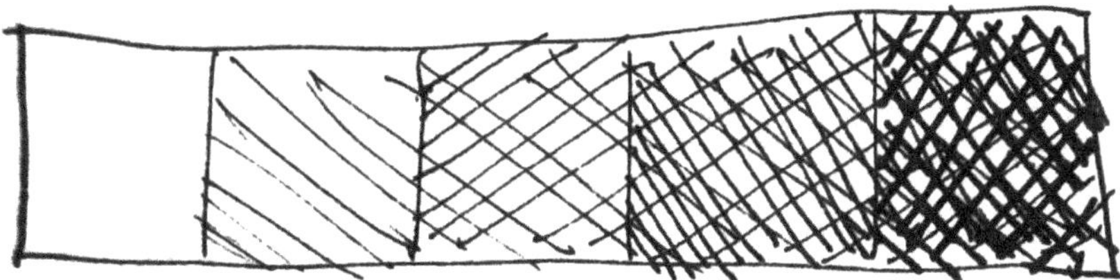

Crosshatching is fun to do and looks great once it's finished. Take time to practise your crosshatching until it feels easy.

You can use crosshatching with a very sharp pencil, too. A retractable pencil is a great choice for this. If you use a normal wooden pencil you will have to sharpen it often to keep the tip small and the lines widths even.

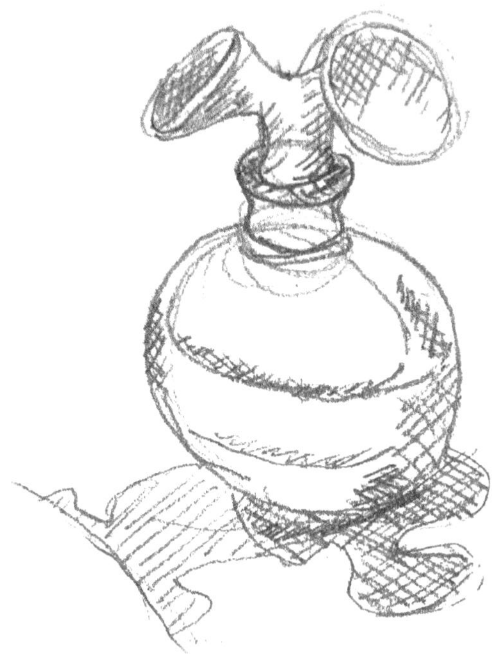

Play Time

Gather all the 'stick' materials you own: pencils, charcoal sticks, pastel sticks.

1. If you have pencils, try using a soft pencil (such as an HB) to make the marks described in the chapter. Then try the same exercise with a much softer (darker) pencil, such as a 2B, 4B or 8B.

2. Charcoal is so much fun to play with for making marks.

    a. If you don't own charcoal, I recommend you get some! It is not expensive to buy. Buy some natural willow charcoal sticks.

    b. Try making the marks described in the chapter using your willow charcoal.

    c. Do you own any compressed charcoal sticks? These perform very differently from the natural willow charcoal. Try the same marks with these sticks and compare the differences from the willow charcoal.

    d. Try blending the charcoal in different spots, using your finger or a torchon[16].

    e. Use a kneadable eraser or a plastic eraser to rub out parts of the charcoal you have drawn.

3. Do you own any sticks of colour pastel? Try making marks with these.

CHAPTER 6
BRUSH MAGIC

*It's all about reprogramming our minds
to focus more on what brings us joy.*

Alaric Hutchinson

CHAPTER 6 CONTENTS

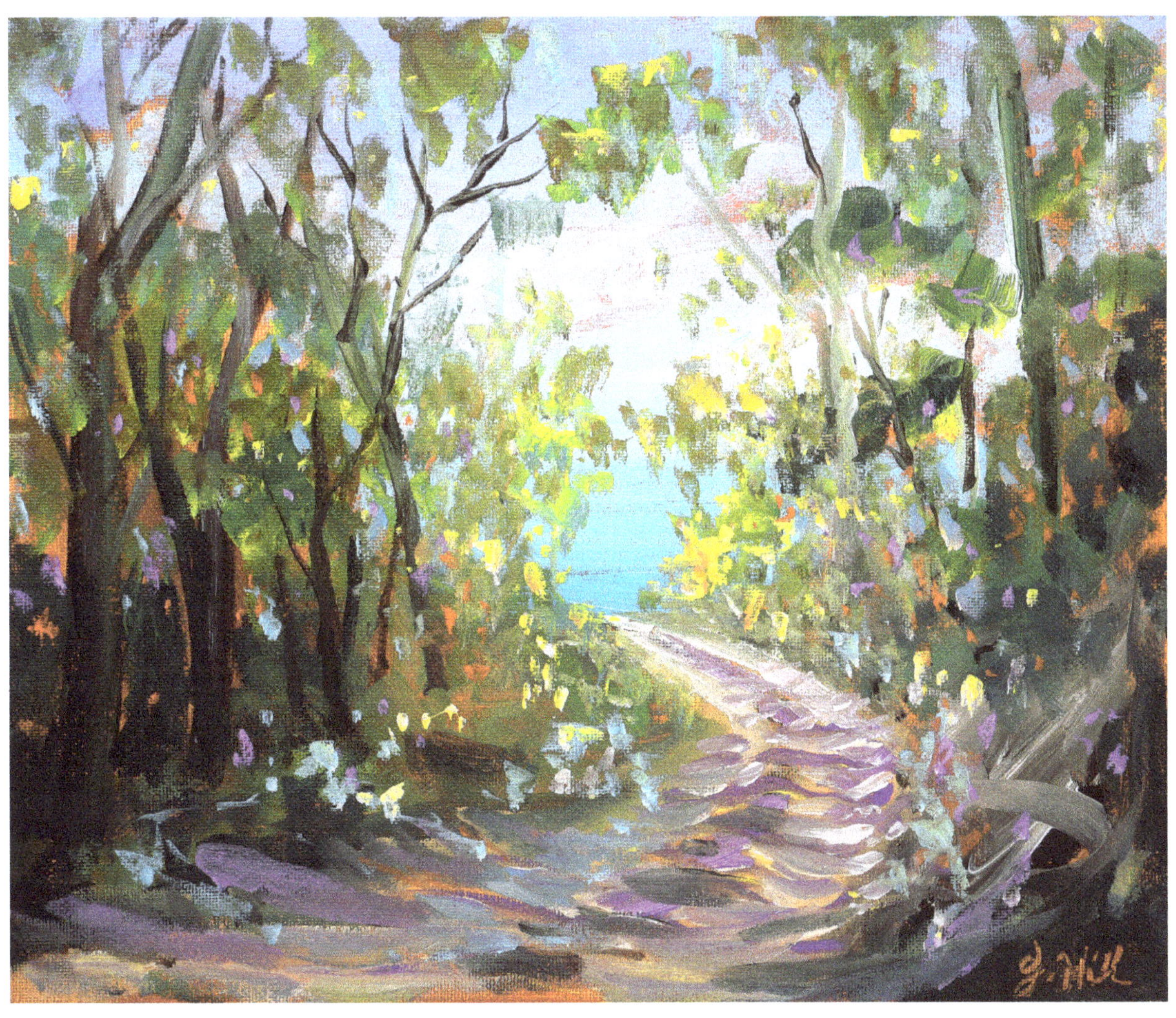

6-1 'Walk to the Ocean' (Fraser Island) Acrylic on Canvas 30 x 25cm (12 x 10")
Daily Artwork No 198 for 2018.

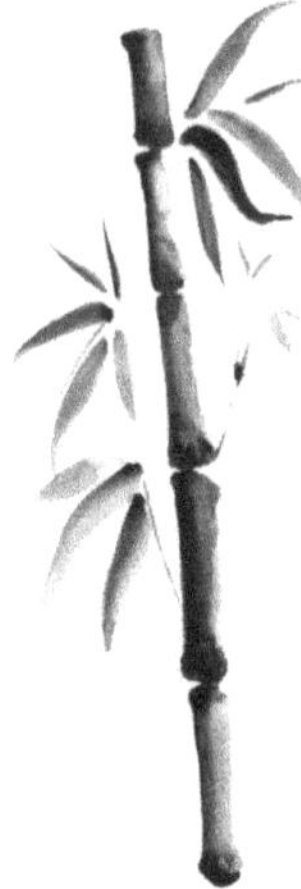

'I love all the marks I can make with the pencil and charcoal,' said Jojo. 'I had no idea such simple tools could do so many things! This is wonderful!'

'You have done well with the stick,' said The Master. 'Now you are ready to learn how to wield the sword. Would you like to learn what the brush is capable of?' he asked, smiling.

'Of course,' answered Jojo. 'I can't wait!'

'Patience, Little Grasshopper. In a moment, I will open your mind to some techniques and you must practise them.

'Eventually, your brush will become an extension of your hand, and your hand an extension of your mind,' he said. 'Your mind will see a stroke and it will appear on the surface without your conscious effort.'

'Do you mean without Modern Mind getting in the way?' asked Jojo.

The Master nodded. 'Zen Mind will see a stroke before it happens. And you will see it appear on the paper without Modern Mind getting in the way.'

'Wow,' said Jojo. 'I'm nowhere near there.'

'Trust that you will be, Little Grasshopper,' said The Master. 'Start with knowing the wood of the brush before you paint the trees.

'Find out how many marks you can make with the brush. Then practise them until they flow as easily as water flows down a mountain.'

All About Brushes

Bristles — Hair types

There are two categories of brush hair, natural hair and synthetic.

Natural hair brushes are made from animal hair, while synthetic brush bristles are made from manufactured materials. The modern synthetic brushes have come a long way. The quality of some of these surpasses the old natural hair brushes. As an added advantage, they don't deteriorate with age or come under the attack of moths!

If you are buying a synthetic brush, don't go for the cheapest one. These sometimes have no spring in the bristle when they are wet.

Bristle Brushes

Bristle brushes are natural hair made from pig (apparently it's the hair from their ears — poor pigs). For this reason they are also known as *hog bristle* brushes.

The Chungking Bristle brush is made from the hair of hogs raised in the region of Chongqing in China.

Bristle brushes are extremely tough. You can use them to really scrub paint on without damaging the brush.

Unfortunately, the term *bristle* is also used to describe the hair on any brush — for example we say synthetic bristles.

Springiness

The spring in the brush is important for you to get a nice crisp brush mark. You don't want to make a mark with paint and have your brush stay in the bent shape. You want it to spring back into its original shape after you've made a mark.

A bright brush (usually flat shape) is one with shorter, springier bristles (hairs). The bristles spring back firmly so you can make crisp 'bright' strokes. You will find it difficult to do long strokes of colour with these brushes though.

The opposite of a bright brush is a long-bristled brush. The bristles are much softer and hold a lot more paint, so you can do longer strokes of colour with these.

The Ferrule

The part of the brush that grips the bristle hairs is called the ferrule[17]. It's often stainless steel or chrome steel in good brushes.

Brush Shapes

Brushes come in many shapes, which all make different marks.

Round		This brush can make so many marks, from tiny dots to lines and broad swoops of colour. It's a good all-rounder brush if you were limited to only one brush. A good round brush will taper to a very sharp point. The cheaper ones that have flatter points are better for stencilling than fine art.
Flat		The flat brush makes sharp, crisp marks. It's one of my favourites. I use it when I want to create loose, impressionist paintings with crisp edges on the brush marks. Left: Bright brush Right: Long-bristle brush

Filbert		This brush makes a rounded paint mark that looks like soft, round fingerprints.
Angle, Dagger, Doe Foot or Deer Foot		These brushes are great for painting into sharp tight corners.
Fan		I'm not a big fan of the fan. Bristle fans are popular for painting textures such as grass, but I find they just don't make the grass random or natural enough for my liking. A natural hair fan brush can be used for soft blending.
Rigger or Liner		A rigger or liner brush is essential to have on hand. It's great for painting long thin strokes, such as boat masts or fence wire or thin branches. It's the one you reach for when signing your art.

Other brushes are usually named for the type of hair in them. Such as:
- the *mop* brush (a soft, very absorbent round brush)
- the *hake* brush (a very soft flat goat hair brush)

Brush Sizes

There is no such thing as an international standard (yet) for the numbering on brushes to give their sizes. Every different brand and different type of brush have their own numbering system.

A Number 10 brush in one brand may be the same size as a Number 5 brush in another.

In most brands the numbers also have no relation to the inches or mm size of the brush. You need the actual measurement of the brush width (which not many websites display). If only websites showed the image of each brush with a ruler alongside!

The best way to compare sizes is to go into an art shop and get the brushes in your hands.

Brush Handles

You can buy short-handled or long-handled brushes.

- Use the short-handled ones when you need to do fine, close-up work, sitting down.

- Use the long-handled ones if you want to paint from further away. Like when you're painting oil or acrylic on a larger canvas, and you're standing up at an easel.

- You can also buy large flat hog bristle brushes that have short handles. Use these when you need to really push the paint onto the canvas and scrub it in. The short handle makes it easier to put muscle into the job.

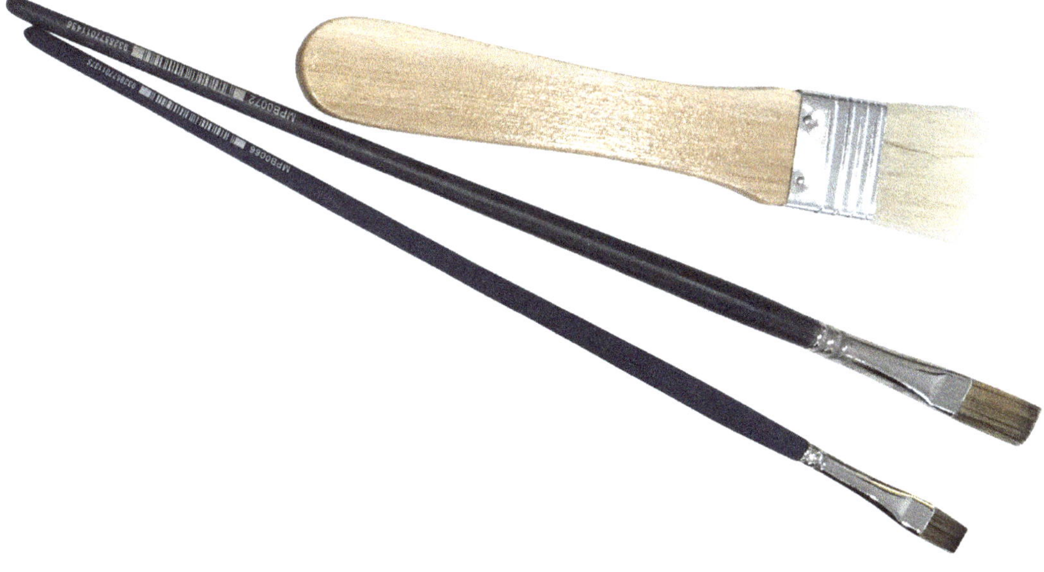

Keep Your Brushes Separate

I love to use synthetic brushes for oil, acrylics and watercolour. The only natural hair brushes I buy now are hog bristle brushes and Eastern Brushes.

I keep my brushes for each different medium separated in labelled brush wallets. I have one wallet for watercolour, one for acrylic and one for oil.

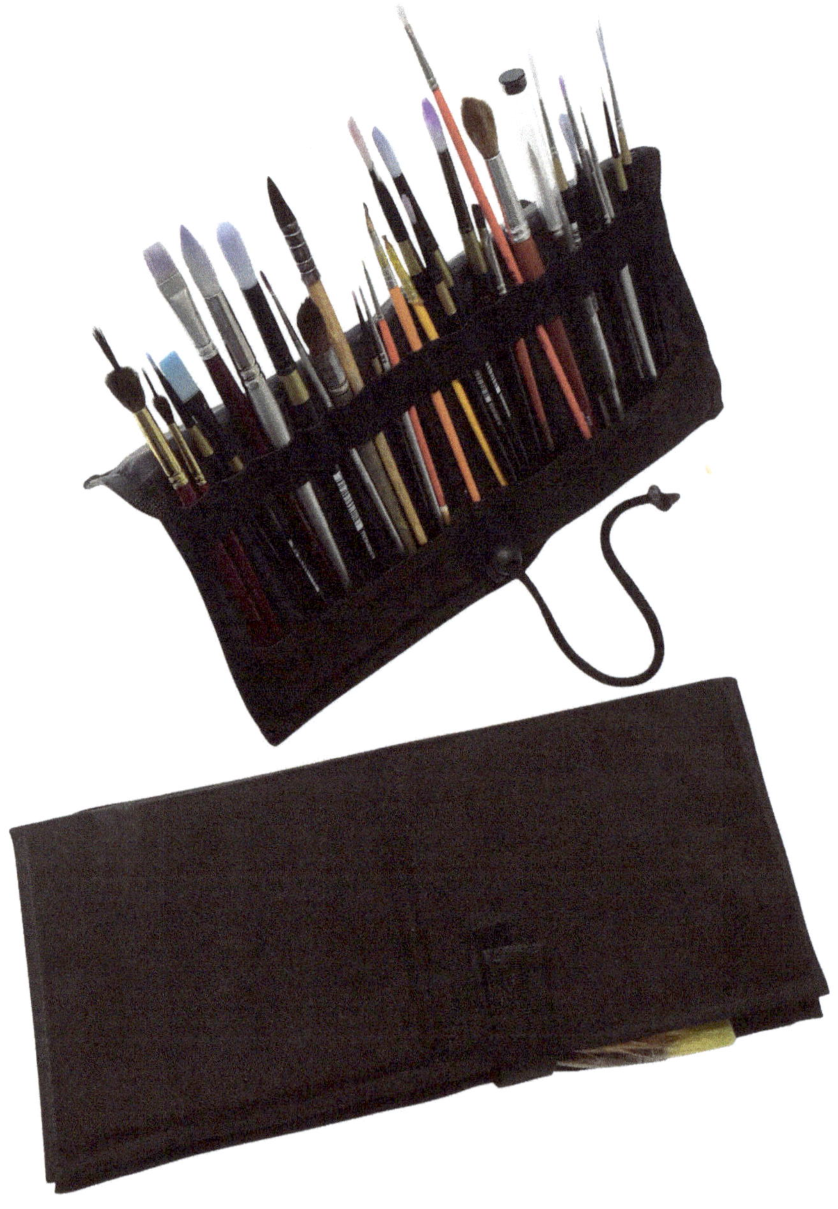

You don't want to use one brush with different mediums, no matter how well you clean it in between.

Making Marks

There are so many marks you can make with a brush! Such as Tip, Flop, Run, Dance, Flick and Floomp.

Yes, I made most of those names up. You probably won't find them in the Academy of Fine Arts dictionary (if there is such a thing).

It's helpful to think of the hairs (bristles) of the brush as fingers and the tips of the bristles as fingertips. The bunch of hair making up the brush end is what I think of as the hand.

Load up your brush with a little paint and try these basic brushstrokes.

Tip

The Tip mark is when you tap the *fingertip* of the bristles on the paper in one spot. Your brush is held vertical, at right angles to the paper.

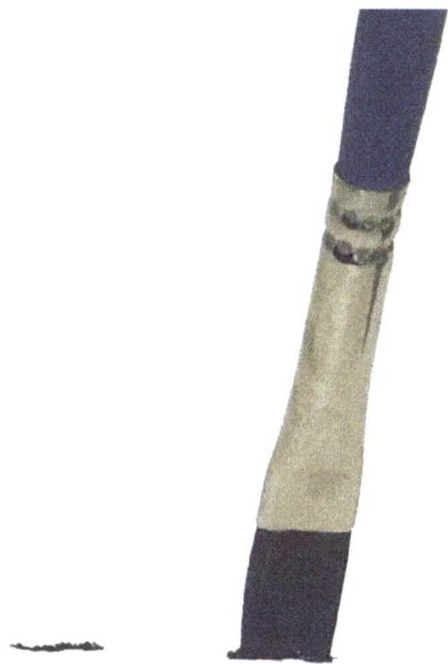

You make this mark on the paper with the *tip* of the bristles, just lightly pressed straight down without moving sideways.

Different shaped brushes will produce different sorts of marks.

Flop

A Flop mark is when you lay the *hand* of the bristles down flat on the paper in one spot. It's like pressing or dabbing the paint onto the paper.

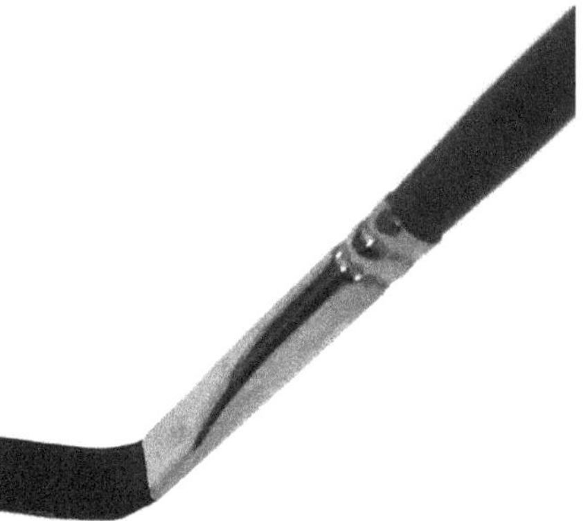

With a round brush there are not too many variations, but with other shapes of brushes it gets more interesting.

Here's a flat Flop mark using a flat brush:

But the Flop can be done a number of ways. You can also turn the brush on its side and Flop:

Here are some other shapes you can make with a flat brush:

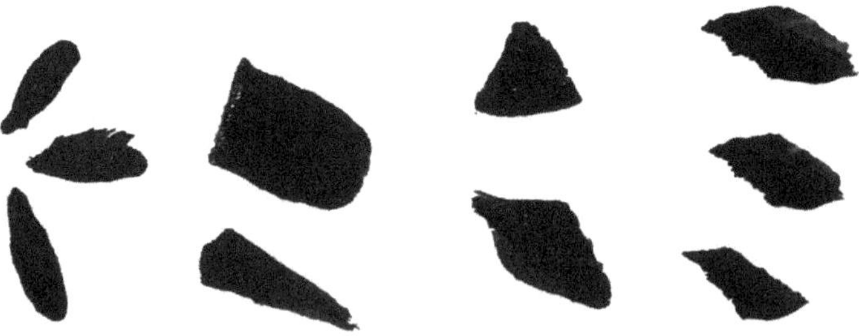

Try it out with different brushes. These daisy petal flops were made with a round brush:

And so were these little tree flops:

Run

A Run is a simple brush stroke that you already know. Draw the brush in a straightish line across the paper.

This simple mark has more options than you may think.

Flat Stroke

This is what the brush is designed for. It's an ordinary brush stroke across the paper.

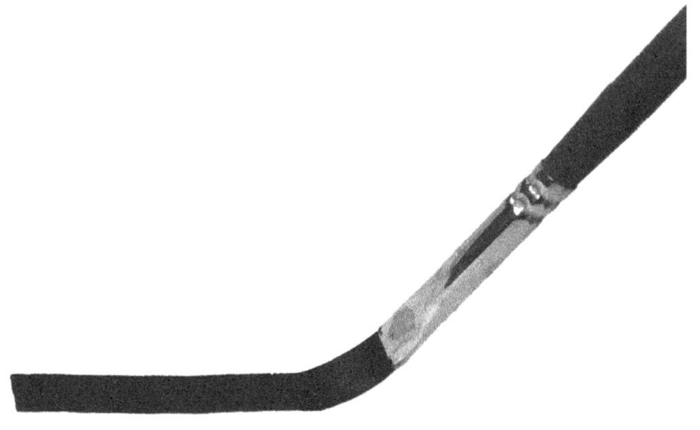

Sword Stroke

That's me making up names again. A Sword Stroke is what I call an icy sharp sideways swish, with the brush held vertically, at right angles to the paper.

Here's that same brush again, making a sideways Sword Stroke:

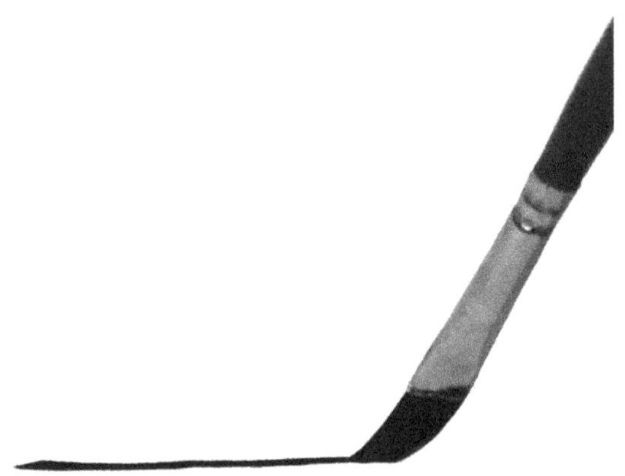

Broad Stroke

This is the name I give to making a broad flat stroke. It's not really what the brush is designed for, but it's an essential stroke to learn if you want to paint trees using the Floomping technique.

This stroke is when you Flop the brush down on the paper and then Run it along, sideways to the bristles. If you have a long-bristled brush, this allows you to use the length of the bristles to get an even wider brushstroke.

You should have the brush handle held low to the paper.

Here's the mark that's made by the same brush, this time making an extra wide Broad Stroke:

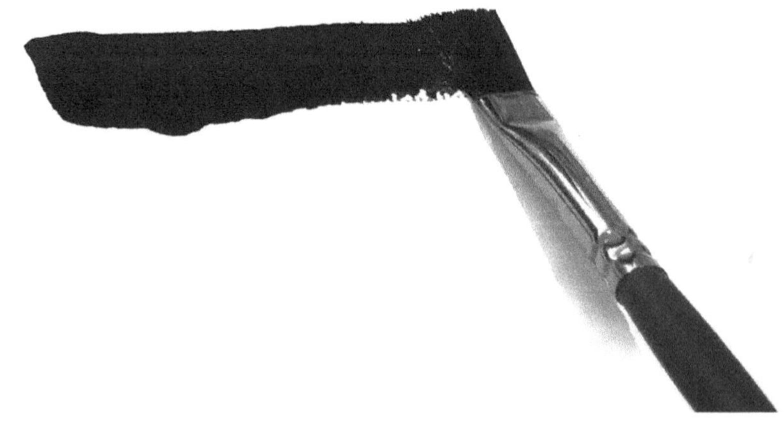

Dance

The Dance stroke is when you Run the brush across the paper, but add some twists and turns, dips and rolls.

Rock 'n' roll the brush across the surface.

Twist and turn your hand as you draw the brush across the paper.

Twist the brush as well — if it is a flat or shaped brush, a different mark is made.

Just like in dancing, you can throw a couple of dips (Flops) in there too! Press and lift your brush as you go to make different width marks.

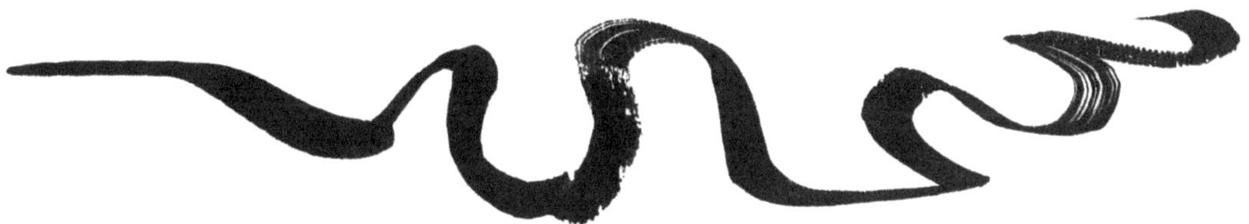

The marks you make can be rhythmic (repetitive) or random (uneven).

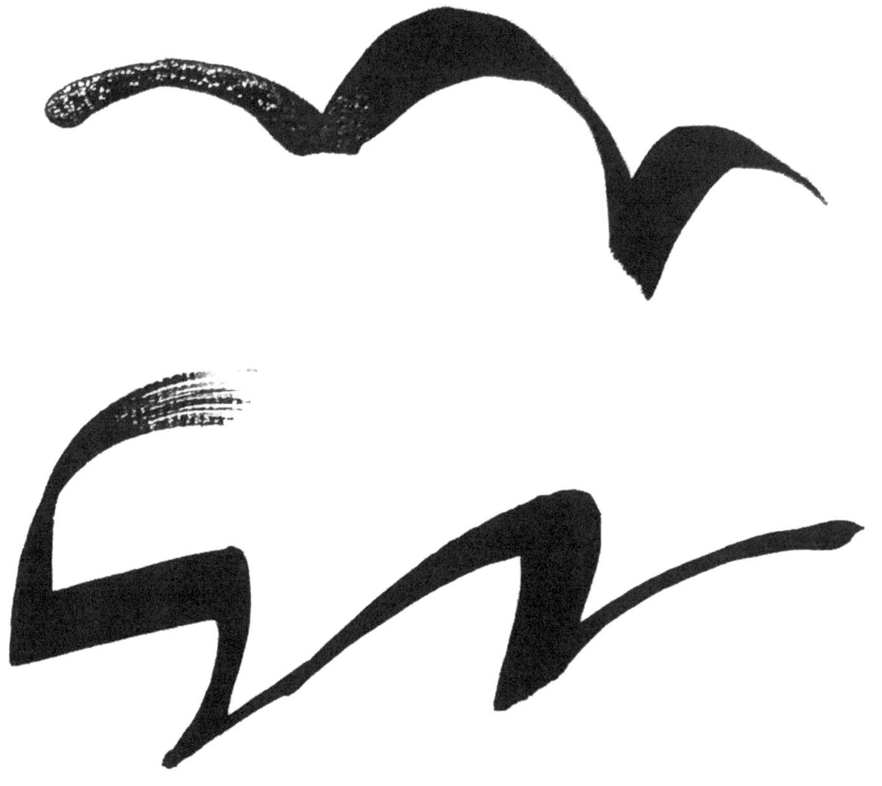

Flick

You can Flick the brush as you lift it off the paper. Choose which direction to go in while you flick to make different marks.

Try adding some Flicks to your Tips and Flops!

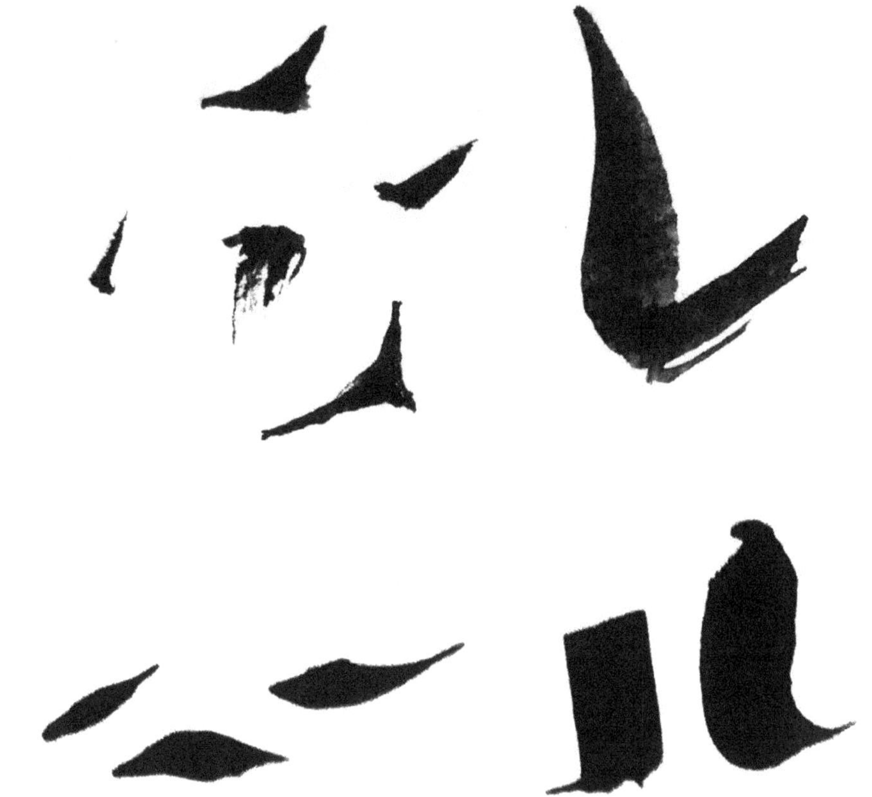

You can also add Flicks to the end of longer brushstrokes like Runs and Dances:

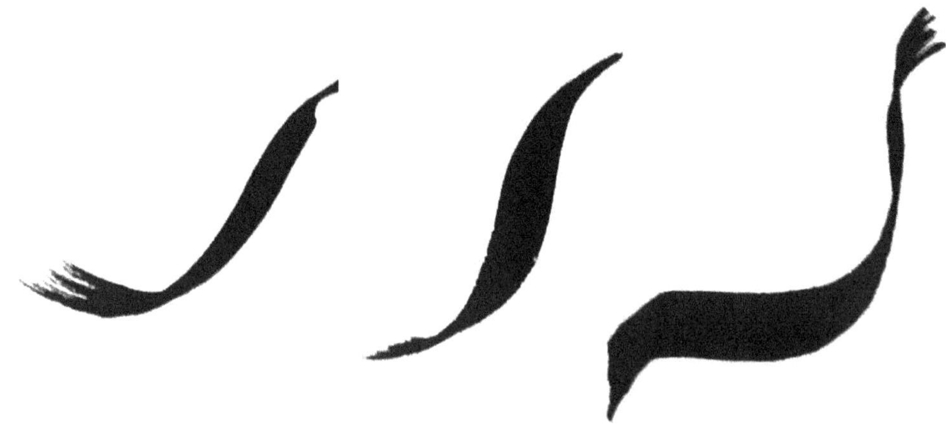

Floomp

Floomping is a word I made up to mean the brush stroke for painting an impressionist clump of foliage.

Here's an example of a Floomp brushstroke with some branches added:

When painting in a loose impressionist style, it is better to paint *foliage* rather than every *leaf*.

The Joy of Eastern Brush

In Eastern Brush, the pressure applied as the brush moves across the paper is all important.

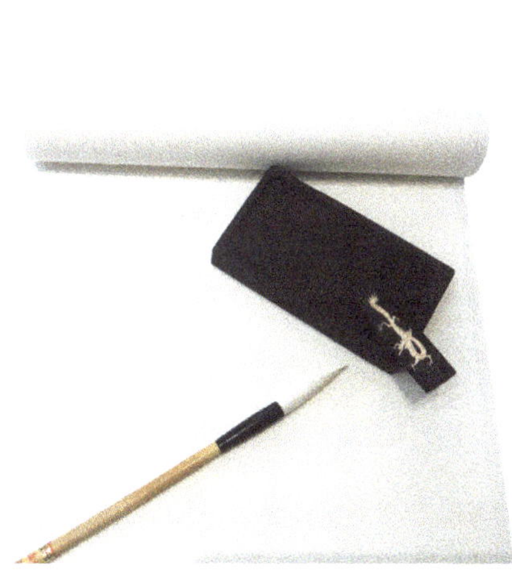

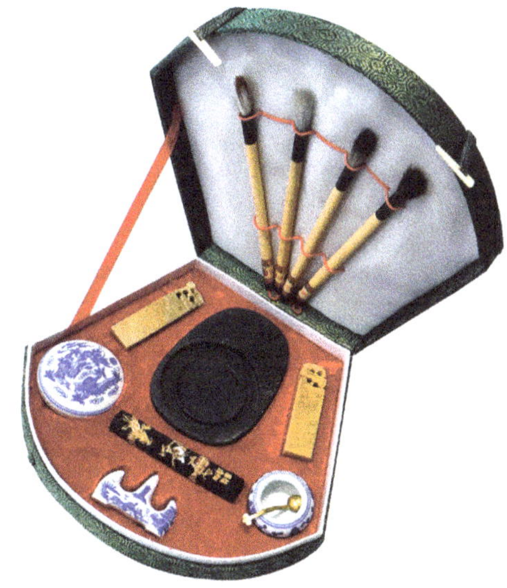

Usually the brush is let down into the beginning of the mark with the tip. Then you press into the paper to make a wider mark as the stroke continues:

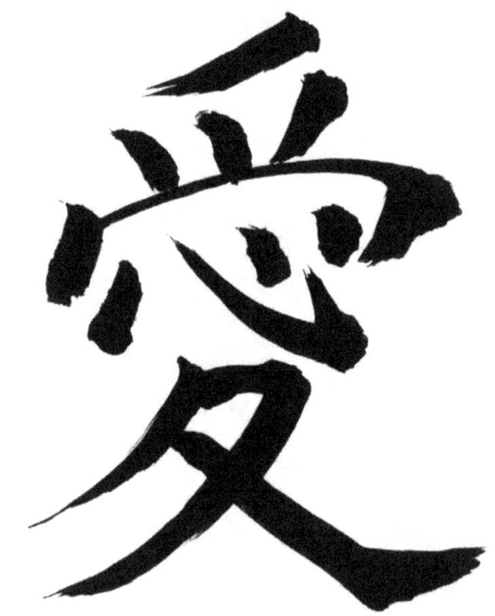

6-2 'Love' Eastern ink on rice paper 20 x 30cm (8x12")
Collection of artist.

Another nuance in Eastern Brush is how the ink is loaded on the brush. This is to achieve a gradient along the bristles from light to dark:

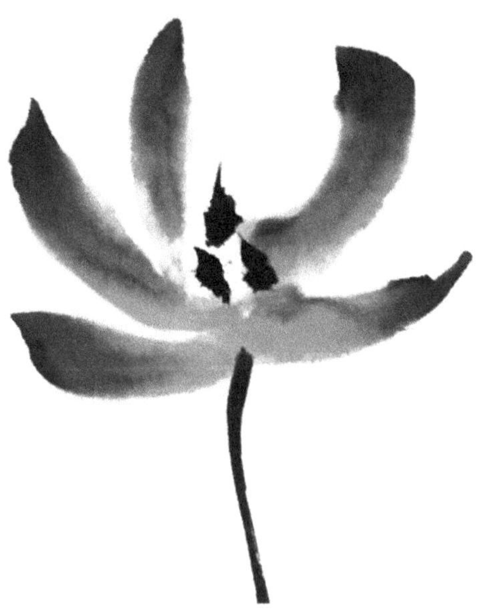

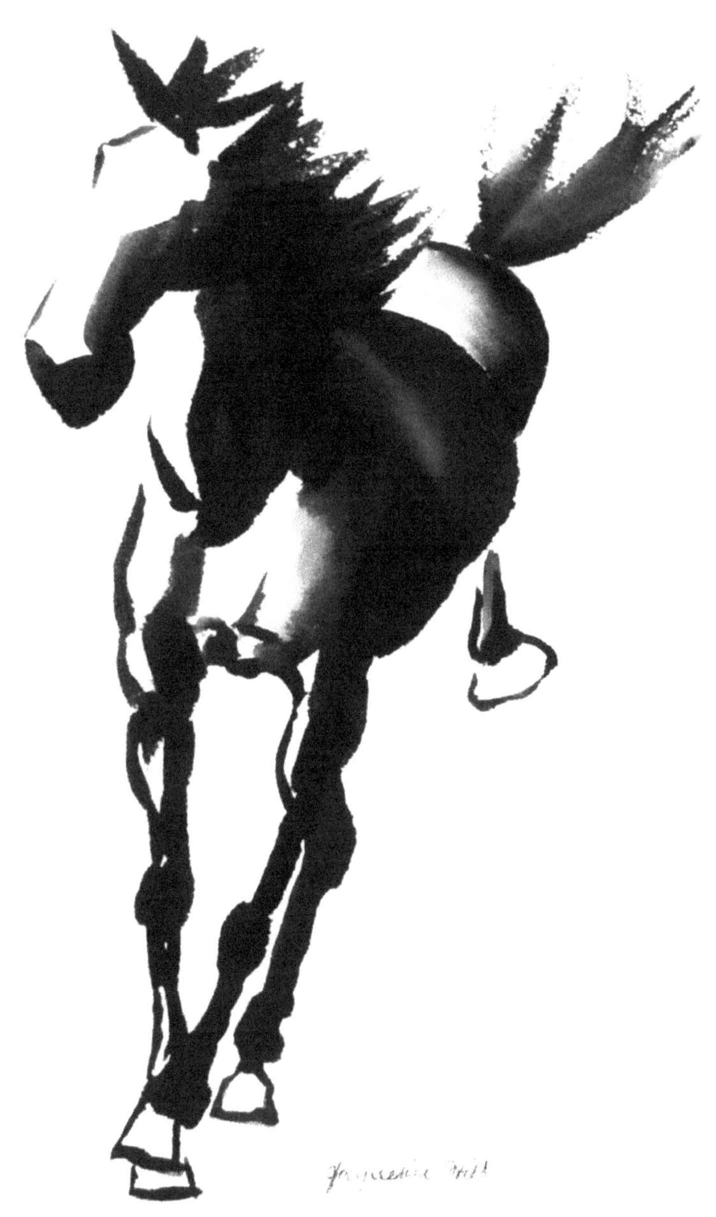

6-3 'Horse III' Eastern-style Watercolour on Cotton Rag Paper 26 x 36cm (10 x 14")
Private Collection, Australia

Your Brush Magic Chart

Mark making is an important skill to practise and it will really pay off in your paintings.

In Play Time you can create a chart of all the marks you can make with your own brushes. We find that in classes, the students get into a lovely relaxed frame of mind when creating this chart, and it is sometimes hard to get them to stop!

See the Play Time at the end of this chapter for a step by step of how to do it.

Ink Brush Magic

With a brush dipped into acrylic artists' ink, you can make all the marks above. You can also try this with an Eastern Brush dipped into traditional Eastern ink.

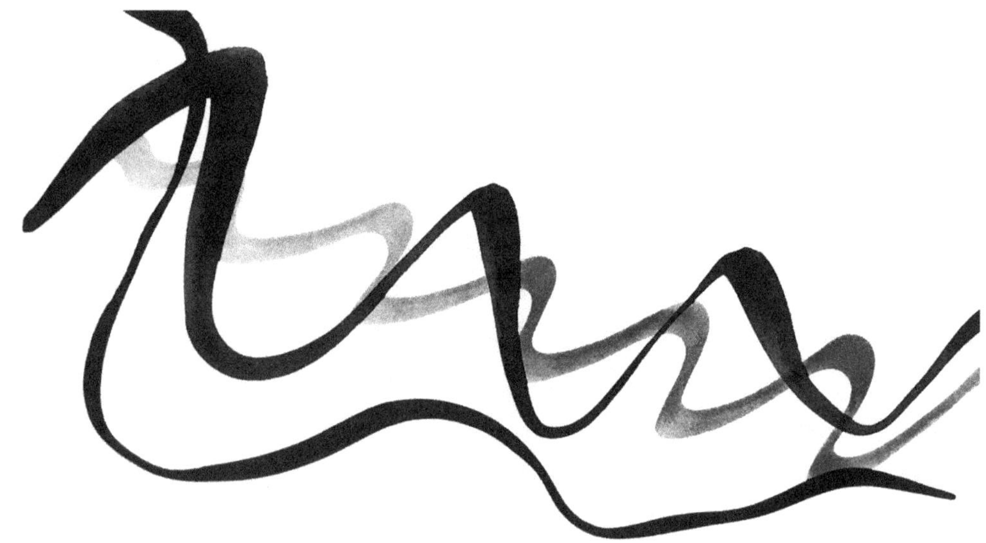

Play Time

Your Brush Magic Chart

In this Play Time you will see how many different marks you can possibly make with each brush.

The goal is to get creative! Play and have fun with making marks. It's a great way to get into Zen Mind. Take a large sheet of sketching paper (A3 or A2 is good).

Brush Marks: Weaving Magic

	Tip	Flop	Run	Dance	Flick	Floomp
Round Synthetic						
Flat Hog Bristle						
Filbert Hog						
Liner Synthetic						

1. Create a grid of brush marks for four of your brushes. Pick a round, a flat, a filbert and a liner / rigger. Or whichever brushes you have on hand. You can also add a row for a fan brush if you have one.

2. Across the top, write the six titles Tip, Flop, Run, Dance, Flick and Floomp. Make sure the area for Dance is the biggest.

3. Down the left side, write the name and size of each brush. Leave lots of space between the rows for you to experiment with marks.

4. Start with the top brush. Load it up with a little paint. Make a mark on the paper with the *tip* of the bristles, just lightly pressing down in one spot.

5. Go to the next column. The Flop can be done a number of ways. How many different marks can you make by pressing the brush down at different angles?

6. Under the next heading, try as many Run strokes as you can. Don't forget the Sword Stroke and Broad Stroke ones.

7. Try making Dance strokes. Have fun playing with this one — the variations are infinite!

8. Continue making as many marks as you can in each column. Complete the Flick and Floomp columns too.

9. Now go back and add Flicks to the brush strokes in each of the previous four columns.

10. Then pick up your next brush and do the same across the next row. Repeat for all the brushes you chose.

When you have finished your chart, look at the clock. Did you notice time passing while you were doing this Play Time? If time flew without you being aware, you were most likely in Zen Mind.

During this exercise, my beginner classes fall silent as people are absorbed in the fun and play and creativity. When it's time to move on to the next learning and I tell them how much time has gone by, they are usually surprised.

Often students don't want to stop because they have so much fun being in this Zen Mind; it's a lovely floaty state of being.

CHAPTER 7
COLOUR SECRETS

If we could see the miracle of a single flower clearly,
our whole life would change.

Buddha

CHAPTER 7 CONTENTS

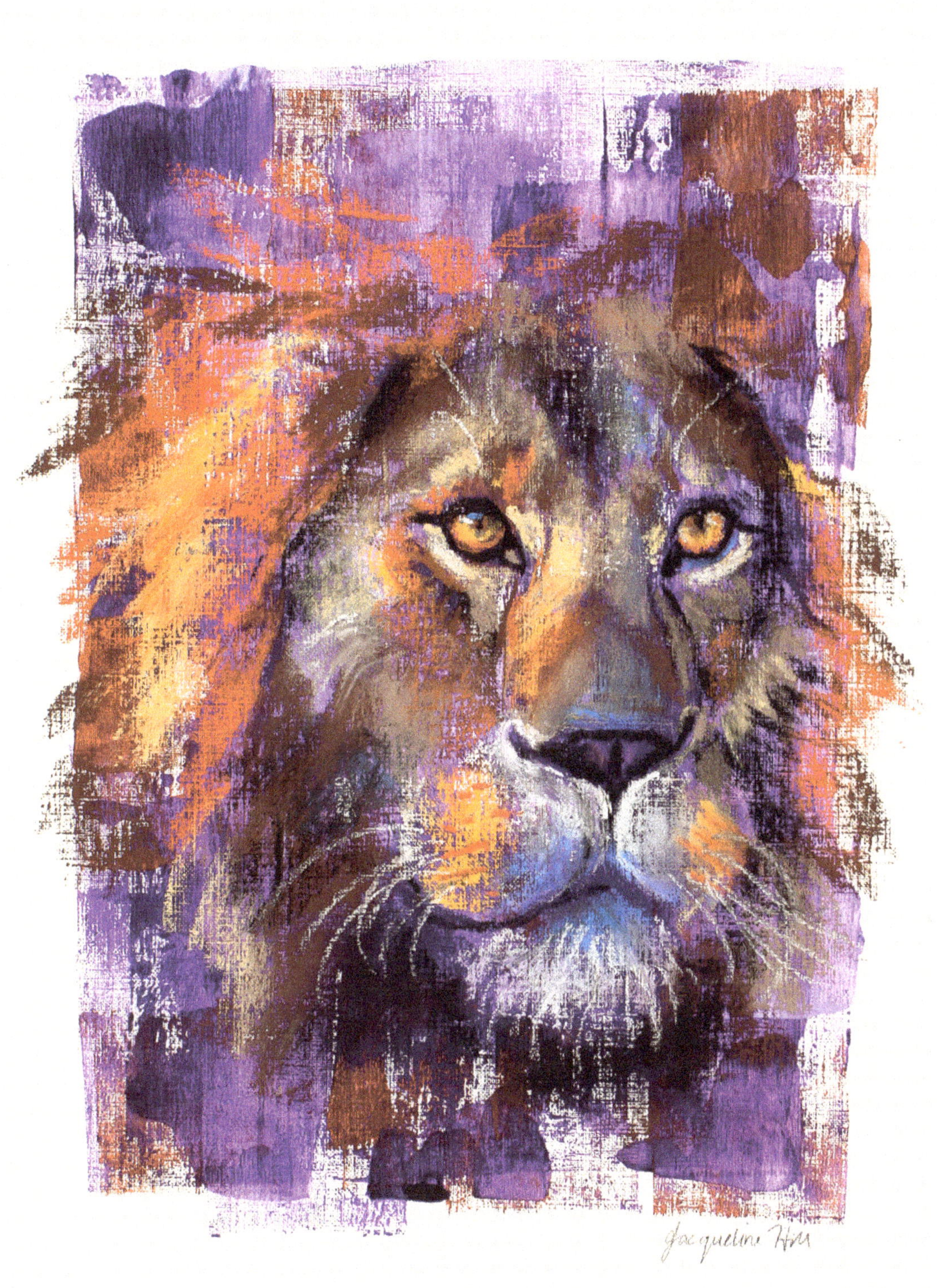

7-1 'Mighty King' (Lion) Mixed Media on Canvas Paper 29 x 42cm (11.5 x 16.5")
Daily Artwork No 240 for 2018.

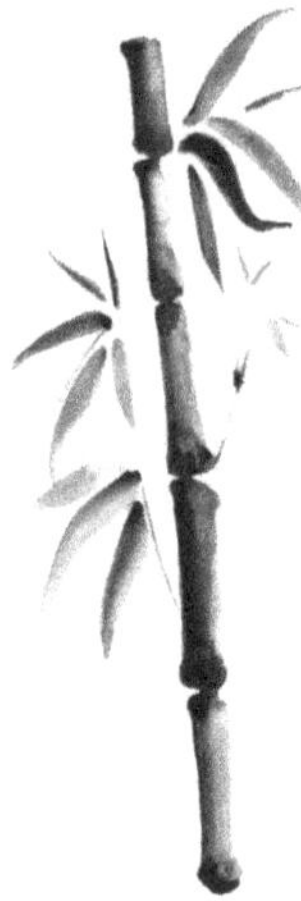

'I wish I could buy all these colours,' said Jojo, flicking through a catalogue of beautiful paint colour. 'Instead I need to mix up all my colours from the tubes I can afford. But I don't know which colours to buy.

'I know basic colour mixing. I know how to make green — with yellow and blue. But anything more complicated...' She sighed and closed the book. 'When I imagine a colour,' continued Jojo, 'I try to mix it up but never get it quite right. I keep adding more and more other colours but never win the battle. What do I need to do?'

'Colour is complicated if you don't know how it works,' said The Master. 'But once you know the secrets of the Magic Wheel, everything is simple and easy.'

'The Magic Wheel?' asked Jojo.

'The Magic Colour Wheel,' said The Master.

'Ohhhh nooooo... Please don't make me do a colour wheel,' said Jojo. 'I've seen it so many times. I already know that yellow and blue make green, and that yellow and red make orange.'

'Ah yes,' said The Master. 'But that's not where the magic of the colour wheel lies. The real magic is in its hidden secrets.'

'What secrets?' asked Jojo.

'Secrets that help you understand how to mix any colour that you can imagine. From the palest, dustiest soft grey of winter snow in shadow, to the blush of cherry blossom pink, all the way to the brightest green of the new shoots at spring.'

'Oooooh,' sang Jojo.

'Secrets to helping colour sing and dance on your art. You will make those who view your art fall in love with your colours,' he said.

Jojo raised her eyebrows. 'All from the silly old colour wheel?'

'All from the simple colour wheel,' said The Master.

Problems with Colour

Have you ever had these problems?

- Bought cheap paints but the colours were awful

- Don't know how to mix colours

- Think of or see a wonderful colour but can't mix it up or buy it (either because you can't afford to buy it or the colour doesn't exist in a tube!)

- Overwhelmed by the huge array of colours at a shop

- Have a limited budget for buying paint supplies

- Want to buy the best quality but can only afford a minimum number of tubes

The solution to all these problems is understanding the colour wheel and knowing the secrets to mixing colour — and making colour sing.

You may have seen the colour wheel before, but it hides secrets that you may not know about! The Colour Secrets unlock everything you need to know about mixing any colour from just a few tubes of paint.

All the Colour Secrets apply when you are talking about paint, pencils, pastels, markers, anything that comes in colour. We will talk about the basic understanding of the puzzle pieces in this chapter. In Chapter 11 Dancing Duets, we put all the pieces together.

Let's start by understanding the colour wheel — because that is where the secrets lie.

Understanding the Colour Wheel

Primaries

A colour wheel starts with the three primary colours. Almost everyone knows that the three primary colours are blue, red and yellow.

Let's put them together in a wheel:

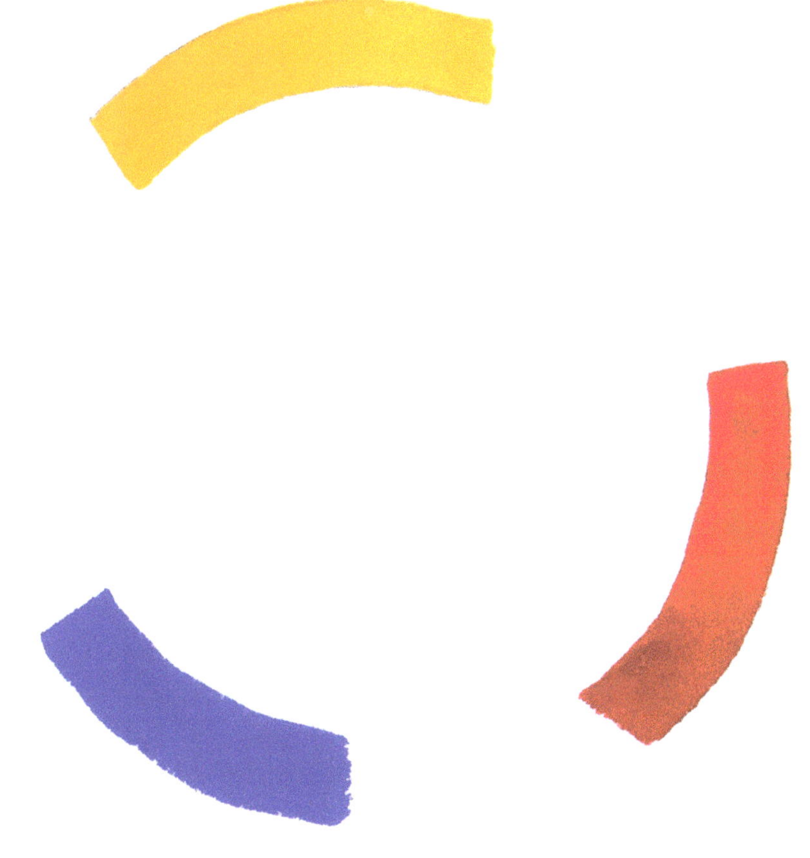

Secondaries

When you mix each primary colour with the one alongside it, you get a secondary colour.

Yellow + Blue = Green

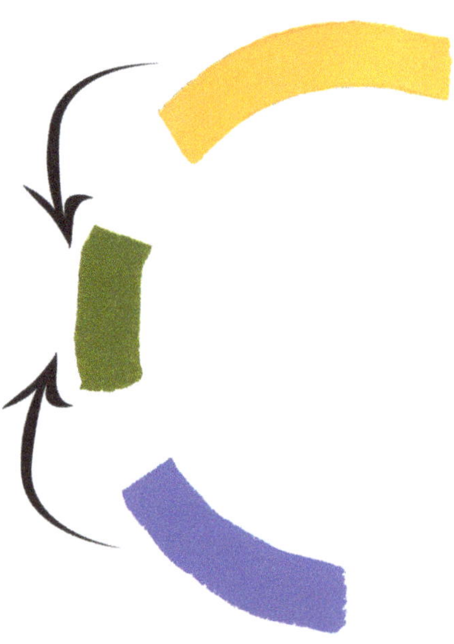

Keep mixing and you will create a six-segment colour wheel.

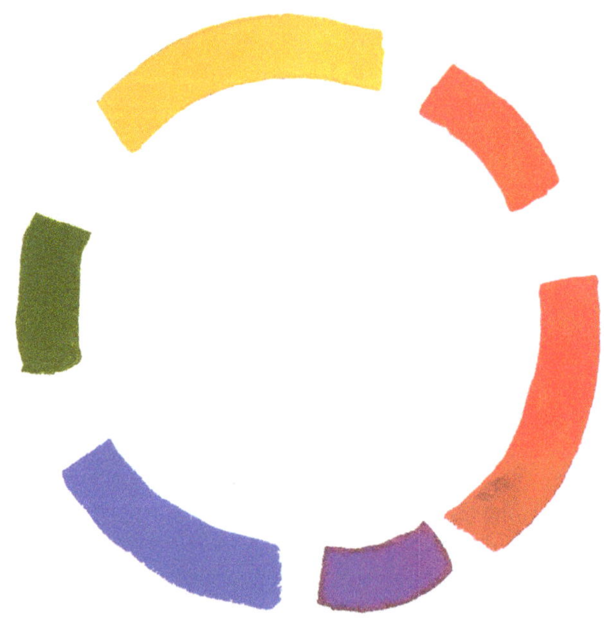

If you were to create a new wheel by blending all these colours a little with the colours on each side, you will see a continuous colour wheel.

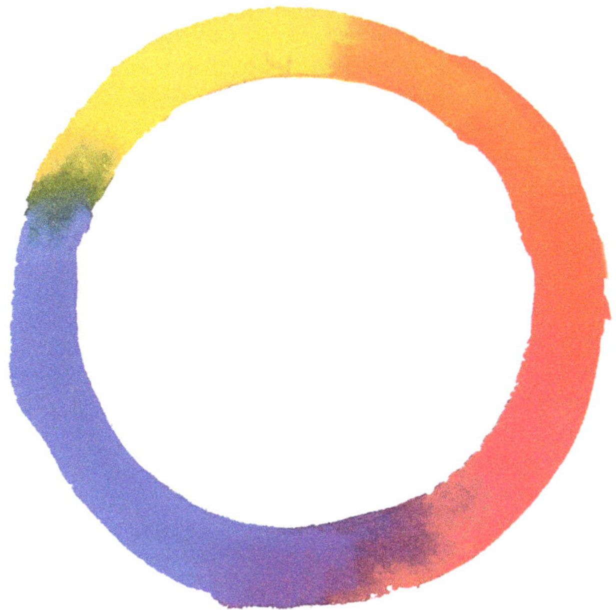

Tertiaries

Tertiary colours are between each of the six segments in the secondary colour wheel. Adding these gives you a twelve-segment colour wheel. I've painted this colour wheel showing the primaries as large blocks and the tertiaries as triangles.

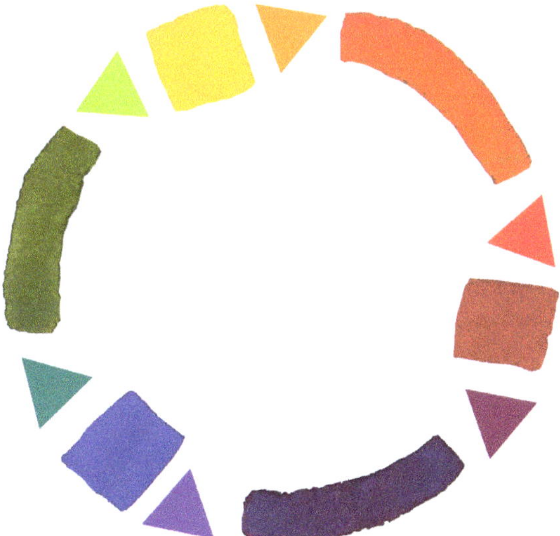

Let's not worry too much about the tertiary colours. They're easy to mix. We'll just focus on the primaries and secondaries. That is where the Colour Secrets are hiding.

Making Mud

When you mix all three primaries together, you would get a mud colour — brown or grey.

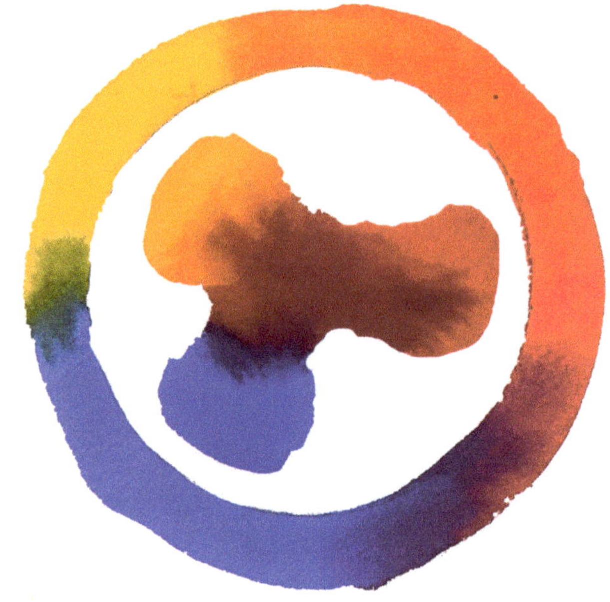

Jeanne Dobie[18] calls these muddy colours 'mouse colours'.

We'll look at the subtleties of mixing muted colours in Chapter 11 Dancing Duets.

Pigments

Students v Professionals

You can buy cheap paints, often called student quality. Or you can pay a bit more and buy professional or artists' paints.

The cheaper paints are usually non-toxic since they are designed for students or children. These colours are made from cheaper pigments, and often mixtures of several different pigments, to approximate the colour. The cheaper paints are almost always duller colours, never as vibrant and bright as the professional paints.

These paints are sometimes cheaper because the manufacturers use less pigment so the colours are weaker.

In the professional range you will often get single pigment colours. That means the colour is not mixed up from a bunch of different ones. A single pigment powder has been ground very finely and mixed with the painting medium. Single pigment colours are so much brighter.

Here is a turquoise in a small professional artist tube above a student-quality tube. You can see the number of pigments being used in each. Look for codes such as PB16, PB15 or PG7.

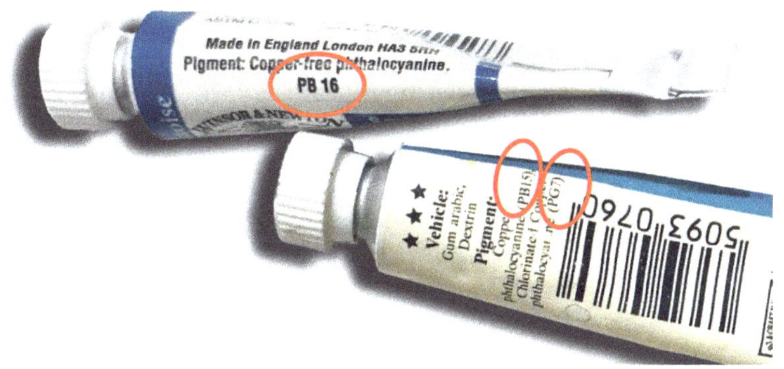

Colour Series

When looking at a range of good quality paints in the art shop, you will sometimes see the prices listed not by each tube of colour but by series.

You will see Series 1, the lowest price, then Series 2, 3 and 4, each increasing in price. Some paint brands go up to Series 6.

This is just a way that the manufacturer has simplified the prices. The cheapest pigments to make are the browns and ochres, which are usually Series 1, the lowest price. You can think of these as simply sand or rock or dirt, all ground up into a nice browny colour and put in the tube.

The most expensive ones are valuable minerals or metals that are mined and cost a lot more. So, the cadmium colours, for example, are in the higher series pricing.

Some Colours are Toxic

In the old days, many paints contained lead and many artists died of lead poisoning. Only recently has lead been taken out of paints, both house paints and artists' paints.

However, the professional range of artists' paints still carry a few nasty pigments.

Some pigments are very toxic. Watch out for the Big Bad Three Cs: cadmium, cobalt and chromium. Don't ingest these in any way.

- Clean your hands after painting and before eating

- Don't blow dust, vaporise or spray paint where you can breathe it in

- Don't put your brush in your mouth, even to hold it by the handle in your teeth

- Don't wash brushes in your kitchen sink or pour art wastewater where you prepare food

I recommend you find a book on safety in the artists' studio[3] that lists the toxicity of some of these pigments.

It's not something to be afraid of — these colours are an absolute delight to use. You just need to be aware and sensible while painting.

Professional paints are worth every cent. I always recommend beginners bypass the student paints and go straight to the professional ones. While they are a little more expensive, the colours are so brilliant they will inspire you to keep on.

I'm also about to teach you how to save money by buying fewer tubes of paint, so you can more easily invest in those great professional colours.

Play Time

1. Take a look at your collection of paints. Are they professional colours or student colours? Can you find out what combination of pigments are in each tube? If they are not written on the tube, you may need to search online for the colour charts[26] to find out.

2. From each of your colour sets (different mediums or brands), choose three tubes of paint (or sticks or pencils) that are a good medium blue, red and yellow.

3. Make three colour wheels, as follows:

    a. Get a small sheet of paper or canvas, enough for three circular colour wheels. Draw up the circle guidelines first, if you like. An easy way to do this is to draw around a small dish or cup lightly with pencil.

    b. Label the top of the sheet with the paint brand and medium (oil, watercolour etc).

    c. Paint a three-segment colour wheel. Label each of the colour segments with the name of the colour.

    d. Now paint a six-segment colour wheel by mixing the secondary colours and adding them in between the primaries.

    e. Finally, try painting a full circle colour wheel. Mix the paint on the paper or canvas.

4. Repeat this process for each set of paints you own, on new sheets.

5. Take a look at the secondary colours created by mixing each pair of primaries. Are they bright and clear or are they a little dull? We'll look at how to control this in Chapter 9 Palette Ingredients.

CHAPTER 8
CHARTING COURSE

Life is available only in the present.
That is why we should walk in such a way that
every step can bring us to the here and the now.

Thich Nhat Hanh

CHAPTER 8 CONTENTS

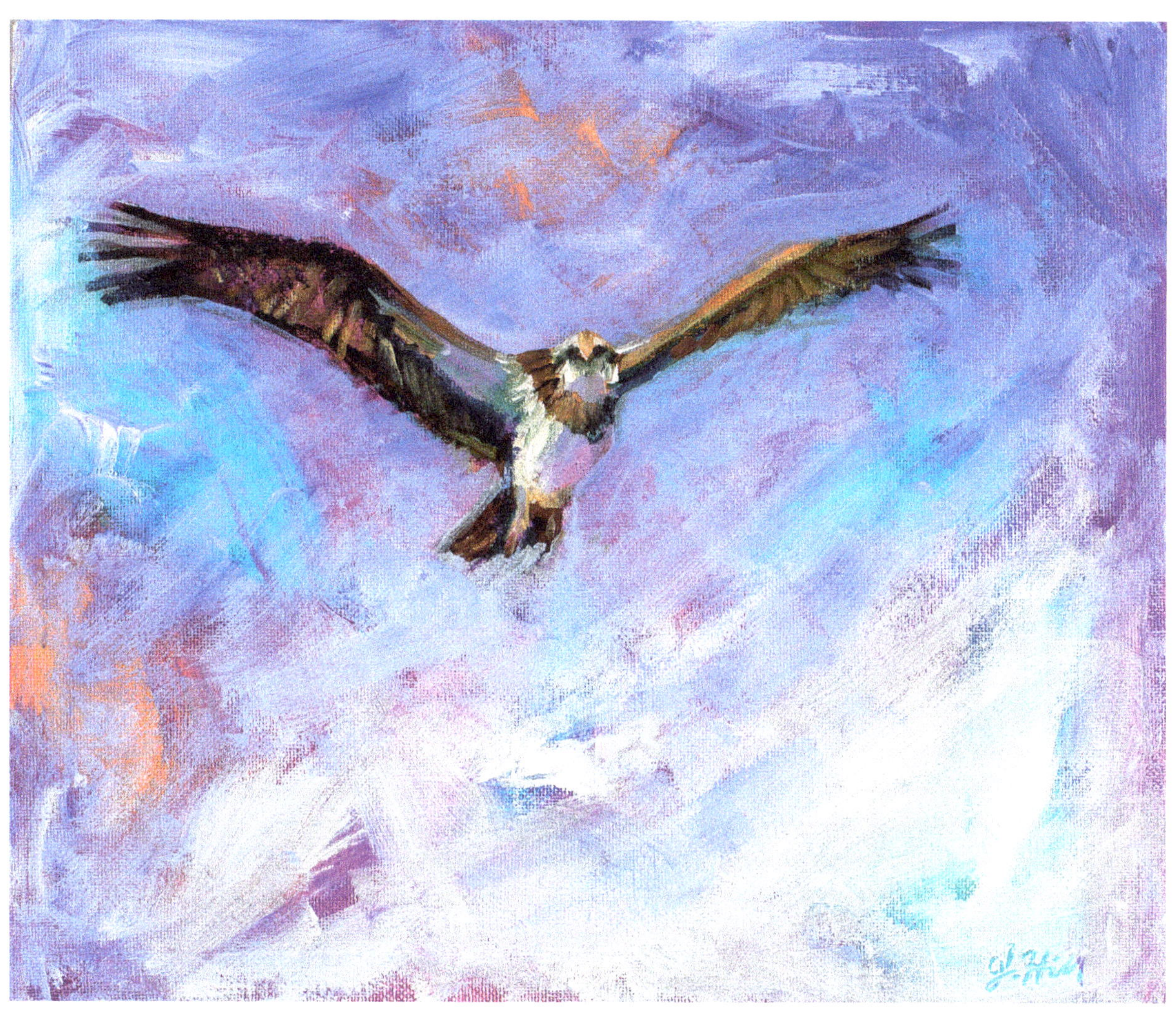

8-1 'Eagle Eye (Sea Eagle, Fraser Island)' Acrylic on Canvas 30 x 25cm (12 x 10")
Daily Artwork No 199 for 2018.

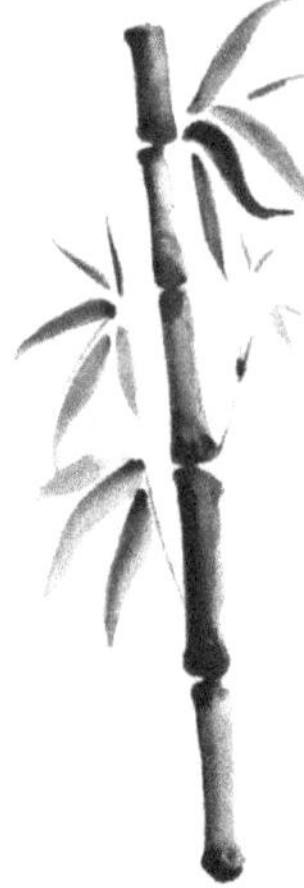

'It's happened again!' Jojo dropped her palette in annoyance. 'This colour looks nothing like the colour on the label. And it's not until I've painted it onto my painting that I realise it's completely the wrong colour.'

'External appearances are not always reliable,' said The Master. 'It's what's on the inside that counts.'

'For people and for paints!' laughed Jojo.

'Yes,' said The Master. 'And a Colour Master would never depend on the label of a paint tube. A Colour Master would have already met the colour and had a conversation with it before using it in a painting.'

Jojo tipped her head on one side. 'What do you mean by that?' she asked.

'You must get to know the colour by using it. You must apply the paint to your surface in a small sample. Then you can trust that as your reference for selecting colours. Not the label on the tube.'

'Do you mean a colour chart? That I paint myself?' asked Jojo.

'If you do not chart your way, how can you know where you will land?' asked The Master.

Why Create a Colour Chart?

You just cannot tell what the real colour is by looking at the paint tube.

The label is usually printed using CMYK printing inks (cyan, magenta, yellow and black). These are nothing like paint. With all the variations that happen during printing, the final colour on the tube may look nothing like the colour inside. You must never depend on the tube label.

You must always create your own colour samples.

Colour charts have been an essential tool for me. I have a rule: when I buy a new tube of paint, I don't let myself use it in a painting until I have added it to my colour chart. I have one colour chart for each medium and each brand.

When the Labels Mislead

Here's an example. In the Atelier Interactive range of acrylics, there are two purples. One is just plain Purple, the other is Dioxazine Purple. 'Dioxazine' is too many syllables to pronounce so I just call it Diox Purple.

Which one of these colours do you think would be the brightest, judging by the colour label on the tube?

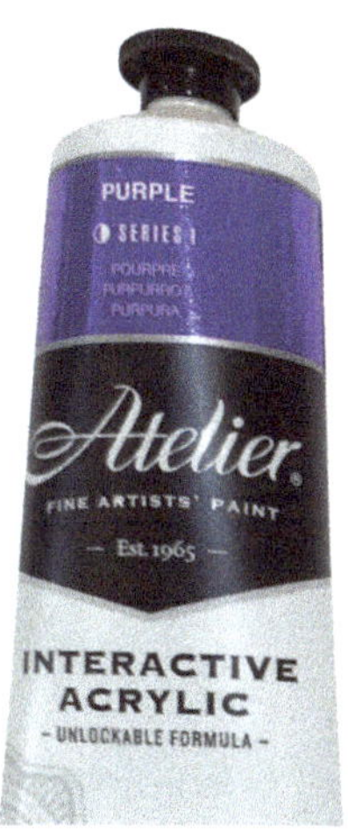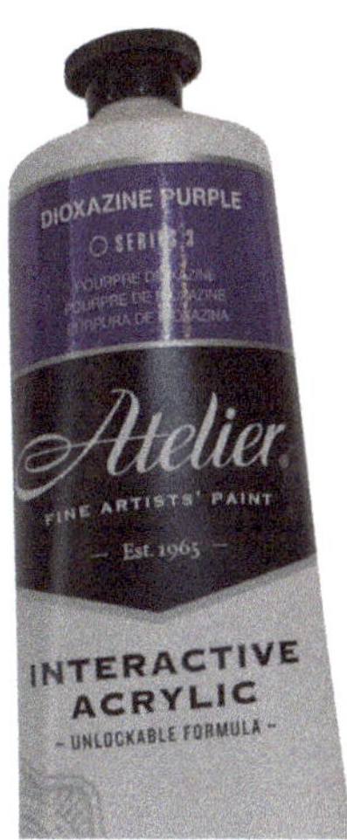

It turns out that the Purple is a dusty muted colour, but Diox Purple is a bright vibrant colour.

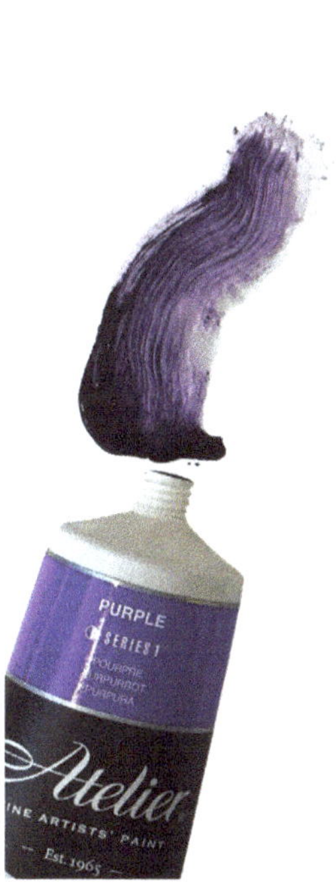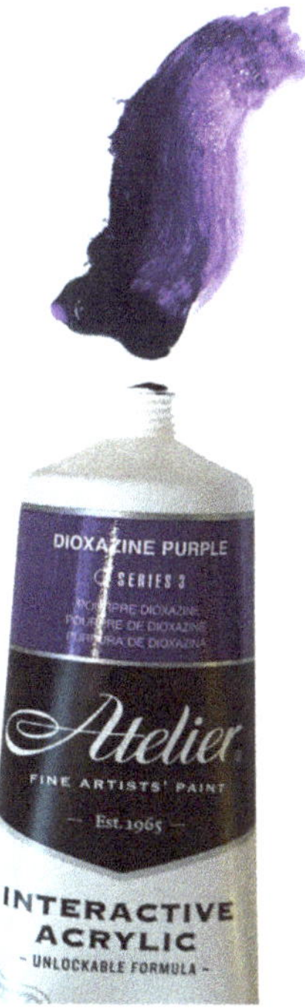

If you were going by the colour of the label, you would pick up the wrong tube to paint from. This is why I always refer to my own painted colour chart when selecting colours to use.

The colour chart step is also vital to your understanding of, and getting to know, a new colour.

What is a Colour Chart?

You can get colour charts in art shops or online. But they don't show you the true colour of the paint. So I always create my own colour chart with the actual paints.

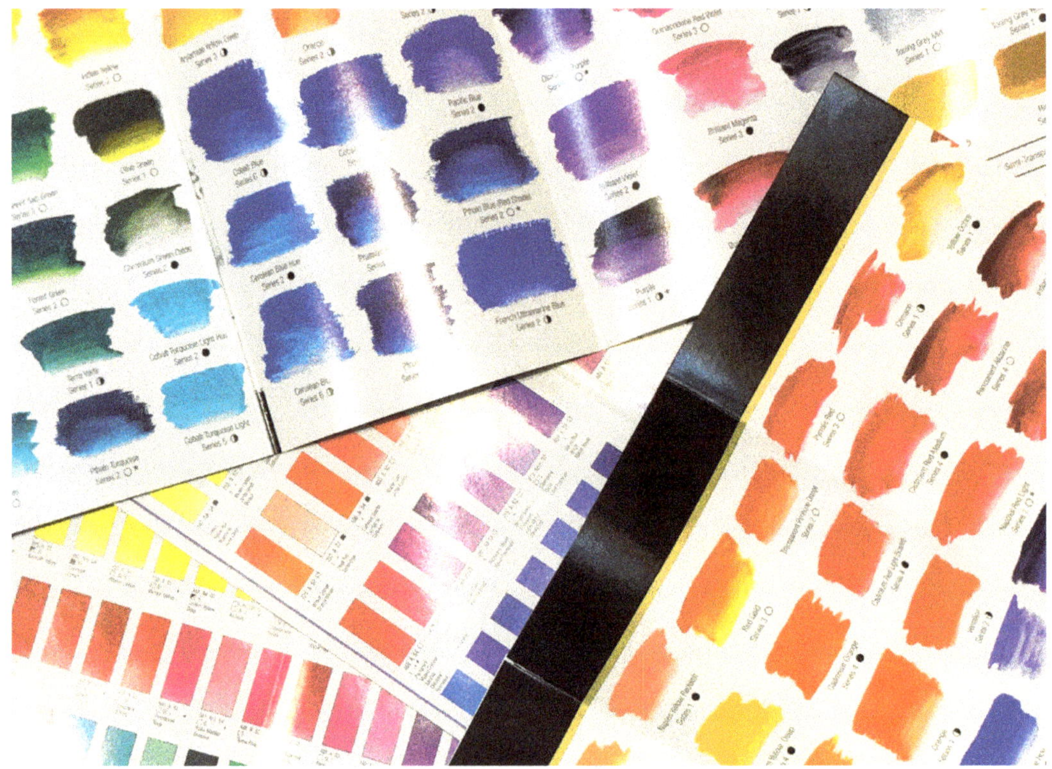

Choose a scrap piece of canvas or paper — whatever you usually paint on to.

Make a whole lot of small 'colour chips' of pencil, stick or paint onto the sample canvas or paper. Label each one with the colour name.

If you usually paint transparently[13] (eg in watercolours, or acrylics with mediums) then make each chip a transparent gradient.

If you paint in an opaque style (eg oils mixed with opaque white) then you would make the chip a gradient mixed with white.

Most colour chips I add to my colour charts using a small gradient of transparent medium on one side and a small gradient with white on the other side. This shows the full range of what is possible with the colour. Mixing with white often makes a completely different colour than making it lighter with transparency.

I try to make each little chip show the full range of the colour, from full (darkest) strength to as diluted as possible. Then I can see what the colour is capable of on my little chart.

I usually put my colours onto the charts in what I call Rainbow Order. Before we do up our first colour chart, let's look at how to lay it out.

Rainbow Order

What is Rainbow Order?

It's what I call laying out all the colours in order, like the colours in the rainbow. Blue blends gradually into purple, purple blends into magenta, then red, then orange, then it fades into yellow, then into green and finally back around to turquoise and blue.

If you lay all your pencils or paint tubes in a circle ordered so that the colours all blend into one another, then you have them in Rainbow Order.

You may find some colours don't really have a place to go. I like to put the browns after the reds, with the reddish browns closest to the red colour, and the yellow browns further away. The whites and blacks and greys go into a spot all on their own. You'll see this later when laying out your painting palette.

Where Do I Start My Rainbow?

It doesn't really matter where you start because the colours go around in a continuous circle and join up.

You can remember the rainbow order by the old imaginary fellow:

ROY G. BIV – Red, Orange, Yellow, Green, Blue, Indigo, Violet.

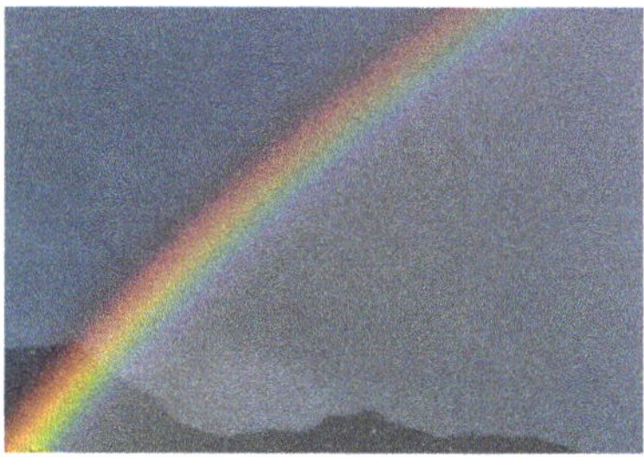

But my favourite order is the way I lay out my painting palette. I start with yellow at the top left corner, then go anticlockwise to blue at the bottom left, then red at the bottom right.

The way my students like to remember this is to think of the

Yellow Brick Road: Y-B-R (Yellow, Blue, Red)

as the order of the primaries on the corners of the palette.

Yellow Brick Road

I love laying out my palette with paint squeezed out on it in this same Rainbow Order. I always lay out my palette exactly the same way, like this:

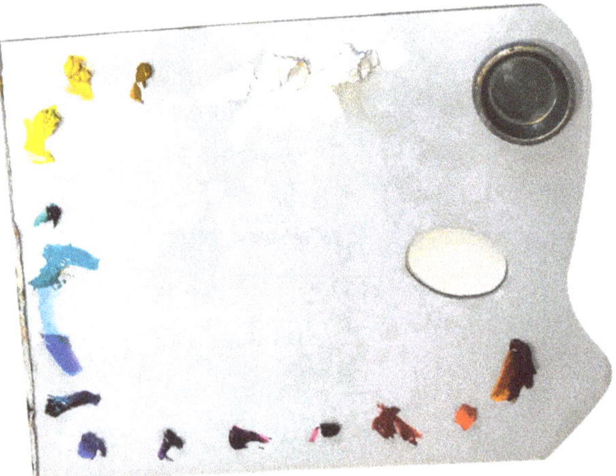

This layout really helps me when I am painting on the fly; I hardly look at the palette. I know exactly where the colour I want is because it's always in the same position.

A set layout is helpful when you are using colours that are so dark they look nearly black when squeezed out of a tube. Each pile of this 'nearly black' could be a blue, a purple, a turquoise, a crimson, but it is impossible to tell by looking at it. If they are in their own set positions on the palette then you'll know exactly which colour is which.

I see so many beginners who haven't organised their palette pick up the wrong colour and paint it onto their painting. It's so easy to avoid!

If you have a travel kit watercolour palette, you can rearrange the order to suit yourself.

How Do I Start a Colour Chart?

First decide where the three central primaries will go.

Mark on your canvas or paper, Y, B and R:

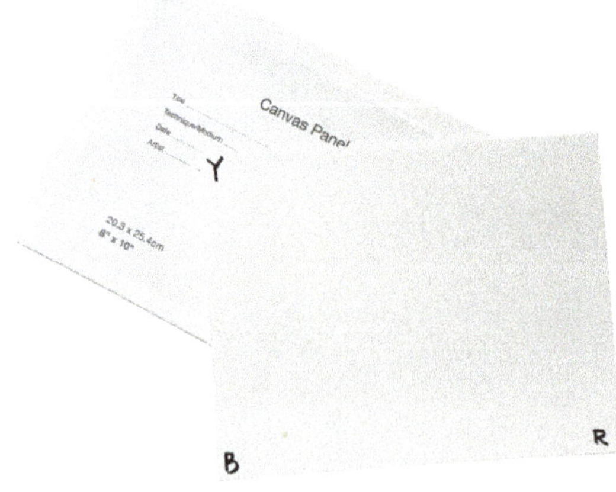

The central primaries are the most neutral primaries that don't seem to lean to any secondary colour.

A central primary yellow, for example, is also known as 'spectrum yellow' or 'pure yellow' or 'neutral yellow'. It's the one that's right in the middle of the yellow range.

Now pick up each colour, one by one, and arrange them with the Rainbow Order in mind.

If you pick up a blue, ask yourself, 'Is this blue greenier or purplier?' Then place it in the right position, where it belongs between two other colours.

With tubes of paint, you may need to squeeze a little paint out on paper to tell what the colour is. We've already worked out that we can't trust the labels of the tubes to tell us what's inside!

Abbreviating Colour Names

I've come up with a system for abbreviating colour names. When you are writing in your little tiny colour chart, there's often not enough room to write the full name, such as Winsor Violet (Dioxazine). I usually abbreviate the name to just the first letters:

WV(D) = Winsor Violet (Dioxazine)

WB(G) = Winsor Blue (Green Shade)

Many colours start with P (Phthalo[19] Blue, Prussian Blue) so I also add the second letter in lower case:

PhB = Phthalo Blue

PrB = Prussian Blue

An awful lot of colours start with a C too, so here are some of my abbreviations to get you going on your own list:

CaO = Cadmium Orange

CaY = Cadmium Yellow

CoB = Cobalt Blue

CeB = Cerulean Blue

ChG = Chromium Green

I don't often use black, so I don't have it in my tubes selection. But if you like using it, the B for Black can get mixed up with the B for Blue. And Bl would be confusing too! So I abbreviate Black to be Bk:

RBk = Red Black

MBk = Mars Black

LBk = Lamp Black

Get the idea? This tip saves so much time writing long colour names.

Make sure each abbreviation you choose is unique, so it can't possibly get mixed up with another colour in the range made by that brand.

Throughout this book I'll add my colour name abbreviations alongside each colour pigment I tell you about.

How to Create a Colour Chart for Paints

Colour Charts for Oils & Acrylics

Take a canvas panel just big enough to fit all your colours. Those little affordable 12 x 18cm (5 x 7") or 25 x 20cm (10 x 8") boards that have gessoed[20] white canvas on one side are ideal.

On the back, in the Title area, write the brand of paint. In the Medium area, write the medium (eg oil).

Lay the board down, choose a corner for each primary colour and write the letter on the corner. I like the layout to be the same as my palette when I'm painting.

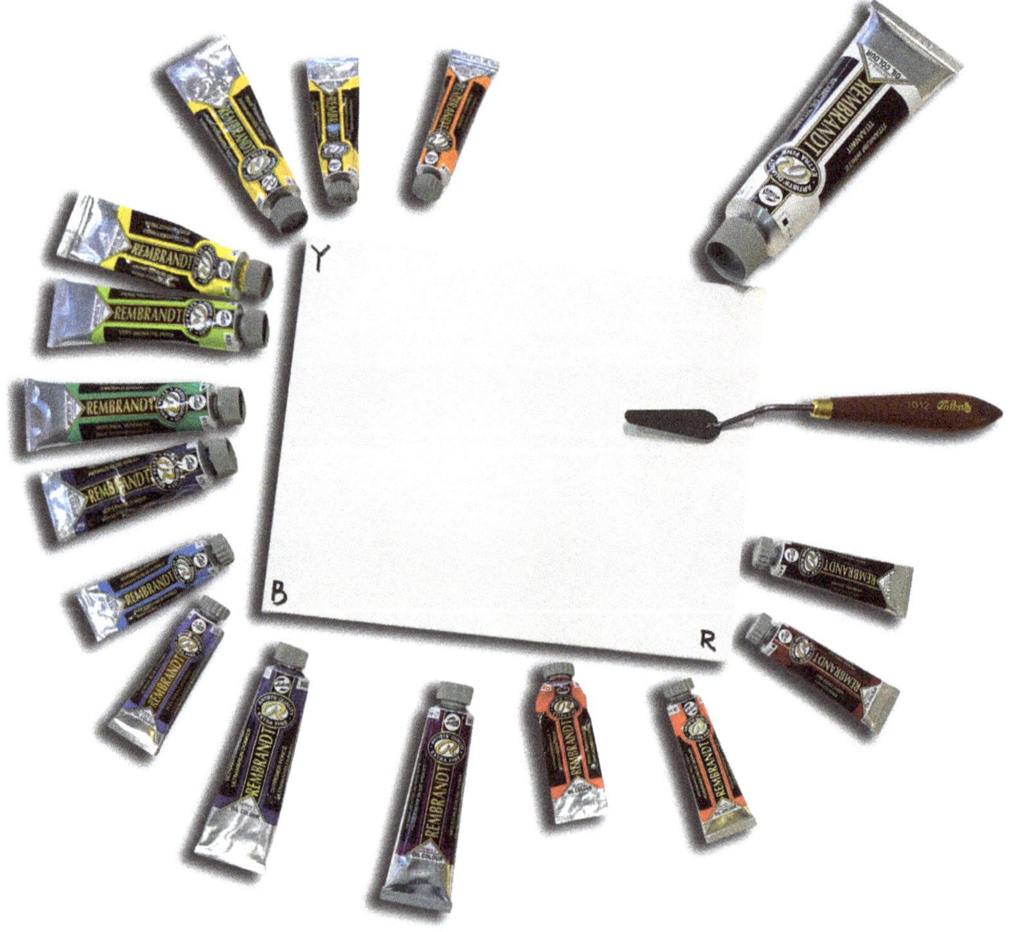

Lay out all your tubes in a circle around the panel, trying to keep them in Rainbow Order. For example, the greener the yellow, the closer it sits to the green on the panel. The more golden the yellow, the further it is around the other side of the Y.

If you are not sure where some paints should sit, try testing them out on a small piece of scrap paper first.

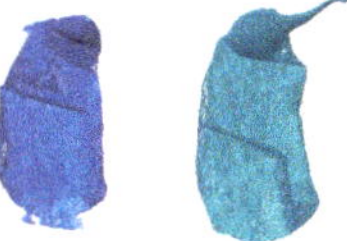

Once you've worked out where each colour should go, write your abbreviation for that colour in the spot on the panel. You can also mark the transparency symbol too.

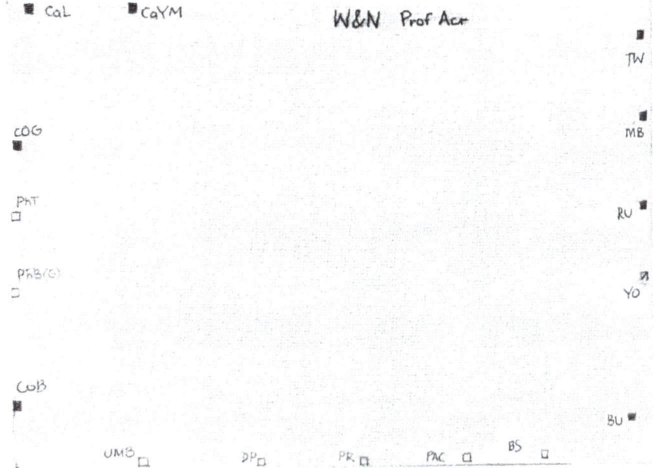

Now you can paint a small colour chip in each position.

After painting each chip, clean your brush thoroughly and then do the next chip.

How to Paint a Colour Chip in Oil & Acrylic

I usually dob the tiniest circle of paint straight out of the tube onto the canvas.

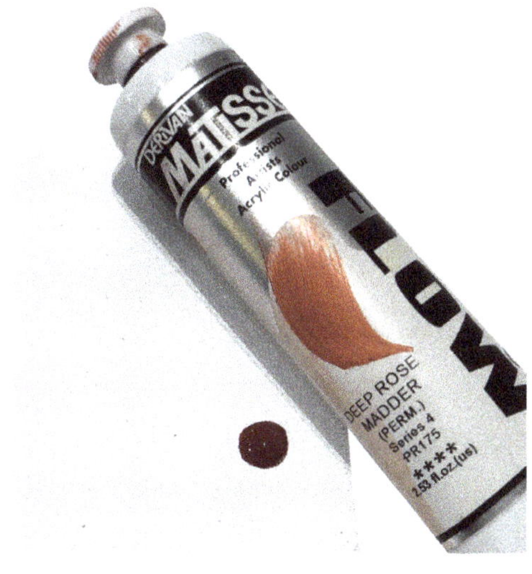

With a small flat brush and a medium (Liquin for oil; clear painting medium or glazing medium for acrylic), I smudge it to one side to get a nice gradient.

I find using the brush sideways across the strip works well to give a gradual gradient.

Try to get it to show the colour from the darkest solid paint straight out of the tube, all the way through to clear. This gets easier with practice.

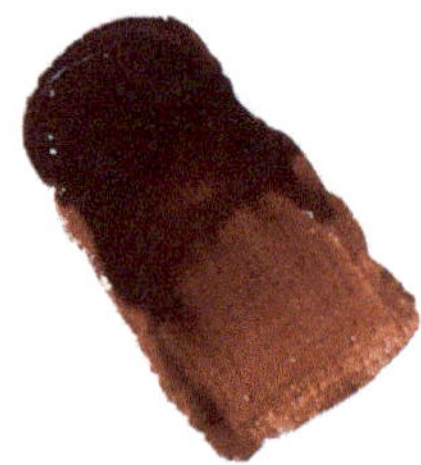

Then pick up a little white and blend it in a gradient on the opposite side of the chip.

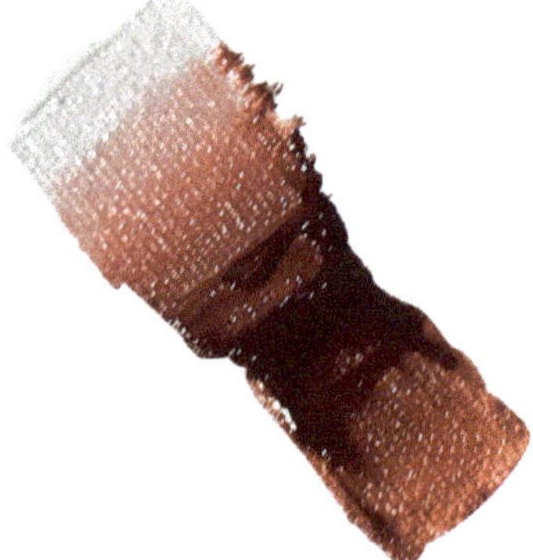

Can you see how different the colour is on each side? Mixing with white makes a completely different colour than making it lighter with the transparent medium.

If you have white in your brush, don't touch the transparent side!

The reason we do the transparent side first is so the brush is clean and untainted with that wicked old chalky, opaque white, which kills any delicious transparency.

So the order is:

1. Squeeze the paint colour on

2. Paint in the transparent side

3. Add the opaque white side

4. Clean your brush ready for the next colour

It's important to do it in this order to keep the colour chips clean and clear.

Here's my finished colour chart for acrylics:

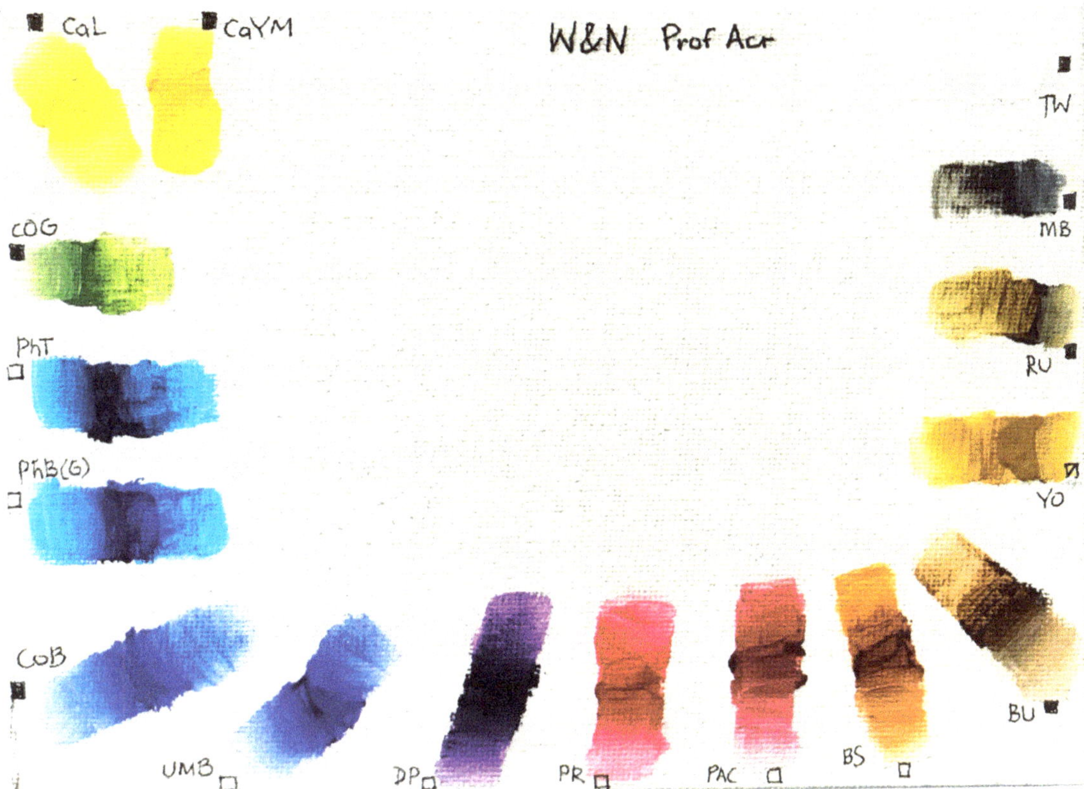

Colour Charts for Inks & Gouache

Do the same as in the above section, except this time your transparent medium is water. Using alcohol inks? Then use water or your normal alcohol medium to dilute the colour for transparency.

Paint your colour chart on a small board of your normal painting surface. If you use cotton rag watercolour paper, then make a chart on that surface. If you paint inks onto Yupo[21] or canvas, then use Yupo or canvas. Some surfaces are a creamy colour rather than pure white. This will affect the colours, so stick with the same surface.

Using your transparent medium, create a transparent side of the chip. Then paint your opaque gradient on the other side of the chip with titanium white.

Colour Charts for Watercolour

Do the same steps as above. But if you never use Chinese White in your watercolours, like me, then the colour chips are really simple. Just do the transparent side, diluting each little chip with water! Easy.

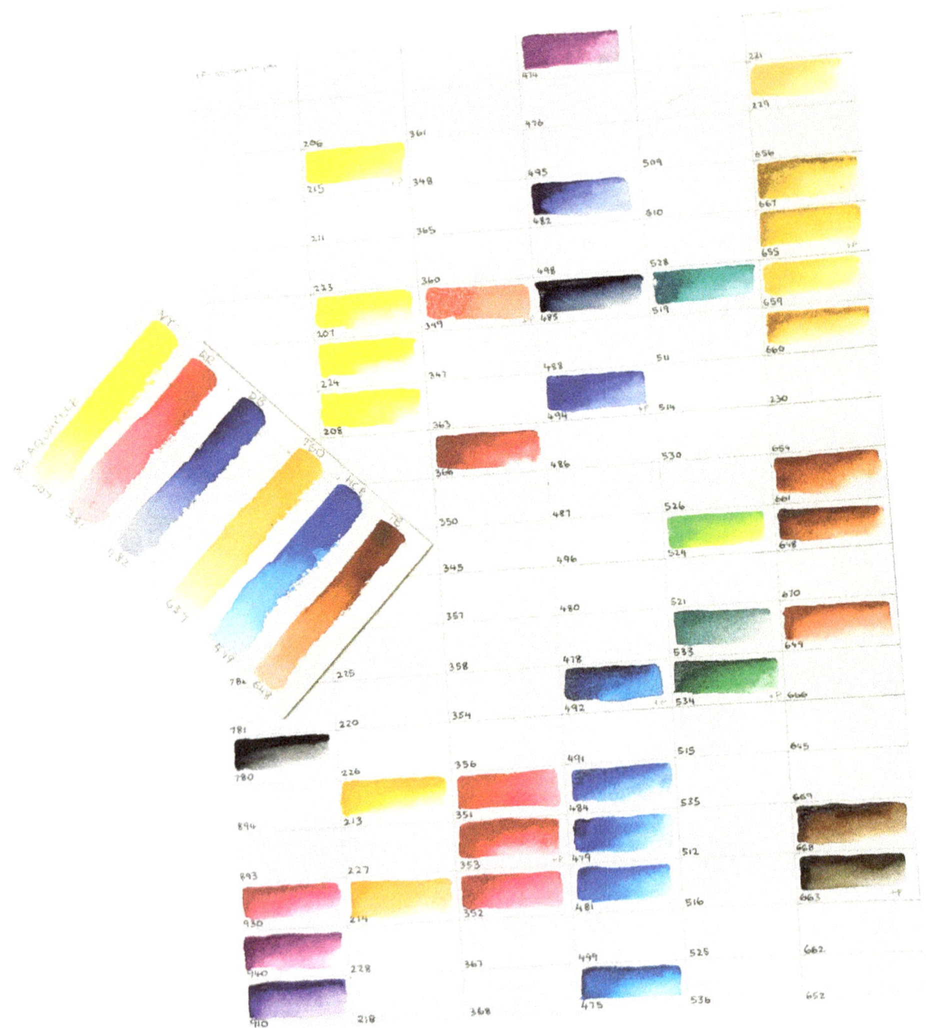

How to Paint a Colour Chip in Watercolour

Using a flat brush, paint a small blob of rich colour on the paper. Then paint a small dot of clear water alongside it. The two blobs should not be too high and 'domey'. They should be flat on the paper and only a little shiny. If you get just the right amount in each tiny puddle, the mingling will work well.

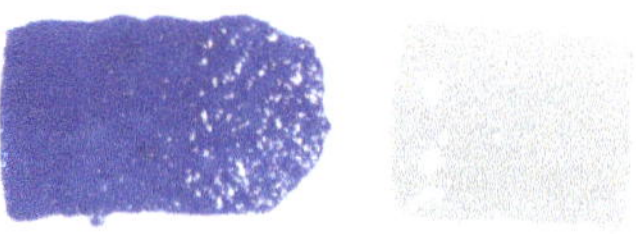

Now push the water pool into the colour pool with your brush, drag back once and lift off. Introduce the two new friends and let them party by themselves!

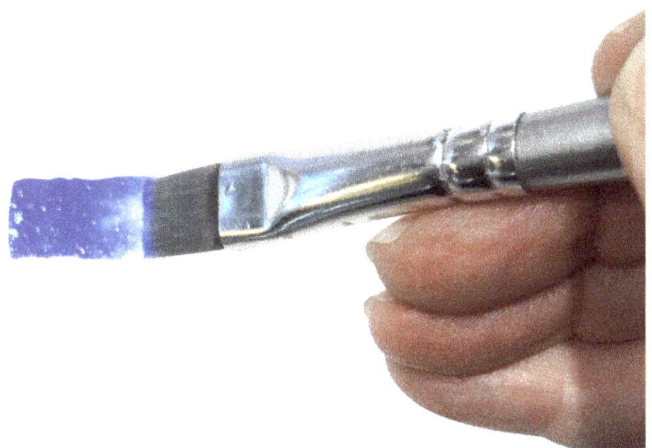

You should now see the gradient of colour from dark to light.

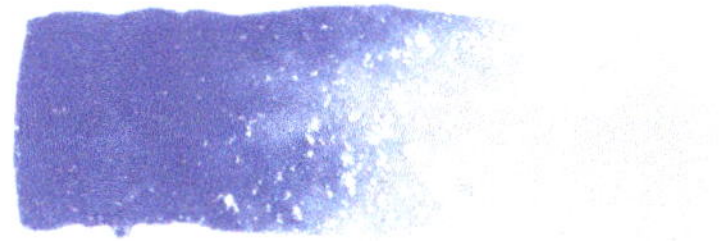

The trick is to use just the right amount of water to get the colour to move the right amount.

A Chart for Your Watercolour Pan Paints

If you have watercolour paint in pans (little tablets of solid dry colour popped into a small paint palette), then the dried watercolour paint often looks nothing like the colour when it is wet and transparent.

In fact, many of the colours are so dark when the pan is dry, you cannot tell them apart — they all look nearly black.

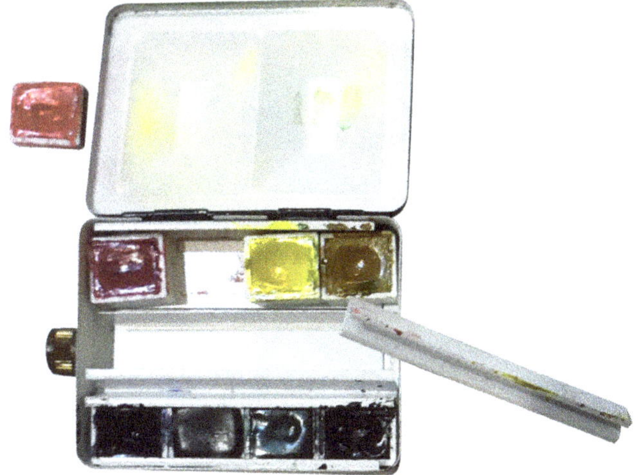

Creating a colour chart to slip into the palette box and keep as a reference can save your sanity. No more picking up the wrong colour to put in your painting!

Before doing anything else, see if you can rearrange the pans in the set so that they are in Rainbow Order. Most professional pan palette kits have removable pans that are held in with little spring clips.

You may need to test each colour on scrap paper so you can see where they fit in the Rainbow Order.

A bonus advantage of doing the Rainbow Order is that if the paints ever spill over into adjacent pans, the mix won't be a disaster because each neighbouring colour is very similar.

Note down the names of the colours in each pan — you should find the colour name written in tiny text on the outside of the tin:

Cut a piece of watercolour paper to fit on the inside of the tin and pencil in the shapes of the pans. Then fill in a little colour chip of each of the colours, reflecting where they are in the palette.

Pencil in the abbreviation of the colour names by each chip.

You will *love* this as a reference card to tell you what colours are where and what they will look like once they hit your paper. Keep the chart inside the tin.

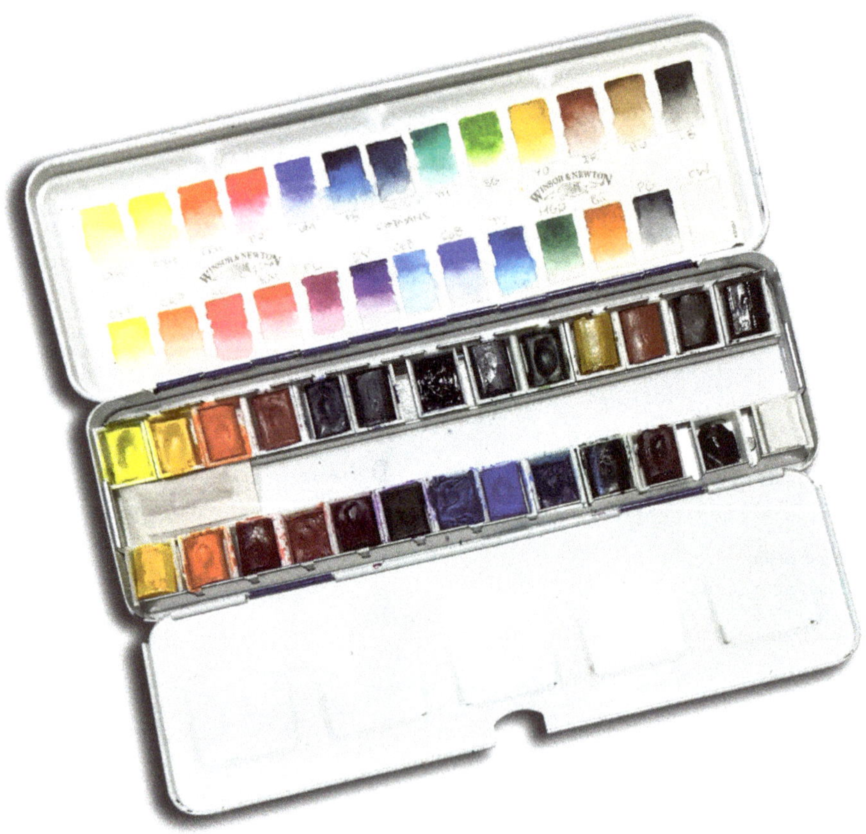

Colour Charts for Pencil & Pastel
This works for both dry pastel and oil pastel.

Take a large sheet of watercolour paper or white pastel card. Lay out all your pencils or pastels in Rainbow Order and make a small shaded mark with each colour. Write in pencil alongside, either the colour abbreviation or the number on the pencil.

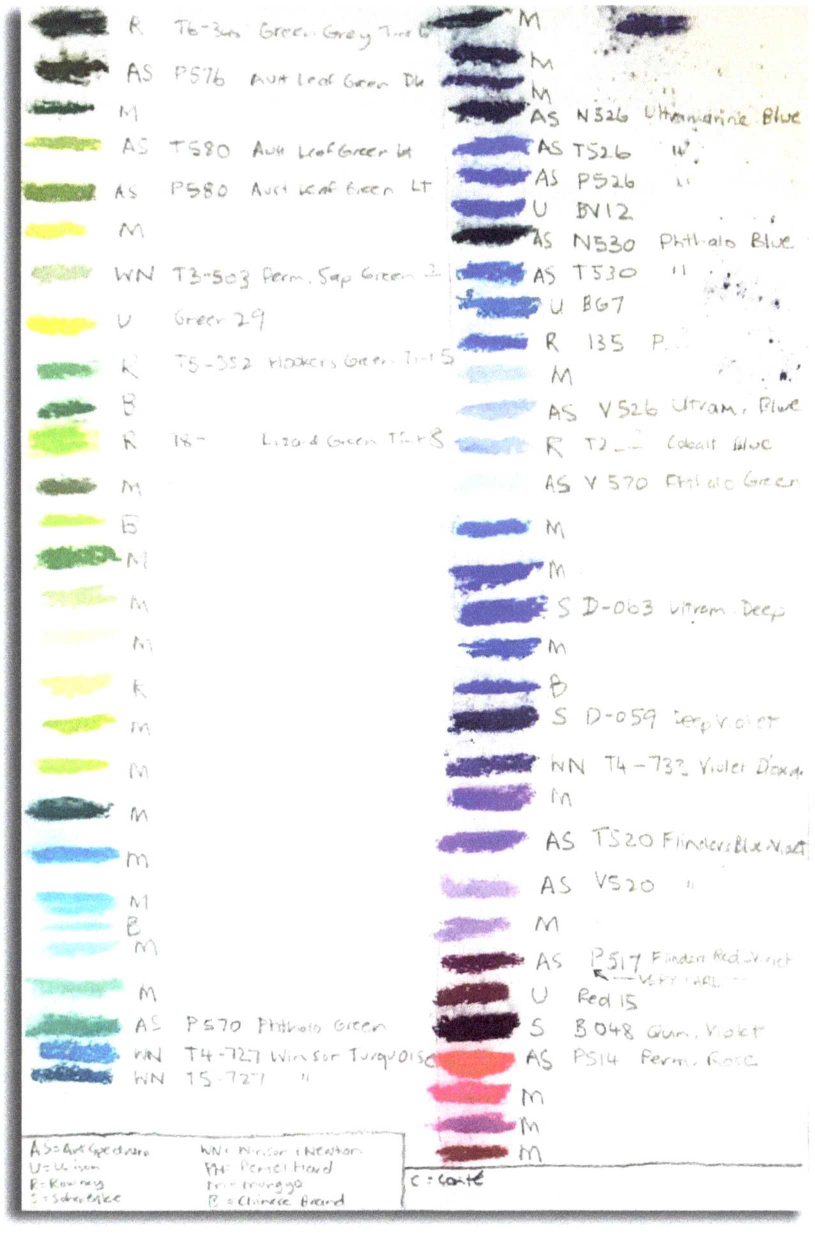

If the sheet is too unwieldy and big, cut it up into sections so you can stack them.

Protect Your Colour Charts

I refer to my colour charts so often that they can get pretty beaten up. In the studio, stacked in with my art materials, the paint can get marked.

Pastel and pencil or watercolour on paper are even more delicate than the little canvas boards for acrylic and oil charts.

I like sealing them up in clear plastic pockets when they're finished to keep them safe. I use the crystal-clear pockets with a sealing strip. These are really clear to see through. I find the plastic of zip lock bags too grey; it dulls down the colours. I want to see the colours clearly without having to take the chart out of the bag.

With my colour charts sealed up in clear pockets, I can handle them even with dirty, painty hands and know they'll stay clean.

I keep my colour charts for each medium as close as possible to where I'll need them. My oil colour chart goes in my oil paint box, my acrylic chart lives with the acrylic paints and so on.

Take Your Colour Charts with You

Don't take the actual charts when you go shopping — that's too much trouble!

Take a photo of your colour charts with your phone. I like to use Evernote[22] and add a text note to the photo. Then I can search for a photo by name, even years later. Having photo backups of your charts will give you extra peace of mind.

So many times I've been tempted to buy a delicious pastel colour in an art shop. Then I get home and find that I already own three of the exact same colour.

The only way I've avoided this is by carrying my colour charts with me as photos on my phone. It only takes a minute to look them up when I'm in the art shop.

Play Time

Colour Charts

Create a colour chart of the colours you own.

- Own more than one medium? Create a colour chart for each!

- For each medium, do you own paints in different brands? Create a separate colour chart for each brand. Label each chart clearly at the top with the medium (eg Oil) as well as the brand and range (eg Schmincke Norma) — in big letters.

- Own a watercolour palette with pan paints in it? Cut a piece of watercolour paper to fit inside your palette and pencil in the shape of each pan. Then add the colour chips and the abbreviated colour names.

- Photograph your colour charts with your phone. Now you can carry them around with you so you don't keep buying the same colours over and over when you walk into an art shop!

CHAPTER 9
PALETTE INGREDIENTS

Your Treasure House is in yourself,
it contains all you need.

Hui Hai

CHAPTER 9 CONTENTS

9-1 'Storm over the Sandhills', Watercolour on Cotton Rag Paper 42 x 30cm (17 x 12")
Daily Artwork No 352 for 2018.

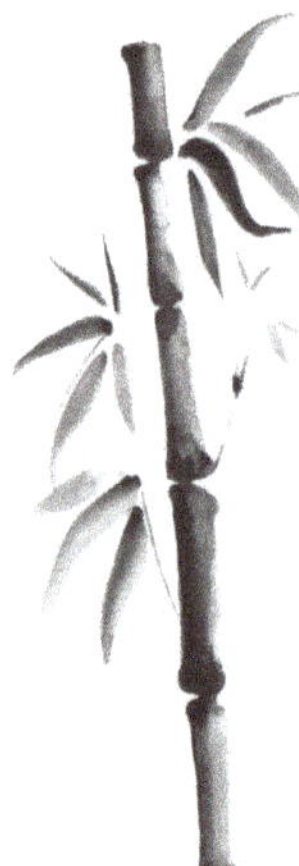

Jojo was admiring the simple watercolours hanging on the monastery walls. 'Some of these paintings are so beautiful but so powerful,' she said. 'They seem to use very little colour. The colour is so subtle, I can't imagine the artist has used as many tubes of paint as I do!'

'You are very observant,' he said. 'These paintings were created with no more than three different colours. Some use only one or two, but none use more than three.

'It is an art in itself to say so much with such minimal strokes and minimal colour.'

'I imagine the tone is even more important in these paintings,' said Jojo.

'Your eyes are opening up to see more already,' said The Master.

Painting with a Limited Palette

Painting with a limited palette means using fewer colours. This technique can create sophisticated, harmonious paintings. You use fewer colours and use your knowledge of mixing to create all the other colours you need. Often you can get away with only three tubes of colour for a minimal palette.

It also saves you money!

How to Select Paint Tubes When You're on a Tight Budget

If you select three tubes of paint very carefully, you will be able to mix all the colours you need. It's a great way to start out in a new medium if you're on a budget!

A Limited Palette Can Work Wonders

Painting with a limited palette is a great exercise. This means using a minimal set of tube colours and mixing all the colours you need from these. It really improves your colour mixing skills.

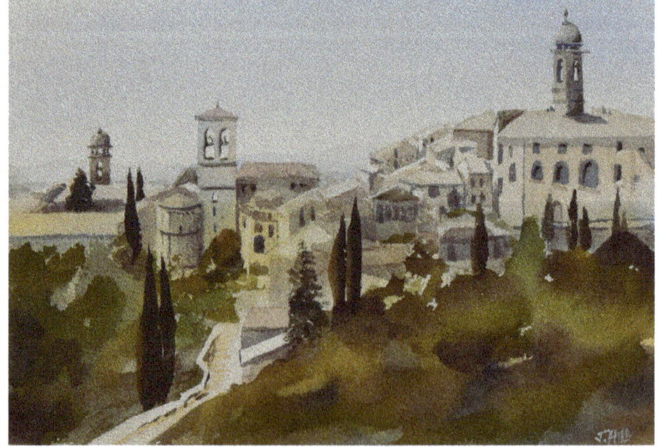

9-2 'Heart of Francis' (Assisi) Watercolour on Paper 30 x 21cm (12 x 8")
Private collection, Brisbane, Australia

I have created some of my favourite paintings with a limited palette.

Plus it takes a lot of confusion away for a beginner — you don't have too many colours to choose from. By mixing colours from a limited set, you get so much better at understanding colours and how they combine.

With practice, you can think of a colour and immediately know how to mix it up.

You Can Get Away with Only 3 Tubes, Plus White

I'll introduce you to a few of my primary colour selections (with only three tubes of paint). Next we'll look at what a good choice might be if you were able to buy six tubes of paint.

All of this colour information applies to every medium, including drawing pencils and pastels.

3 Colour Sets (Triads)

Traditional Primaries

I remember in school days we received a set of five colours in a box. It included black, white and three primary colours:

- Bright golden yellow

- Mid-blue

- Fire engine red

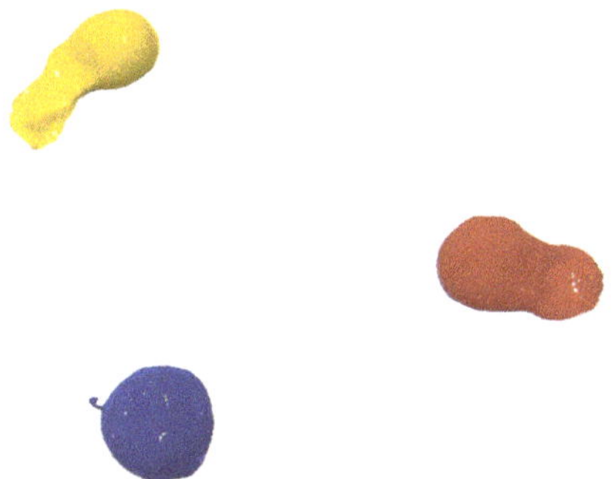

I remember being able to mix a nice orange from the yellow and red, and an ok sort of green from the yellow and blue.

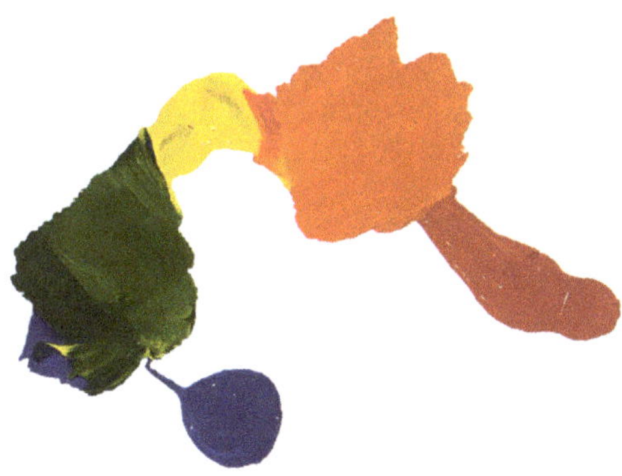

But every time I tried to get a nice purple colour with the red and blue, I was disappointed and frustrated. The colour always turned out a yucky brown! I could never get a pretty purple.

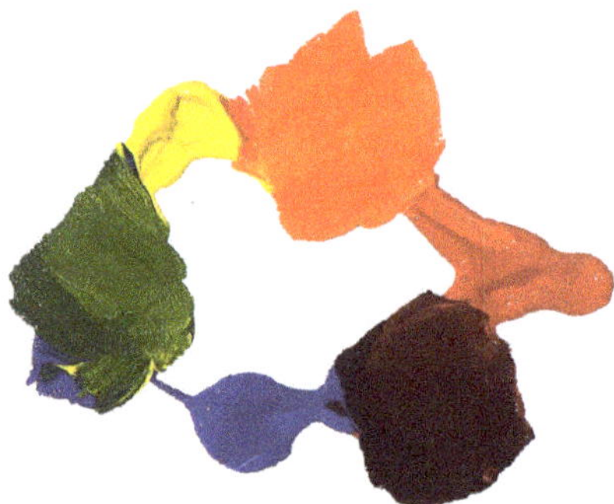

The red in these packs was a really bad choice. It had too much yellow in it, so mixing the red and blue resulted in brown instead of purple. In effect I was mixing three primary colours together, which gives brown.

Now that I'm all grown up, I can choose my own primary colours and I've worked out a better red to pick.

My Favourite Basic Primaries

Here's a really good set to start out with if you've only got enough pocket money to buy three tubes of paint:

- Golden yellow, eg Cadmium Yellow (CaY)

- French Ultramarine Blue (FUB)

- Pure Magenta or Rose, eg Permanent Quinacridone Magenta (PQM) or Permanent Rose (PR)

Here are the watercolours:

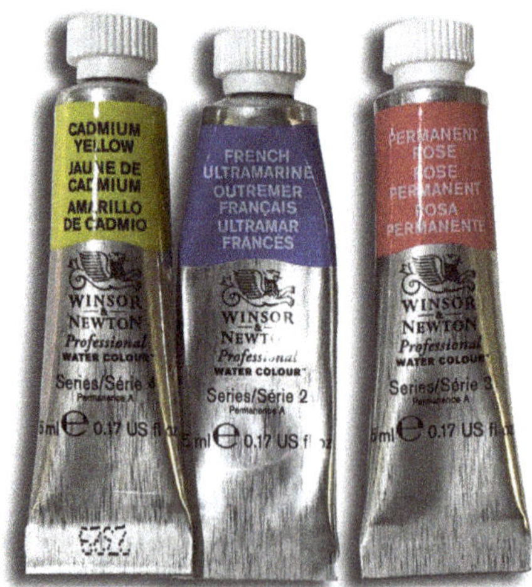

The equivalent colours in acrylic are delicious when laid out in a colour wheel:

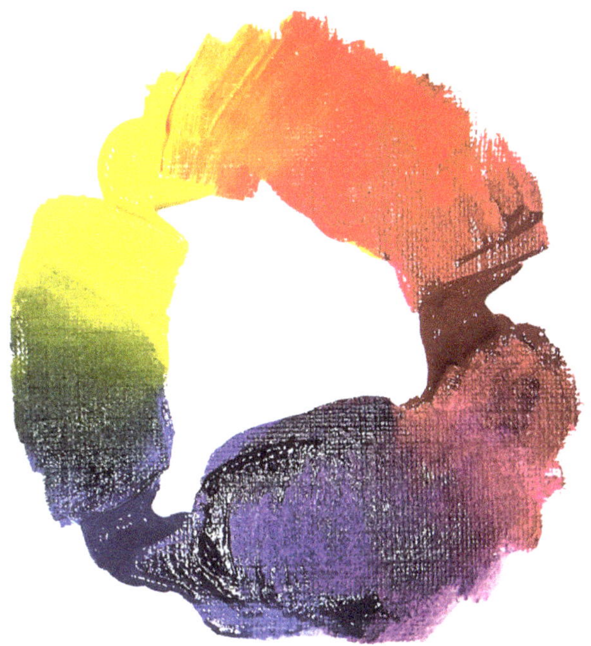

This set gives pure, clear secondary colours, except for green.

This blue is warm, meaning it has hints of red or purple in it. You'll learn more about warm and cool colours in Chapter 10 Heated Hues. The yellow is warm too. It has hints of orange or red in it. So when mixing the two we get a browny tinge to the green, because all three primaries are present in this mix.

I quite like having a muted green in a basic set of paints because greens in nature are often muted. It's very rare to see an acid green or pure green in trees and grass.

The other thing I like about this mixture is that the French Ultramarine Blue (FUB) is a nice strong dark. So you can use it to darken colours and get better tonal variation in your paintings.

So you get clear secondaries except for green. But a dirty green is more realistic in nature. And you can get nice strong darks with French Ultramarine Blue (FUB).

Bright Primaries

In printing processes, there is a term called CMYK. This stands for the colour set Cyan, Magenta, Yellow and Black. Colour printing on paper often creates the full range of colours using only these 4 colours of ink. Let's look at the three primaries:

- Yellow — Transparent Yellow (TY) or Lemon Yellow (LY)

- Cyan — Cerulean Blue (CeB) or Manganese Blue (MnB)

- Magenta — A Magenta or Rose colour, same as in the Basic Primaries

This combination gives you very pretty, clean bright secondary colours.

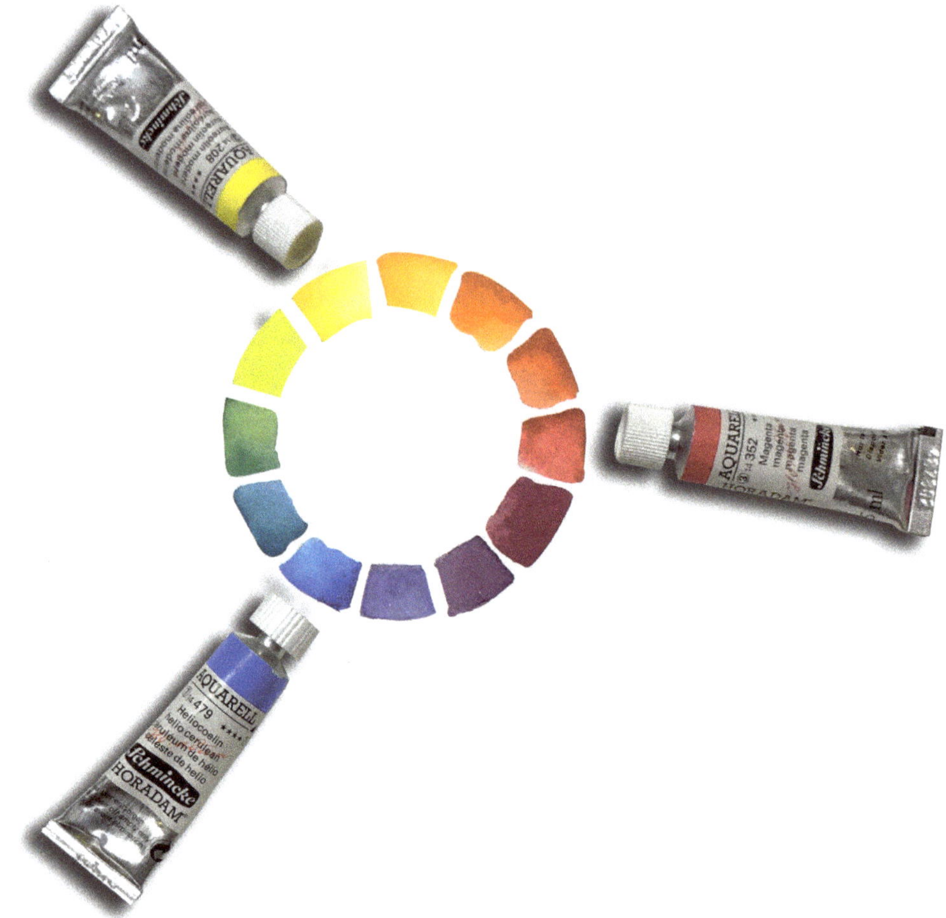

Unless you are using very strong pigments like the Schmincke colours above, it is sometimes difficult to get strong darks with this colour set.

6 Colour Sets

Let's look at a minimal set of colours that will allow you to paint any colour under the sun, from bright to muted and everything in between.

Maybe you have more pocket money and can extend your collection a little. A six colour set is perfect.

Of course, you can also add white to make it seven. But I usually don't think of white as a colour. Here let's just look at the six colours.

Don't forget that white is unnecessary to buy for watercolour — instead the blank paper is the white.

Split Primaries

We get the best six colours by splitting the three primaries into two colours each.

If you were to take the basic primaries:

- Cobalt Blue (CoB)
- Winsor Yellow (WY)
- Winsor Red (WR)

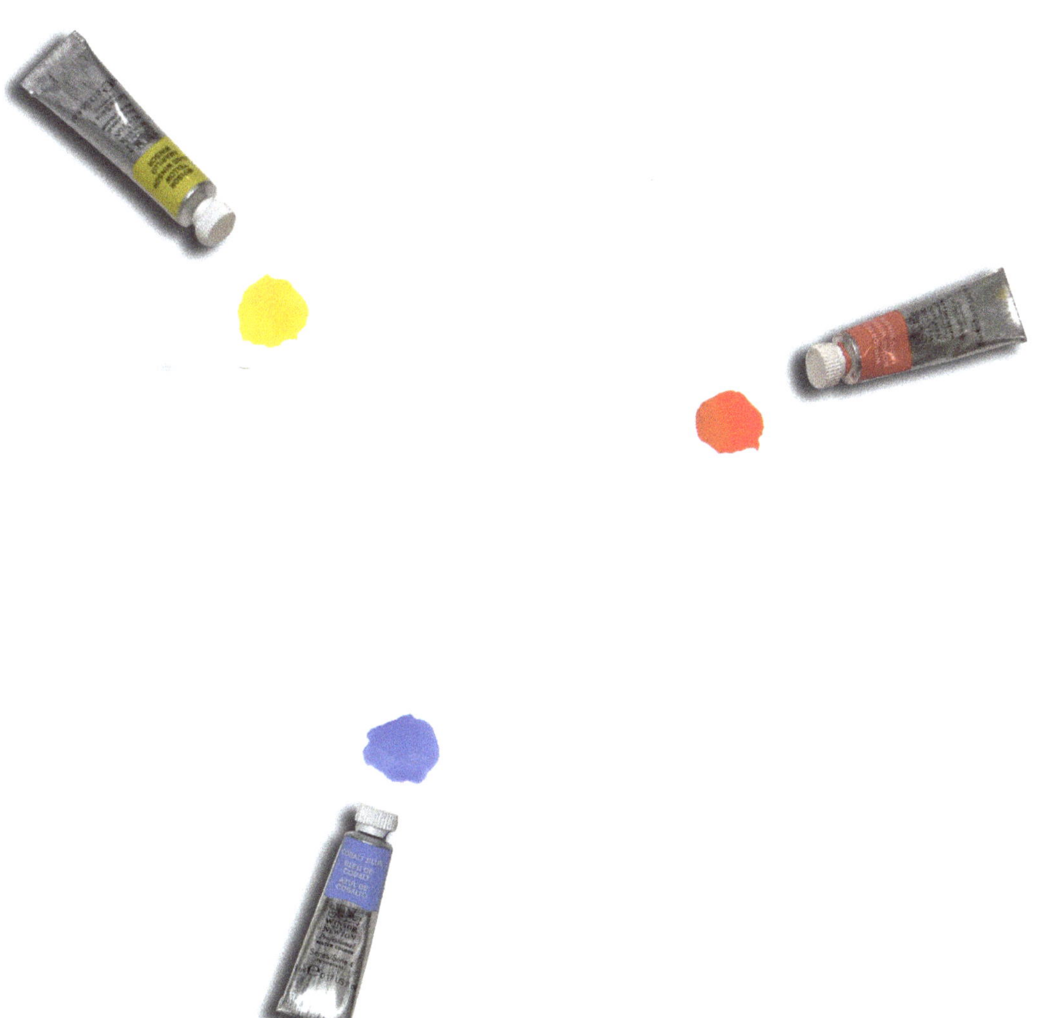

and then split each into two, you would have a set of six colours that would mix the most pure, clear secondary colours you could imagine.

I call this set of six my Split Primaries colour set.

It's my favourite set to buy when I am starting out on a new medium or brand.

To see how to do it, let's look at each primary one by one.

How to Split Yellows

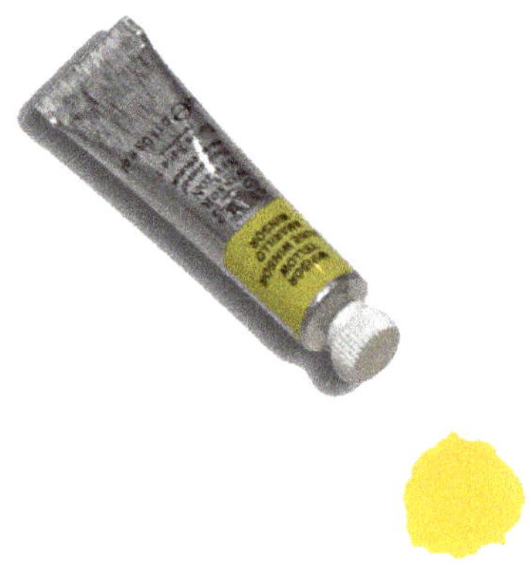

Yellow sits between two secondary colours.

On one side is orange, which *leans towards* the red side of the wheel.

On the other side of yellow is green, which is off on the blue side.

We could take a simple 'middle' yellow (a 'primary yellow' or a 'spectrum yellow') that sits right between the secondaries. It wouldn't *lean towards* orange. By that I mean it doesn't have an orangey tinge to it. It also wouldn't *lean towards* green; there's no hint of green in the yellow. So it's right in the middle. It's just yellow.

Instead of using a middle yellow, you can split it into two yellows, each sitting to either side of the middle. That's what I call a Split Primary.

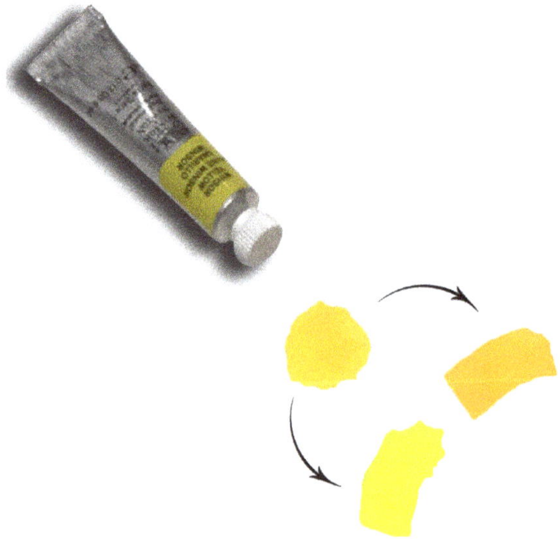

Choose a yellow that *leans towards* green a little. A Transparent Yellow or Lemon Yellow is a good choice for this one.

Also choose a yellow that *leans towards* orange a little. Such as a Golden Yellow or Cadmium Yellow. These have the tiniest hint of orange in them.

To compare the two colours, lay out a little sample of each side by side on some paper. Then you can see which secondary colour they lean towards and you can see the difference between the two of them.

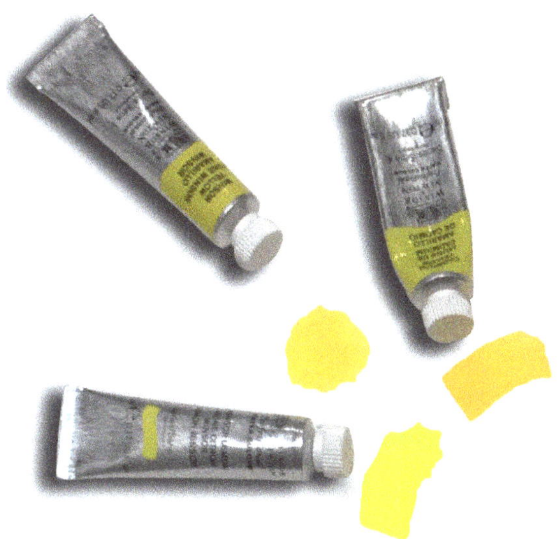

So now we've got the two yellows chosen.

How to Split Blues
We do the same process for blue.

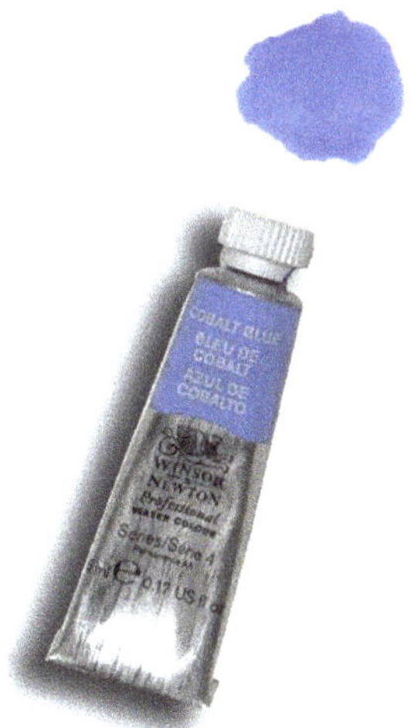

I would call Cobalt Blue a 'middle' blue. In some paint ranges you will find a Spectrum Blue.

To split the primary blue, we need a blue that *leans towards* purple — French Ultramarine Blue (FUB) is a good choice.

A blue that *leans towards* green is something like Phthalo Blue (PhB).

You can see the difference when you lay samples of these split primaries next to one another. One *leans towards* green, one *leans towards* purple.

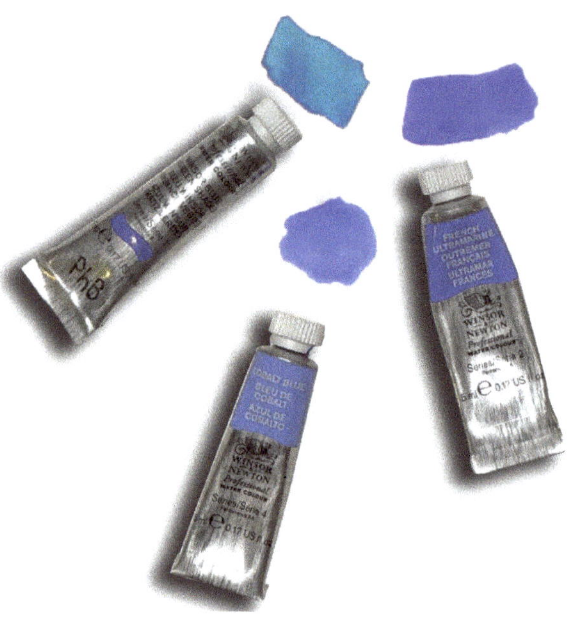

How to Split Reds

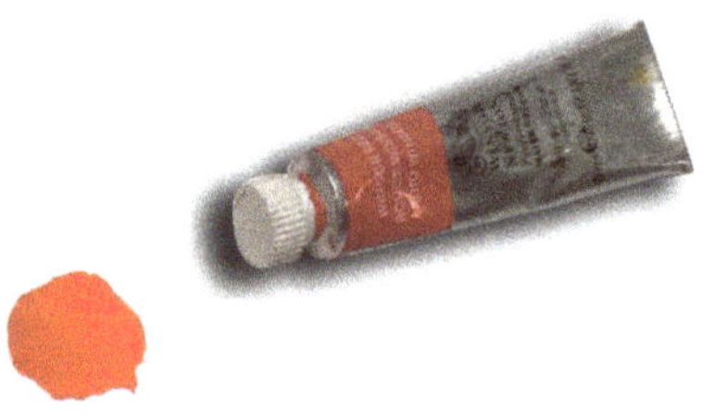

In Winsor & Newton the middle red is Winsor Red.

One of the primary red splits is an orangey red, which I call Fire Engine Red. A Napthol Red Light (NRL) or Cadmium Red (CaR) is a good choice for a red that *leans towards* orange.

The purply red would be Magenta or Rose. I like the permanent versions of these colours, which are lightfast (see Chapter 12 Mixing Maestro). So I choose Permanent Magenta (PM) or Permanent Rose (PR).

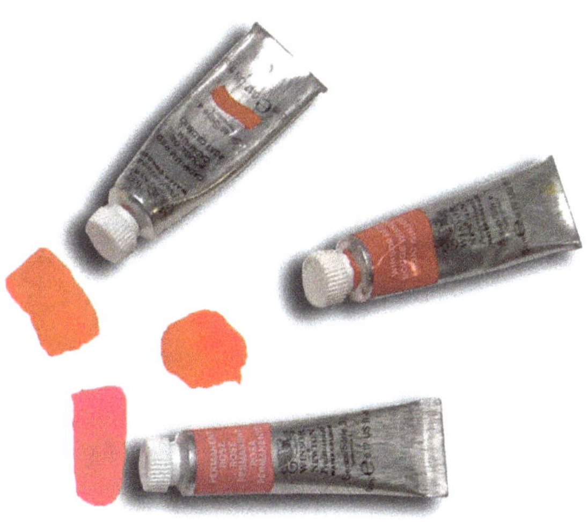

Now we've got a beautiful set of split primaries. Let's put them into a new colour wheel.

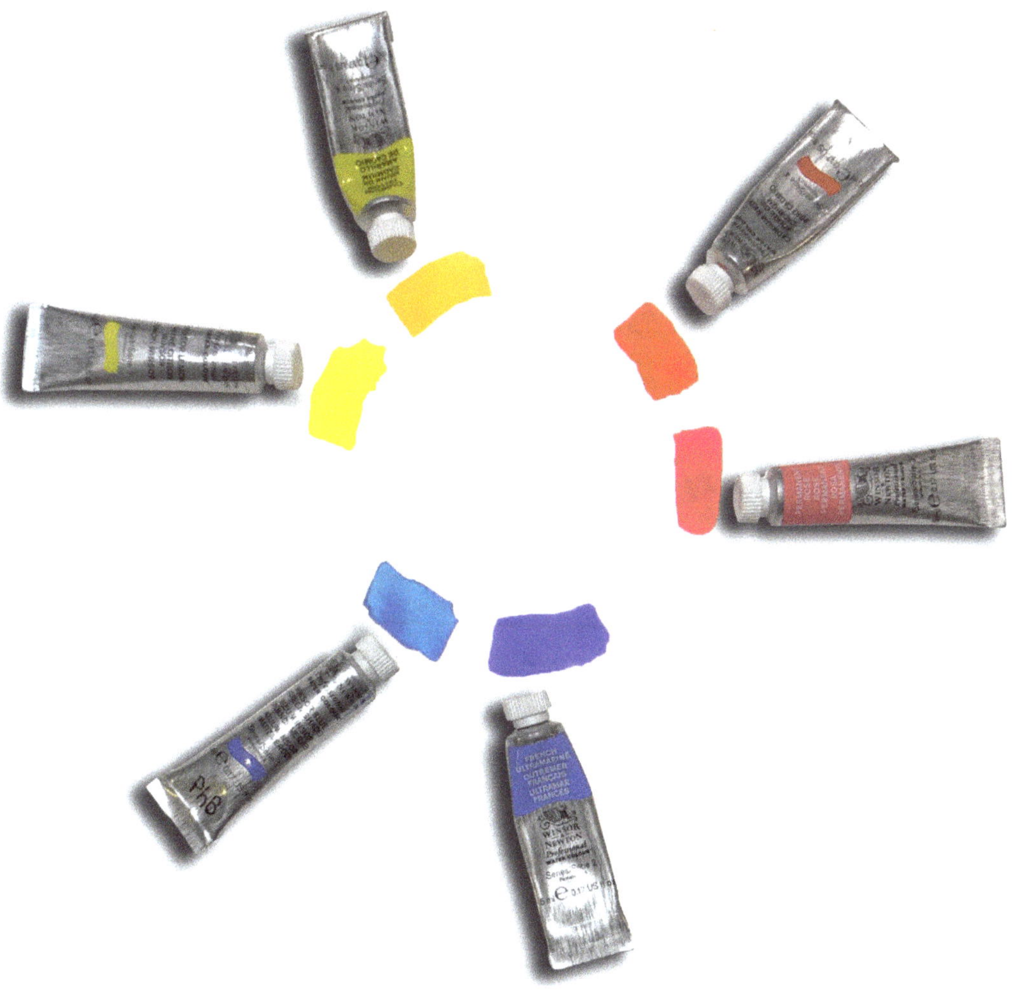

The Clear Secondaries

When you use a set of split primaries, the most exciting thing is that you will get really pure, clean, bright secondary colours.

By choosing two of the split primaries that lean towards the colour you want, you get a brilliant version of that colour.

For example, mix a greeny yellow with a greeny blue and you will end up with a very greeny green!

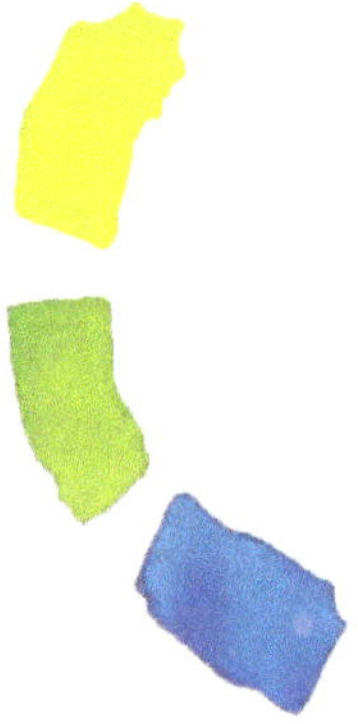

Why is the colour so clean? Because none of that wicked old third primary, red, is coming in to give you brown. It's just not in the mix.

All the secondaries will be bright and beautiful.

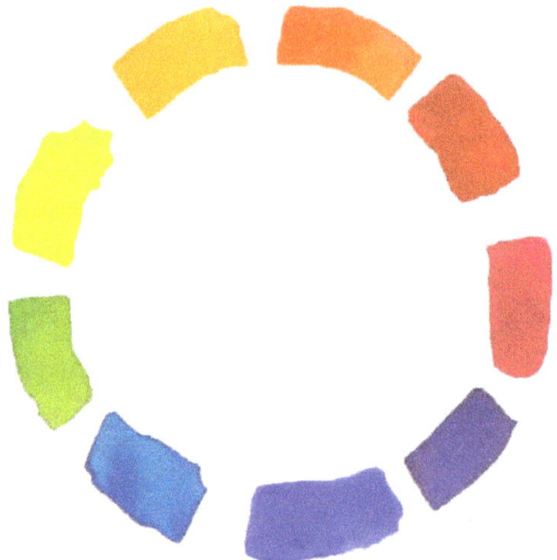

You can compare these bright, clean secondaries with the secondary colours we get by mixing the original three primaries below. The original mixes are the small dots. Can you see they are duller colours than our new ones?

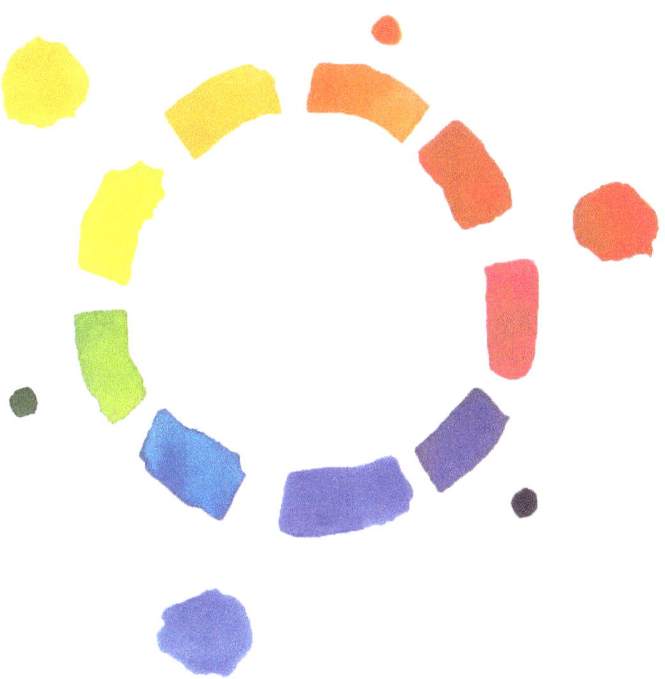

Once you can mix pure clean colours of any part of the rainbow, you can learn how to knock back colours into more muted versions really easily. We'll look at how to do this in Chapter 11 Dancing Duets.

With the full range of pure colours, and knowledge of mixing muted colours, you can create any colour you will ever need from just six tubes of paint! Isn't that exciting?

Play Time

Colour Wheels

1. Select the best set of six Split Primaries from your current paint set.

    a. Lay them out in the correct order around the wheel.

    b. Create a colour wheel with these colours.

    c. Check that you get really clear clean secondary colours. (If you don't, check your choice of split primaries.)

2. Choose your favourite set of three CMY colours (Bright Primaries).

    a. Lay them out in the correct order around the wheel.

    b. Create a colour wheel with these colours.

    c. Make bright and clear (not dusty, dirty and muted) secondaries. (If you don't, check all of your primaries are pure and neutral.)

CHAPTER 10
HEATED HUES

Every day we are engaged in a miracle
which we don't even recognise:
a blue sky, white clouds, green leaves...
our own two eyes. All is a miracle.

Thich Nhat Hanh

CHAPTER 10 CONTENTS

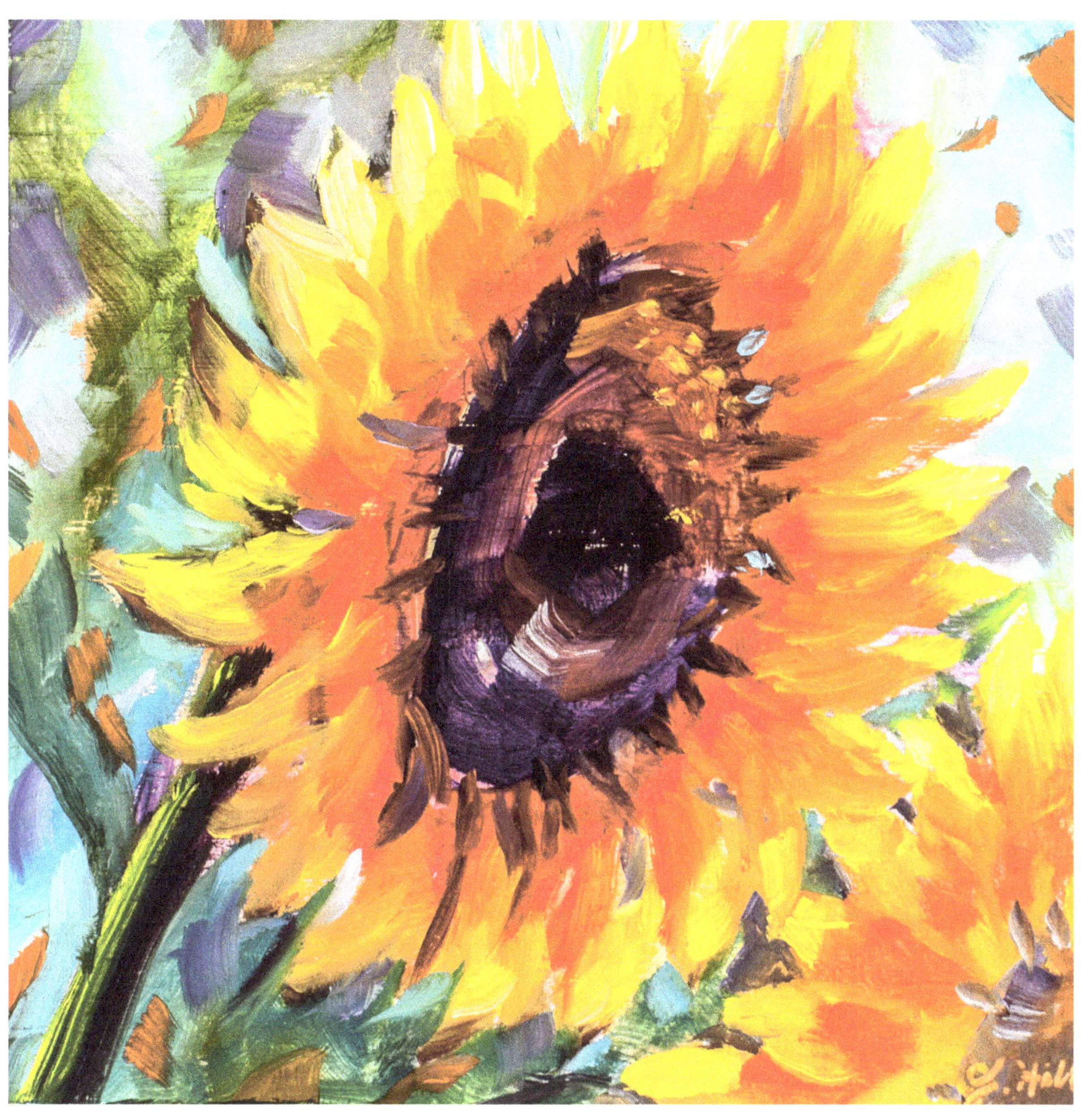

10-1 'Summer Smile (Sunflower)' Oil on Wood Panel 15 x 15cm (6 x 6")
Daily Painting No 346 for 2015. Brooks Collection, Stirling, Perth, Western Australia

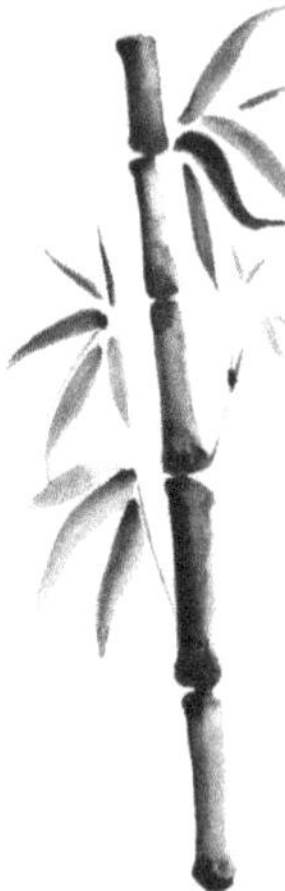

Sitting in the clearing with The Master, Jojo looked around and breathed deeply. The air in the shade was cool and the large stones they sat on were cool to touch. The sunshine filtered through the canopy of leaves above to warm Jojo's upturned face. The bamboo leaves above were backlit by the sun. She saw greens that looked almost fluorescent with sunlight.

'I've heard that different colours have different feelings,' said Jojo. 'That's true, isn't it?'

'It is true that every different colour evokes a feeling,' answered The Master. 'Some colours are high energy. Some are peaceful energy.'

'How do I know which is which?' asked Jojo.

'If you quiet your thinking Modern Mind and peacefully explore your inner feelings with Zen Mind present, you may find what the feeling is.

'Make sure that you are truly in Zen Mind — in the present. Allow any memories that you have of that colour to float on by and disappear.'

'I'm going to try that,' said Jojo. 'It sounds fun.'

She thought for a moment, looking around at the shade and sunshine, dappled all around the clearing floor.

'I've heard of warm and cool colours before,' she said. 'But I've never really understood what it means. I've got a vague idea that red makes you feel warm, and blue makes you feel cold. But I'm sure there's more to it than that.'

'You are right,' said The Master. 'There is often much confusion around warm and cool colours. We'll do some exploring so that you will really see. It is very important in your painting.'

'I'm excited,' said Jojo. 'It will be so good to finally understand.'

Warm & Cool

If you look at some paintings by the old masters, you can get a feel of the painting being warm or cool.

For example, scenes of winter are painted in a particular colour palette of blues and greens that makes the painting look very cool.

The impressionists were particularly good at contrasting the warmth of dappled sunlight against the cool of soft shadows in the one painting.

Degas painted ballet dancers in the wings off stage with blue in the cooler light of the shadows.

In my painting of an old pier in the Far North of Australia, I contrasted the cool of the water with the burning sunlight on the jetty above and the warm red bucket.

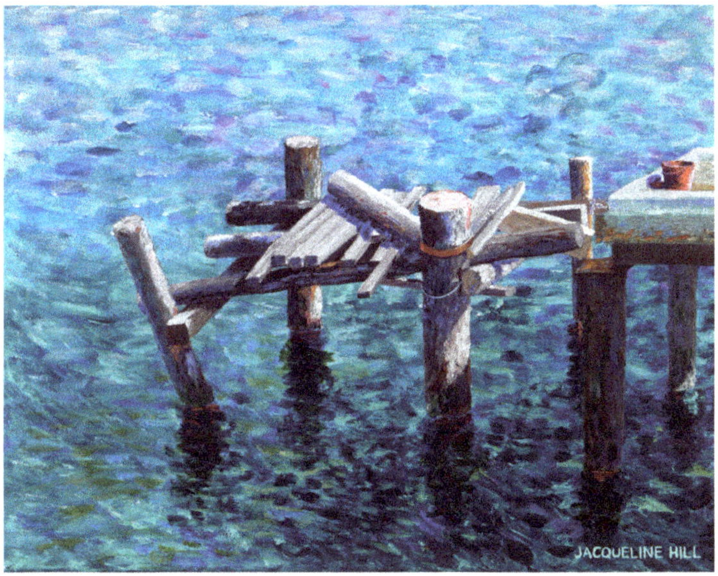

10-2 'Old Pier at Karumba' Acrylic on Canvas 59 x 40cm (23 x 16")
Painted on location in Far North Queensland, Australia

Here's a painting where the warm colours dominate. The cool background helps to contrast with warm fruits.

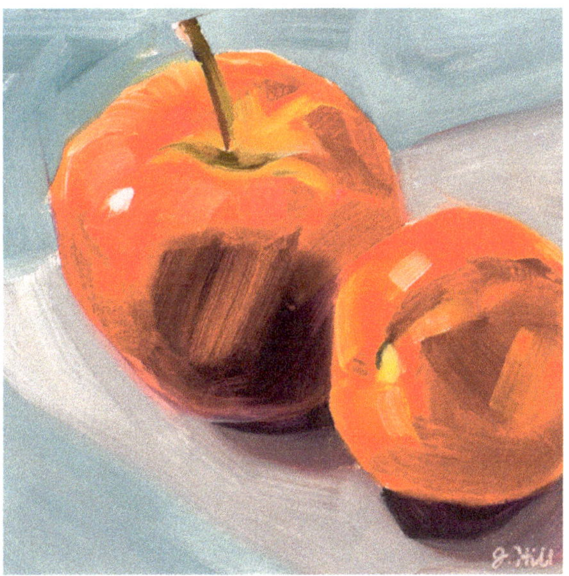

10-3 'Red Army' (Apple and Tomato) Oil on Wood Panel 15 x 15cm (6 x 6")
Daily Painting No 246 for 2015. Private Collection, Australia

Which Colours are Which?

Here's how you remember what colours are warm and cool:

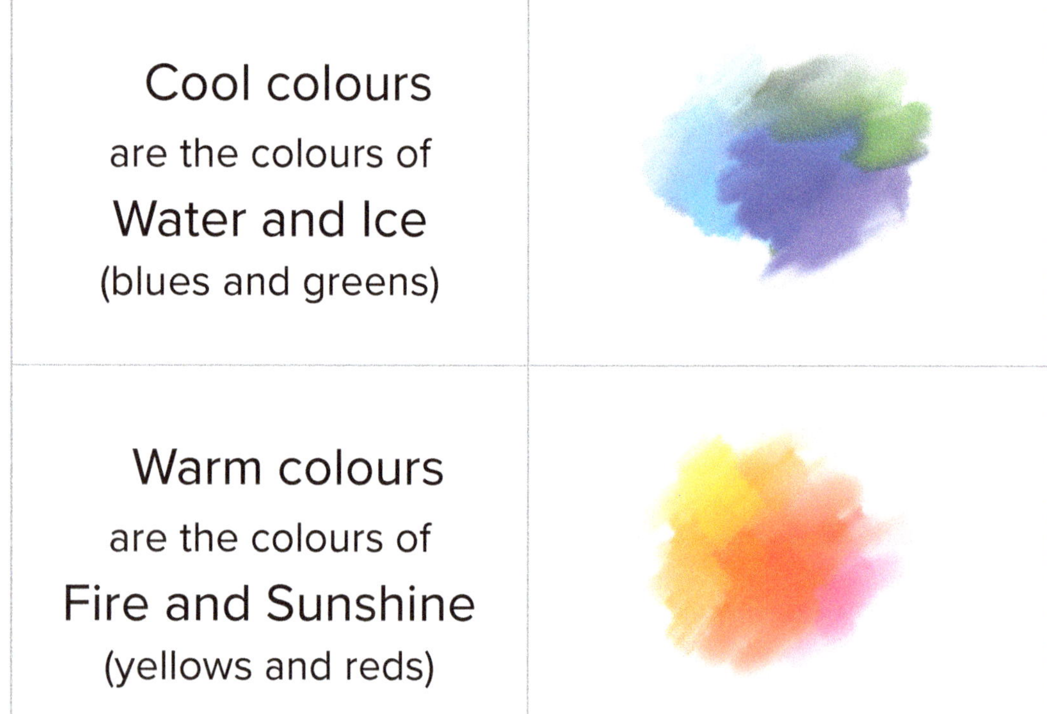

<table>
<tr><td>

Cool colours

are the colours of

Water and Ice

(blues and greens)

</td><td></td></tr>
<tr><td>

Warm colours

are the colours of

Fire and Sunshine

(yellows and reds)

</td><td></td></tr>
</table>

You can label colours as warm or cool in two different ways.

First Method: Zones in the Overall Colour Rainbow

This is the method for the chart of warm and cool colours above.

If you look at the overall colour wheel, you can label part of it as cool and part of it as warm.

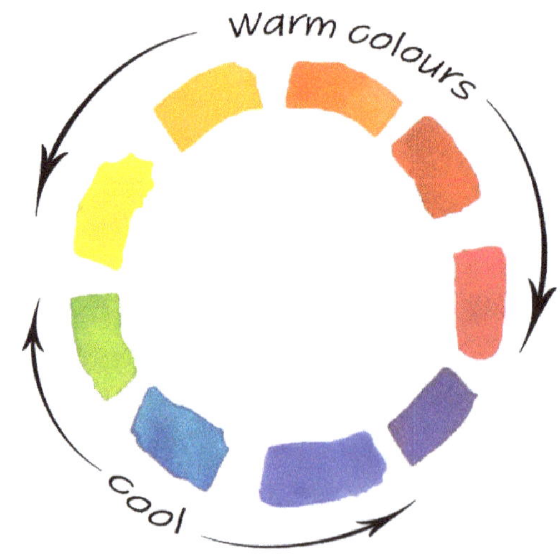

We usually say that 'red is a warm colour' or 'blue is a cool colour'.

Can you see where the two zones meet? Purple is difficult to label as either warm or cool. You could call it a 'neutral' colour. Neutral colours, when talking about the temperature of colours, are neither warm nor cool.

Second Method: Comparing Individual Colours

Sometimes we refer to a 'warm yellow' or a 'cool yellow'. This is when we compare two versions of a colour and decide which one is warmer or cooler than the other.

Remember when we split yellow into two colours for our Split Primaries? We actually took each neutral primary and split it into a *warm* and *cool* version of that colour.

Warm & Cool in the Split Primaries Set

From a neutral yellow, which is neither warm nor cool, we split it into a warm yellow and a cool yellow. The warm yellow *leans towards* red (a hot colour), and the cool yellow *leans towards* green (a cool colour).

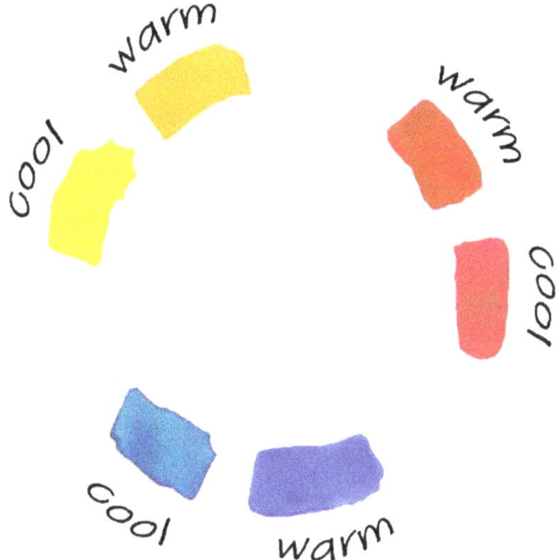

Blue was split into a warm blue (the purply-red blue) and a cool blue (the greeny blue).

Red was split into a warm red (closer to orange) and a cool red (the purply one that's closer to blue).

You can also talk about warm and cool secondary colours when you compare them.

It's difficult to say whether an orange can be warm orange or a cool orange because all the oranges sit between the two warm colours, red and yellow! But it's good to know that red is a hotter colour than yellow. So if you really want to, you can even talk about a warm orange or a cool orange depending on whether it *leans towards* red (warmer) or yellow (cooler).

Why are Warm & Cool Important?

- Warm colours advance in your painting and cool colours recede. You can create the illusion of depth by putting the warmer colours in your foreground objects and the cooler colours in your distant, background objects.

- Objects in sunlight are often warm and objects in shadow are often cool.

- You can create cool wintry paintings by using mostly cool colours.

- You can create warm, cosy fireside paintings by using a lot of warm colours.

- You can make warm feeling or cool feeling abstracts.

Using your Zen Mind with your eyes open to see what's truly there will help you to discern.

'Oh I love that simple explanation of warm and cool,' said Jojo. 'Now I understand why I was confused before — I didn't realise there were two ways of labelling warm and cool.'

The Master smiled. 'It is wonderful for a teacher to have such an enthusiastic Little Grasshopper so keen to learn,' he said.

'Can you teach me some more about colours?' asked Jojo, bright-eyed.

'Do you remember the Notan, the Lord of Light and Dark?' asked The Master.

'From the Three Emperors,' said Jojo. 'He was the Lord of Tone.'

'Yes,' said The Master. 'There are some secrets that his armies know that may help you with your painting.'

Jojo looked at him and waited.

'Would you like to know some advanced secrets about darks and lights?' he asked.

'Well of course!' laughed Jojo.

Darks & Lights

Extending your tonal range to the extremes is important for bringing punch and interest to your paintings. Here are some tips to help you.

Naturally Dark Colours

Some colours are naturally pale (like most of the yellows), while others are naturally dark.

When you are aware of the naturally dark colours (strong darks), you won't get too heavy handed when mixing them.

I love having one or two dark colours in my minimal palette so I can mix up a colour as close to black as possible (without using black). This way I include the whole tonal range in my painting and keep that punch and sparkle in the artwork.

Pure white and pure black are fairly dead colours. I prefer to have shimmers of other colours in them, but still stretch the tones out to the full range.

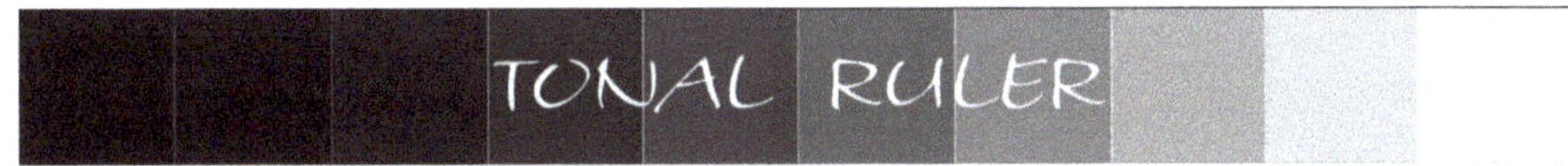

Here are a few of my favourite strong darks:

- French Ultramarine Blue (FUB)

- Permanent Alizarin Crimson (PAC)

- Burnt Umber (BU)

- Phthalo Turquoise (PhT)

- Dioxazine Purple (DP)

I've found these pigments consistently dark in all types of paint, whether watercolour, acrylic or oil.

Good professional pastels often have five sticks of tones for each colour, ranging from very pale to mid-tone (fully saturated colour) to dark.

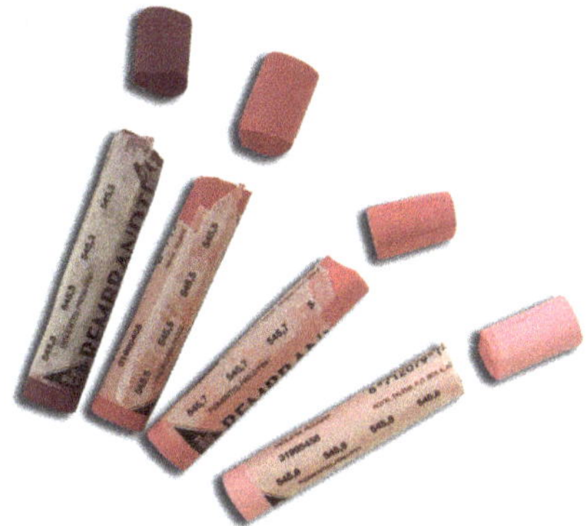

In pastel I have a few particular colours that I reach for to paint my darkest darks. One of my absolute favourites is in the Art Spectrum range; it's called Flinders Blue Violet Deep.

If you need to start with a strong dark drawing before you add pastel, then charcoal is great. But I find this Flinders Blue Violet Deep sometimes goes on even darker than charcoal.

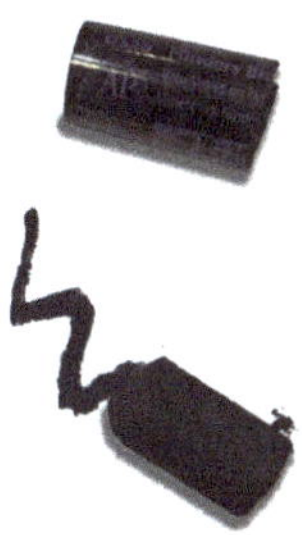

The Brightest, Purest Whites

In Pastel & Pencil

While we're on the topic of *tones* in pastels, I'll let you in on my secret for bright white. For a soft pure white, you can't go past a stick of Schmincke Titanium White. It's a beautiful soft pastel and will go over everything without pressing too hard.

It's perfect for putting in those final pops of highlights in your pastel painting. Remember the 'ting' in the crystal, from Chapter 1 Three Emperors?

In Watercolour

With watercolour painting, it is traditional not to use any white paint. Instead, leave the white of the paper untouched for your brightest highlights.

You can buy tubes of Titanium White (TW) and Chinese White (CW) in watercolour paints. But they don't look anywhere near as fresh and lovely as just leaving the white paper.

In Oil, Acrylic, Gouache & Ink Paints

In these paints, I've tried using all the different whites available.

My go-to white is always Titanium White (TW). It keeps things simple.

In the old days it used to be Lead White, but of course this is far too toxic to use any more.

Titanium White is very opaque and very strong.

Other Whites

There are lots of other whites you will find on the shop shelf.

I have tried Zinc White and Mixing White, which have a lot less white pigment in them and so are more transparent than Titanium White. But I tend not to use these any more. I find that sticking with one white makes it easier to work out proportions when mixing colours. Your process becomes smoother when you are familiar with the mixing strength of one white.

Particularly when you are starting out, jumping between different whites can be confusing.

Transparent v Opaque with Whites

Remember that *adding white to any transparent*[11] *colour will make it opaque and chalky.* All the transparency will be lost.

If you want to lighten the colour, but you want *to keep the transparency, add clear medium* — and keep well away from the white. Don't even allow any white to sit in your brush!

Black Without Black

I love having darks in my painting without using a black from a tube. I find the tube black makes a very dead, dull colour. It's the same as pure white: I much prefer to have some subtle shimmery colours hiding in both these extreme tones.

Sometimes I use undiluted Diox Purple (DP) as a strong dark. But if I want a neutral black, then I mix it.

I much prefer a shimmering black with subtle hints of other colours in the darkness of the paint.

Here is one of my top-secret formulae from the Secret Lab[23] to mix a black.

My favourite (and the easiest one) is:

- French Ultramarine Blue (FUB) + Burnt Umber (BU)

These are two lovely dark colours and mixing them together in the right quantities makes a beautiful black.

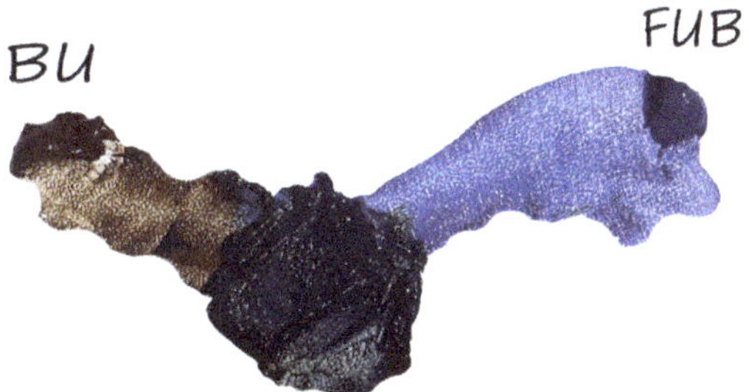

I also use Diox Purple (DP) with a lovely dark and a very transparent yellow, such as Indian Yellow (IY). You need a transparent[13] yellow so that the yellow (one of the lighter colours) doesn't lighten the dark of the purple. I find this mix still tends to look a bit brown so I add blue to make it neutral.

Just using French Ultramarine Blue (FUB) and Burnt Umber (BU) is the quickest way. This colour combination works in all painting mediums I have tried, including oil, acrylic, gouache[12], ink and watercolour.

When you're mixing two darks together, sometimes it's hard to see what colour you're getting. You can check how neutral your dark is by testing a tiny touch of the mixed colour with a bit of white. Looking at the resulting grey, you know whether it is learning towards blue or brown. Once it is right in between, then you've got the right black.

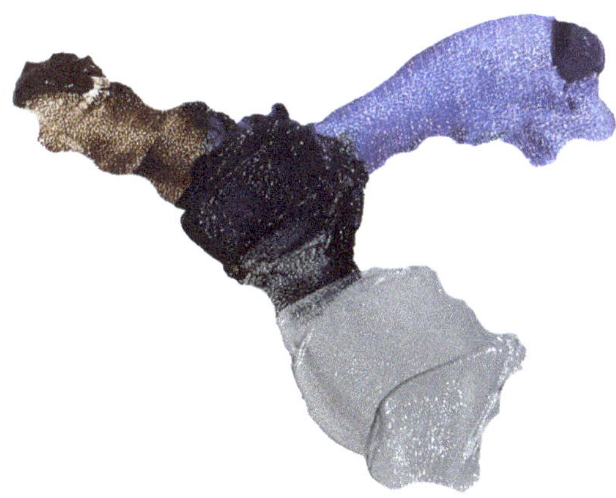

However, I prefer to not get white mixed in my brush. So I either smear the dark paint mix across the palette with my mixing knife or mix it with a touch of clear medium to see a grey.

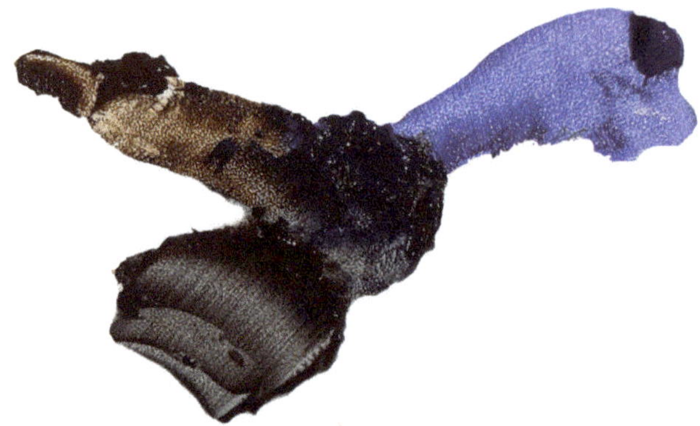

Once you've mastered mixing black, you can make any tone of grey by adding different amounts of white. This grey will not look as dull as a blacky grey from a tube but will show subtle hints of the delicious other colours through it.

You can also make your darks *warmer* by adding more brown or *cooler* by adding more blue. In small, subtle quantities of course!

Play Time

Warm & Cool Colours

If you've already made a colour chart with your paints laid out in Rainbow Order, use that to answer the following questions. Otherwise, take all your tubes and lay them out in a colour wheel circle, in Rainbow Order. Leave the browns, blacks and whites out of this game.

1. Remind yourself of the Overall warm–cool method.
    a. Can you see the two areas in your circle? Do they *feel* warm and cool to you?
    b. Can you spot the neutral colours where the two overall areas meet? Which colours would you label neutrals?
2. Remind yourself of the second warm–cool method for comparing individual colours.
    a. Look at the centre of the Yellow area. Which ones are on the cool side and which ones are on the warm side?
    b. Can you see any neutral 'spectrum' primaries in there?
    c. Repeat the above two steps for the other two primaries.

Mixing Black

Look up the list of dark colours in the section above called Naturally Dark Colours.

If you have any of these colours in your collection, try mixing up a few combinations to see if you can create a neutral blacky black.

CHAPTER 11
DANCING DUETS

Awareness is the greatest agent for change.

Eckhardt Tolle

CHAPTER 11 CONTENTS

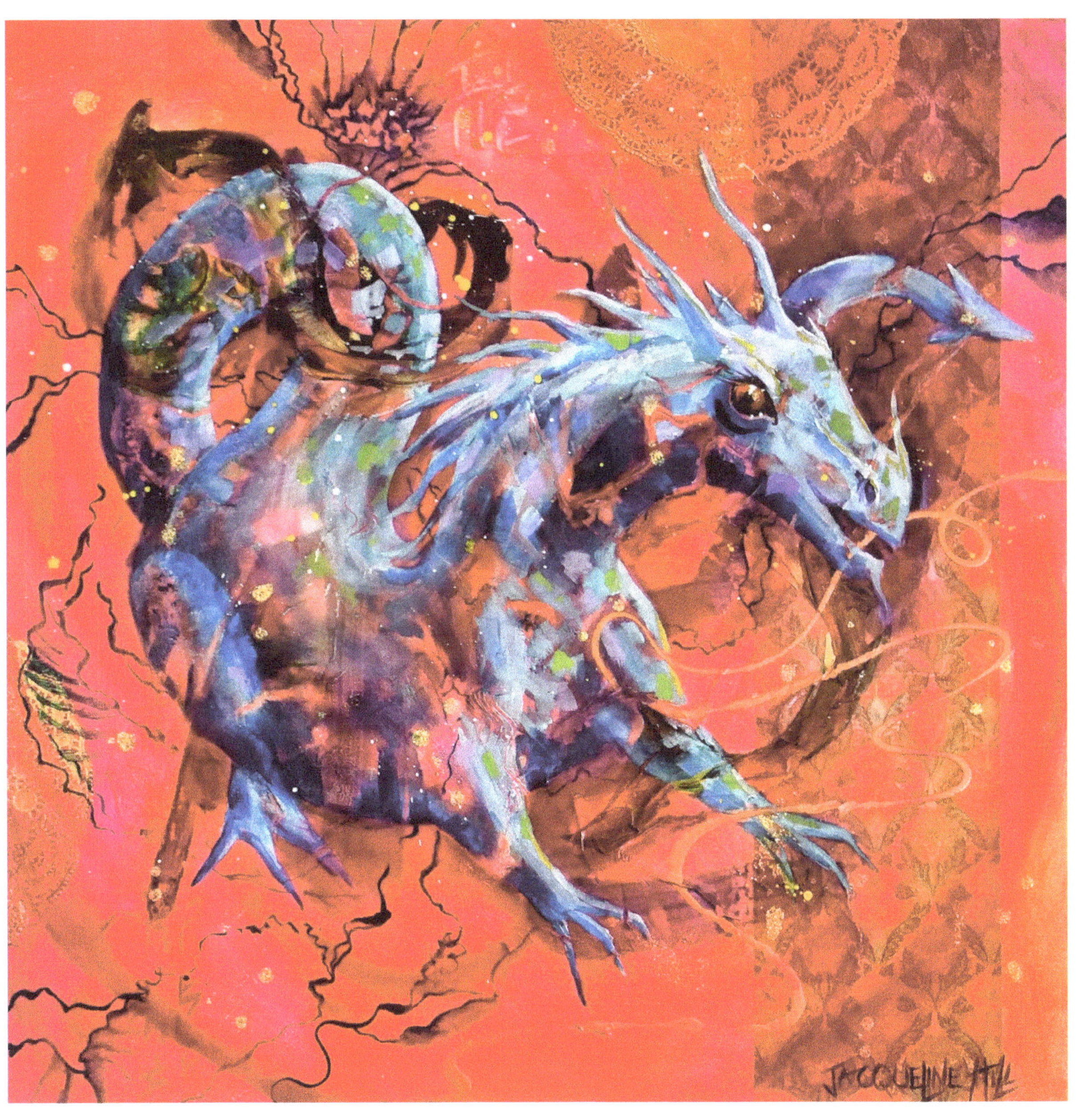

11-1 'Dragon II' Acrylic and Mixed Media with Japanese Paper, Gold and Copper on Canvas 60 x 60cm (24 x 24")
Vandervalk Collection, Cashmere, Queensland, Australia

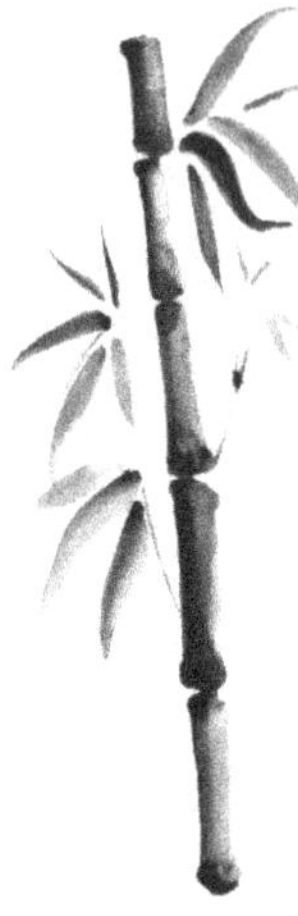

'I thought I knew all about the colour wheel,' said Jojo, 'but now I know so much more.'

The Master smiled. 'You still haven't uncovered the best secrets of all,' he told her.

'Really?' asked Jojo.

'You haven't yet learnt how to make colour sing,' said The Master.

'Oh, yes!' said Jojo, clapping her hands together.

'Now you understand the basics, you are ready,' said The Master. 'Let's begin. Have you heard the story of Blue-Kun and Orange-Chan?' he asked.

'No...' said Jojo. 'What are they?'

The Master smiled. 'Not what, but who. In the West you would call them Mr Blue and Miss Orange.'

Jojo shook her head. 'I definitely haven't heard of them,' she said, smiling, and settling down to listen.

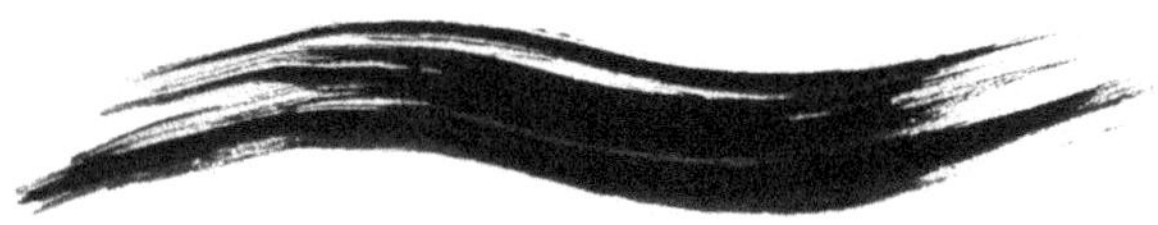

Blue-Kun and Orange-Chan

Blue-Kun was a young man who lived in a village with his family in the misty mountain forests of the Distant East. It was traditional in his village to wear blue. Everyone wore blue. The flags were blue. People painted their doors blue. Their favourite flowers were blue.

As Blue-Kun grew up he became dissatisfied with seeing nothing but blue. He wanted to see more!

Wise old Aunty had an idea. 'Perhaps it's time for you to travel a little, my boy!' she said.

He said goodbye to his parents and went travelling to explore other places in the region.

One day he came across the village of Orange, which was the furthest village away from his own. The whole village loved everything to be orange. Blue-Kun found it the most exciting place he had ever been to. The colour was so different from what he grew up with.

As he was walking along the village path, he met the most beautiful young woman named Orange-Chan.

She wore a kimono layered with beautiful shades of orange. She was smart and cheeky. She took no nonsense from him but she also found him terribly attractive — he was so different! She had never before seen such amazing shades of blue as those he dressed in.

Of course, they fell in love and decided to marry.

The marriage ceremony was held in a large forest clearing, halfway between the two faraway villages.

The two villages turned out to decorate everything in their blues and their oranges. It was the most spectacular display with lanterns, origami, ribbons, flags and flowers. Everyone agreed with Aunty that the contrasting blues and oranges had never looked so bright and cheerful.

Blue-Kun arrived in his most brilliant blue tunic and stood beside Orange-Chan in her fabulous orange wedding kimono. The two colours shimmered and sang against one another. Guests from both villages gasped and talked about how beautiful the couple looked alongside each other.

The Wise Monk from the monastery smiled as he married the two and blessed them.

Blue-Kun and Orange-Chan moved into their own little cottage in the forest. Then reality set in. They discovered they were very different people.

Blue-Kun loved cooking, so Orange-Chan agreed to help by washing the clothes (which she still didn't love doing). She didn't like having to wash the blue clothing and orange clothing separately to keep the colours looking like new. It was twice the work!

Orange-Chan was a little busy-bee and ran around doing lots of things. Blue-Kun preferred to sit in a comfortable chair and read peacefully.

Orange-Chan was annoyed when she didn't get enough help from Blue-Kun. And Blue-Kun was annoyed when Orange-Chan buzzed around fussing and working when he just wanted to relax.

'Why can't you be more like me?' they shouted at one another. 'And why can't you ever wear my favourite colour?'

Orange-Chan started to care a bit less and hurried through the washing chores to get onto more fun things to do. She would throw the tunic and kimono in the washing pot together and clean them all at once.

After a while, without them noticing, their bright clothes began to be a little bit duller; they lost their brilliant colour. They became more brown and grey.

When Aunty visited, she saw that their clothes looked very sad and dull and their faces were too.

'Are your hearts not happy?' she asked them. Blue-Kun and Orange-Chan glanced at each other then looked down at the ground, silent.

Aunty suggested they visit the Wise Monk in the monastery to get some advice.

At the monastery, the Wise Monk looked at them kindly and sat with them.

'I have been waiting for this visit,' he said. 'When you first fell in love, you fell in love with your differences. The stark contrast in your colours made your two colours sing. But there will always be vibrations and tremors when two are so opposite.

'You must remember this as you move on together. If you allow each of your colours to shine, you will sing together a happy song. If you smash your colours into each other, you will be dull, unhappy and sad. Your life will be grey and brown.

'Can you allow each other to be the bright person you married, and still love each other?'

Blue-Kun and Orange-Chan looked at each other.

'Yes, of course,' they agreed and kissed each other like new lovers.

The Monk blessed them again and they went home, much happier.

They also took Aunty's suggestion to wash their clothes separately.

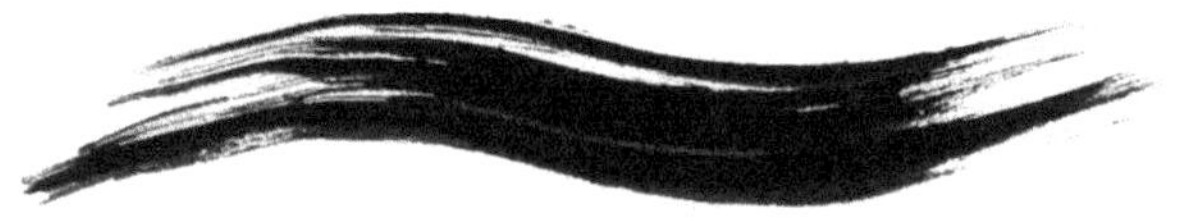

Jojo stared at The Master. 'That just sounds like marriage counselling,' she said. 'Or laundry advice!'

The Master laughed. 'But did you hear the story underneath the story?'

'About the colours, you mean?' asked Jojo.

'Of course.'

Jojo looked at the colour wheel she had painted. 'So blue and orange are complete opposites,' she said. 'And when they stand next to each other they look beautiful?'

'Even more beautiful than when they are on their own,' added The Master.

'And when they smash into each other, they knock each other out?' joked Jojo.

The Master smiled too. 'Now you understand,' he said.

What are Complementary Colours?

Complementary colours (spelt with two e's) are pairs of colours that sit opposite each other on the colour wheel.

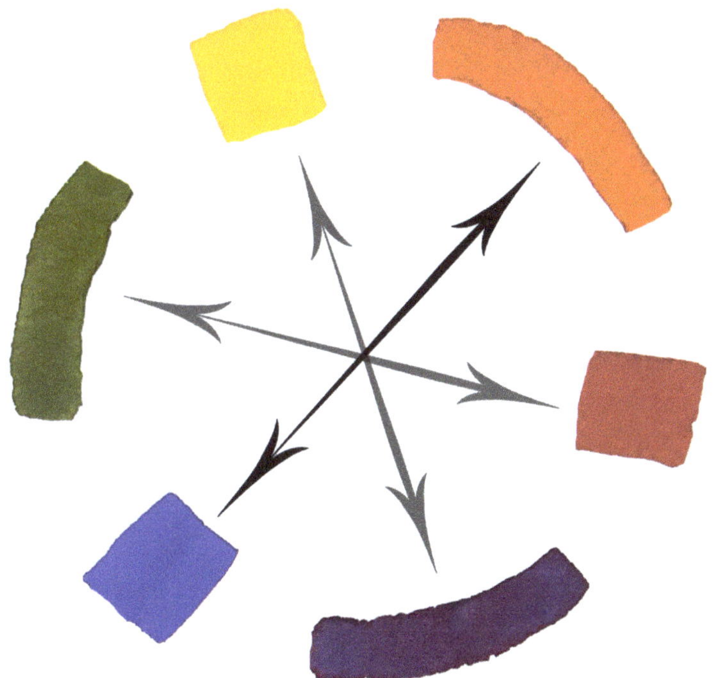

We say that 'orange is the complement of blue' and that 'blue is the complement of orange'. And that 'blue and orange are complementary colours'.

Here are the main pairs of complements. They must be pairs of colours that are directly opposite each other on the colour wheel.

- Yellow – Purple
- Blue – Orange
- Red – Green

Can you see that a primary colour's opposite is a secondary colour?

You can also find complements *anywhere* on the colour wheel, just by dialling the clock arrow around.

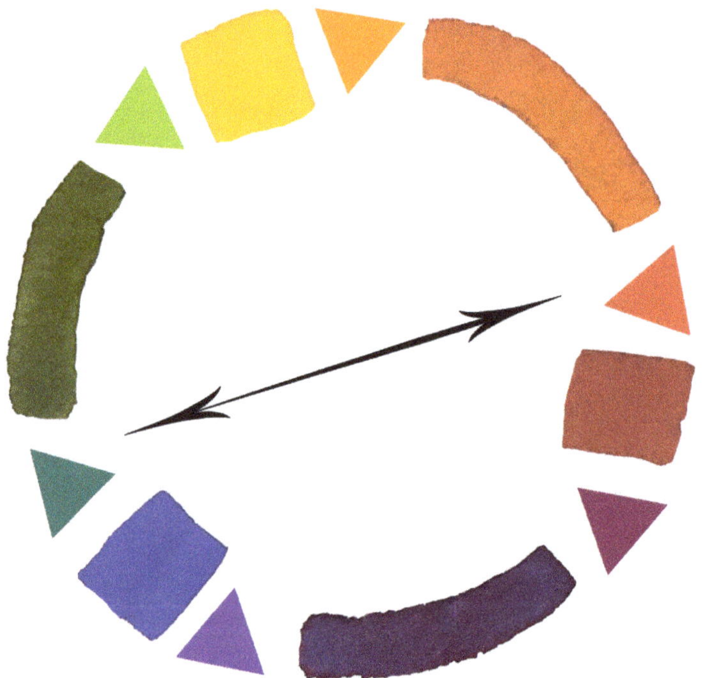

Can you see the complements of reddish orange and turquoise in the Dragon painting at the beginning of this chapter?

Why Complements are So Important

You need to understand two things about complementary colours:

1. When you put them *alongside* each other, they *dance*
2. When you *mix* them together, they *knock each other back*

Dancing Colours

When you put a pair of any complements alongside each other, they seem to vibrate. The two colours look brighter than they usually do when they are on their own.

I often use pairs of complements in my paintings. The colours end up looking so vibrant I often have people ask me what brand of paints I use! They are so excited about the colours in my artworks that they think I use some magical type of paint.

The fun part is that the brand is *irrelevant*. The key is getting the colours to dance and sing by combining them in this special way that makes them *look* brighter.

There's a wonderful book by Jeanne Dobie called *Making Color Sing*[18]. It's worth checking out. Jeanne talks about mouse colours and jewel colours.

Examples of Artworks Using Colour Dancing

It's a bit like companion planting in gardening — two plants that help each other grow stronger when planted alongside each other.

Here are some examples of paintings that make colour dance and sing by putting complements alongside one another.

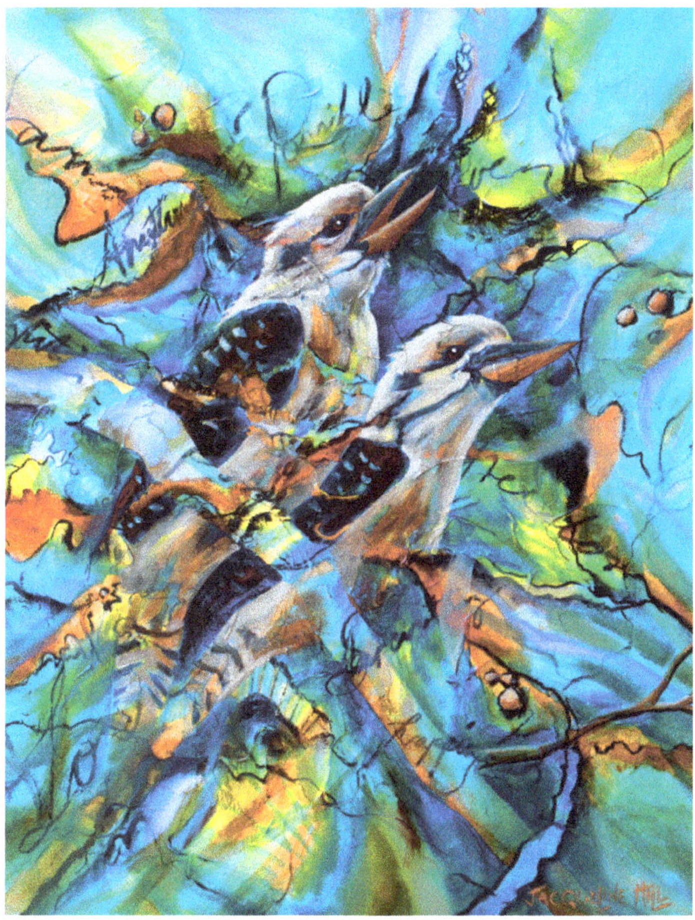

11-2 'Kookaburras II (The Lads)' Acrylic on Canvas 70 x 90cm (28 x 36")
Gentle Collection, Brisbane, Australia

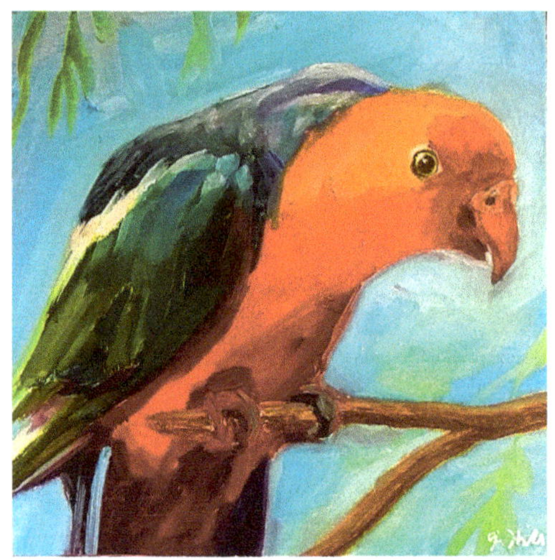

11-3 'King Parrot II' Oil on Wood Panel 15 x 15cm (6 x 6")
Daily Painting No 229 for 2015. Stephenson Collection, Anstead, Queensland, Australia

Knocking Back Colours

You also use your new knowledge of complements to mix muted or dusty colours. You can make muted colours by combining bright colours straight from the tubes. By understanding how to mix these muted colours, your art will go up another notch.

It doesn't mean that you can't still use your lovely bright pure colours! You can still have them in your painting, but a muted backdrop allows them to really shine. You will be able to control your focal points in your painting better with this knowledge.

How to Knock a Colour Back

A knocked back colour is slightly duller or less saturated than the original bright colour.

Take a good amount of the colour you want to knock back. Then add a tiny amount of its complement into it.

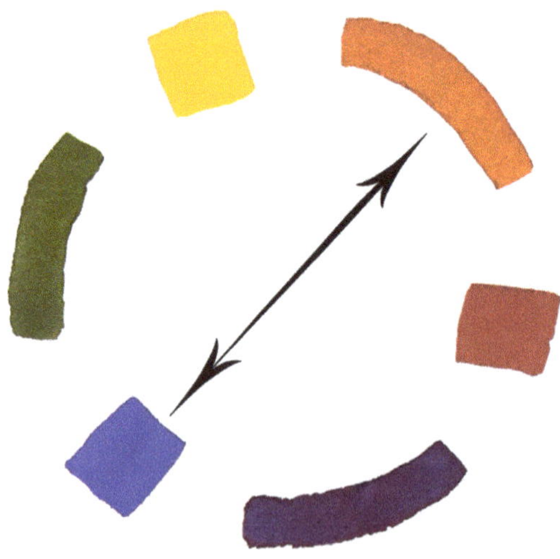

You need a lot of the original colour and only a tiny, tiny amount of the complementary. I tell my students the amount you want to add in is only the size of a bee's bum[24]. Sometimes it might be as small as the size of an ant's bum[24]!

Can you see how the tiniest amount of orange knocks back the bright blue into a duller version of blue?

How Using Complements Improves Your Paintings

Let's look at a couple of examples for when you may want to knock colours back.

Say you wanted to paint a little farmhouse on a green field. Here's what it would look like if you took the paints straight out of the tube:

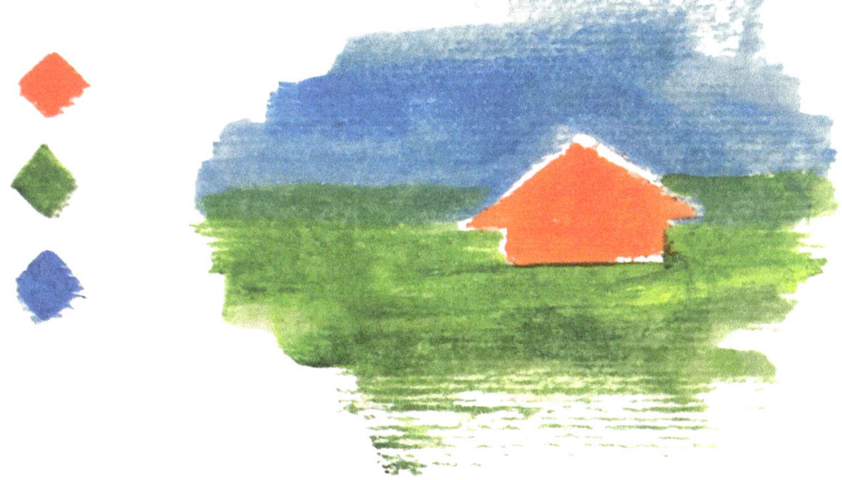

It looks a little naïve, doesn't it? Definitely a beginner's painting.

How about we start again, and think about what the colours need to be.

The red roof of the farmhouse might be a more rusty red, like a corrugated iron or terracotta roof tiles. So we would knock the red back.

Red is knocked back by its complement, green. Take a small puddle of red paint and add the tiniest little amount of green.

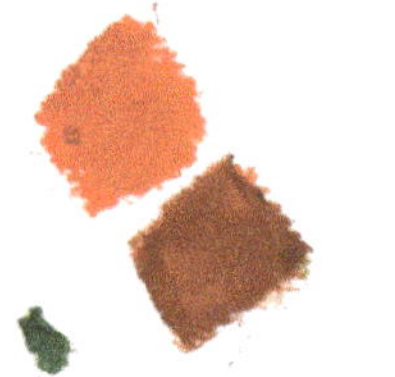 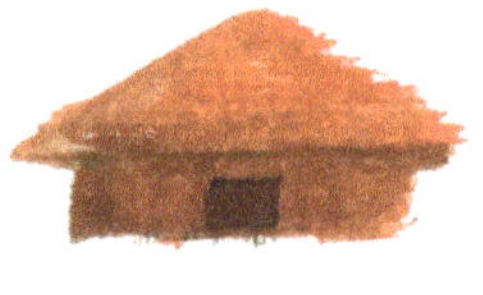

Then the green of grass is always a much more muted green than the viridian colour straight from the tube. Let's take an orangey red to knock back the bluey green and make a nice natural grass colour.

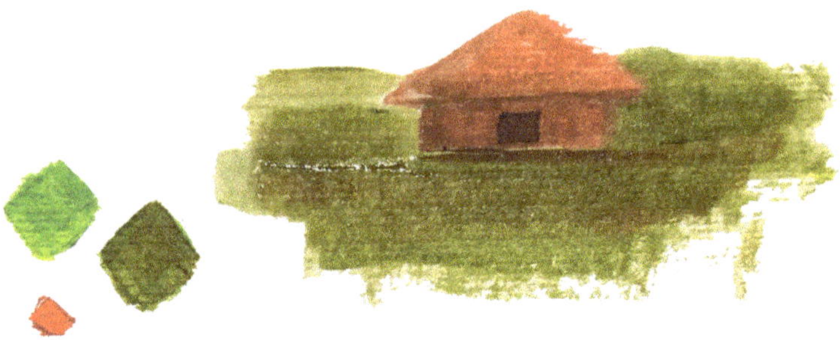

Then maybe we want a stormy wintery sky above. A stormy sky is usually greyer than a bright blue summer sky, so we need to knock back blue.

The complement of blue is orange — remember you just need to look at the colour opposite it on the colour wheel. So a tiny teeny amount of orange mixed into the blue gives a nice muted blue to put in the sky.

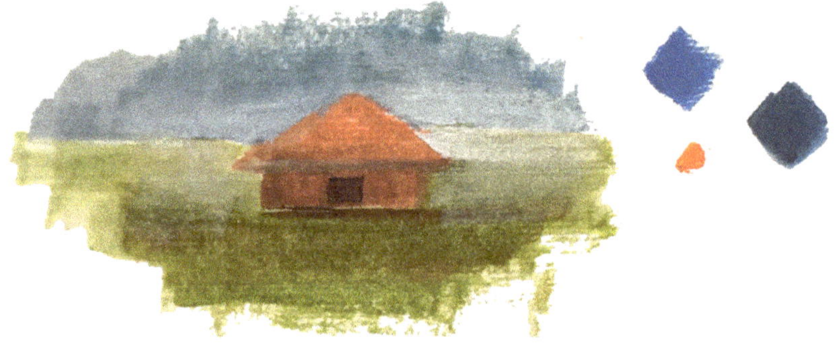

Here's our new painting (with some white added too) — pretty different from the previous one! I think the colours in this version of the painting are more sophisticated than in the first one.

Making Shadow Colour

Another reason for knocking back colours is when you are adding shadows.

Imagine you are painting a lovely alfresco scene in Paris or Rome. Perhaps there is a yellow tablecloth.

Where the sun hits the top of the table, the colour is bright and clear, so let's put the pure yellow on the top of the table.

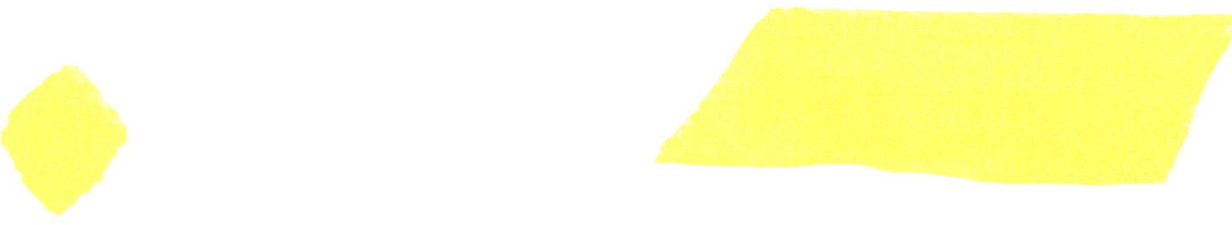

But on one side of the table, the tablecloth is draped into the shadow, so all the brightness of colour drops right down. The full saturation of the colour doesn't happen because the sunlight isn't on it. So we need to knock the yellow back.

Can you remember what the complement of yellow is?

Hint: it's directly opposite yellow on the colour wheel.

It's purple of course. So we mix the teeniest weeniest amount of purple into the yellow.

Watch out! Yellow is often a light, weak colour (unless you are using cadmium), and if you are putting Diox Purple (DP) into it, that is a very strong dark colour. So I recommend only an ant's bum[24] worth of purple mixed into your yellow. You don't want to mix a brown colour. You want a colour that is definitely yellow, but a shadowy version of yellow.

When you mix the right colour, it might look a bit like a mustard yellow. Paint it into the shaded part of the tablecloth and your table will start to look quite three dimensional.

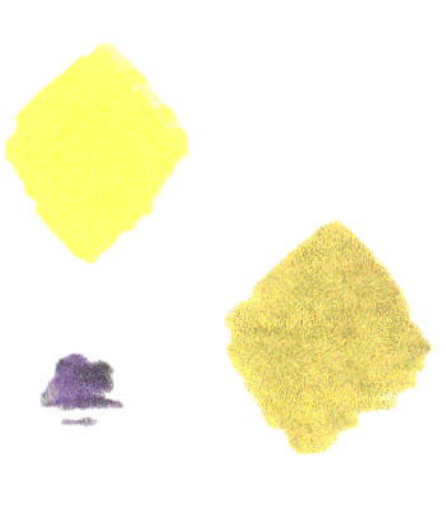

Let's add one more side of the table. This one has a bit of sunlight on it (but not as much sun as the top). Mix a little pure yellow with some of the knocked back yellow and paint it in.

Look at how much this looks like a yellow tablecloth in the sunlight!

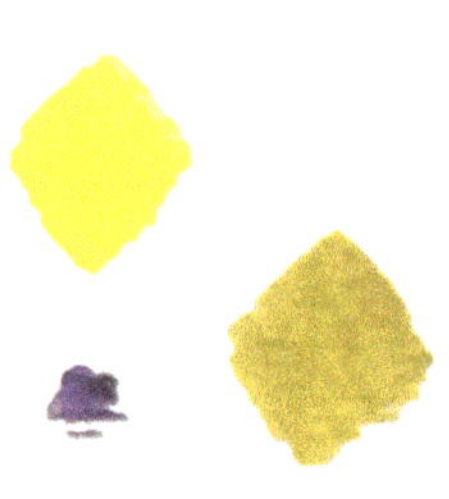

So now you know that you can drop any bright colour into shadow by knocking it back with its complement. Isn't that groovy?

Mouse Colours

Mouse Colours are the browns and grey colours. You can mix them, in fact any shade of them, by combining pairs of complementary colours.

You need to fall in love with mouse colours. If you are brave enough to include mouse colours in your painting, your art will go up to a new level.

How to Mix a Mouse Colour

Start by taking enough blue and enough orange and mix together until you get a dull, middle sort of brown or grey.

The final mix shouldn't have a hint of blue, and it shouldn't have a hint of orange — it should be right in between.

When you are mixing this colour, it's not an exact formula of equal amounts of each colour. Some colours are stronger than others. Keep bringing the colours until you get the middle colour that doesn't lean toward either blue or orange.

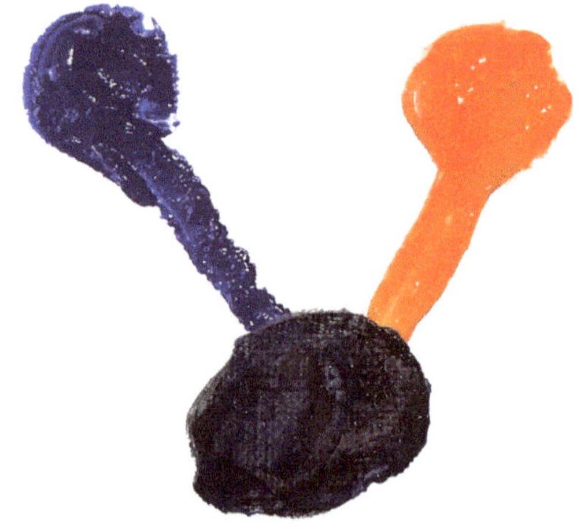

If it looks too bluey, add a tiny amount of orange. If it looks too orangey, add a tiny amount of blue. Do this until you get a colour that is right in the middle.

Play Time

Knocking Back Colours

We're going to play with colour complements — mixing knocked back colours and mouse colours.

You will need a colour wheel handy for this Play Time. Ideally it will be one you have painted.

It doesn't matter what paint medium you use. You can even use coloured pencils or pastel if you like.

1. Take a small piece of canvas or paper, around 12 x 18cm (5 x 7").

2. Write these column headings across the top with pencil:

Primary	Knocked Back Primary	Mouse Colour	Knocked Back Secondary	Secondary Complement

3. Label all the primary colours down the first column. Do it in the Yellow Brick Road order.

4. Label the complement of each primary on the right column.

5. Make sure you put the right secondary colours in the right rows! Use your colour wheel as a reference to check each colour's opposite. You need to make sure the colour in the fifth column is the complement of the colour in the first column.

6. Paint all those six primary and secondary colours in.

7. Just for fun, let's start with the middle row. While you've got the story of Blue-Kun and Orange-Chan fresh in your mind!

    a. *Knocked Back Primary:* Take a portion of blue paint and mix the tiniest little amount of its complement (orange) into it. You want to get a blue that is still blue, just a muted version. It might look like a denim or a navy blue. When you get that colour right, paint it into the box alongside blue in the second column. This is what I call a 'knocked back' blue.

b. *Knocked Back Secondary:* Repeat the process with orange using the tiniest amount of blue to get a muted, duller sort of orange. It should look clearly like orange, but a slightly more brown version of orange. It should *not* look like brown! Paint this muted orange in the box alongside the pure orange.

c. *Mouse Colour:* Now mix enough blue and enough orange to get a dull, middle sort of brown or grey. It shouldn't have a hint of blue and it shouldn't have a hint of orange — it should be right in between. Put this 'mouse colour' in the centre box for the blue and orange row.

Don't worry if you get a brown instead of a grey. The result depends on which colours you start with.

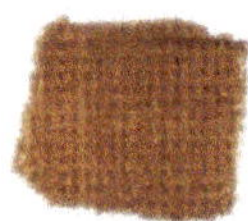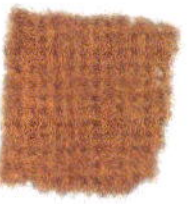

d. Repeat this for each row until the entire grid is filled in. Keep working each row in the order described above.

When you've finished, take a look at a finished example over at *www.zenartart.com*[25]

Farmhouse Scene

Paint the farmhouse scene first described in this chapter as the naïvely painted image.

Then paint it again using muted knocked back colours, as described.

Can you see the difference between the two? Which one do you like best?

Tablecloths in the Sun

Paint a scene with a yellow tablecloth in the sun as shown in this chapter. Use knocked back colours for the shadows.

Paint some plates and cups on the table too! Make sure to drop some little shadows under the plates. Add a chair or two if you are feeling brave.

If you like, paint another table with a pale blue tablecloth and give it shadows.

Then try painting a third table with a pink or red tablecloth.

CHAPTER 12
MIXING MAESTRO

*Stay in the center, and you will be
ready to move in any direction.*

Alan W. Watts

CHAPTER 12 CONTENTS

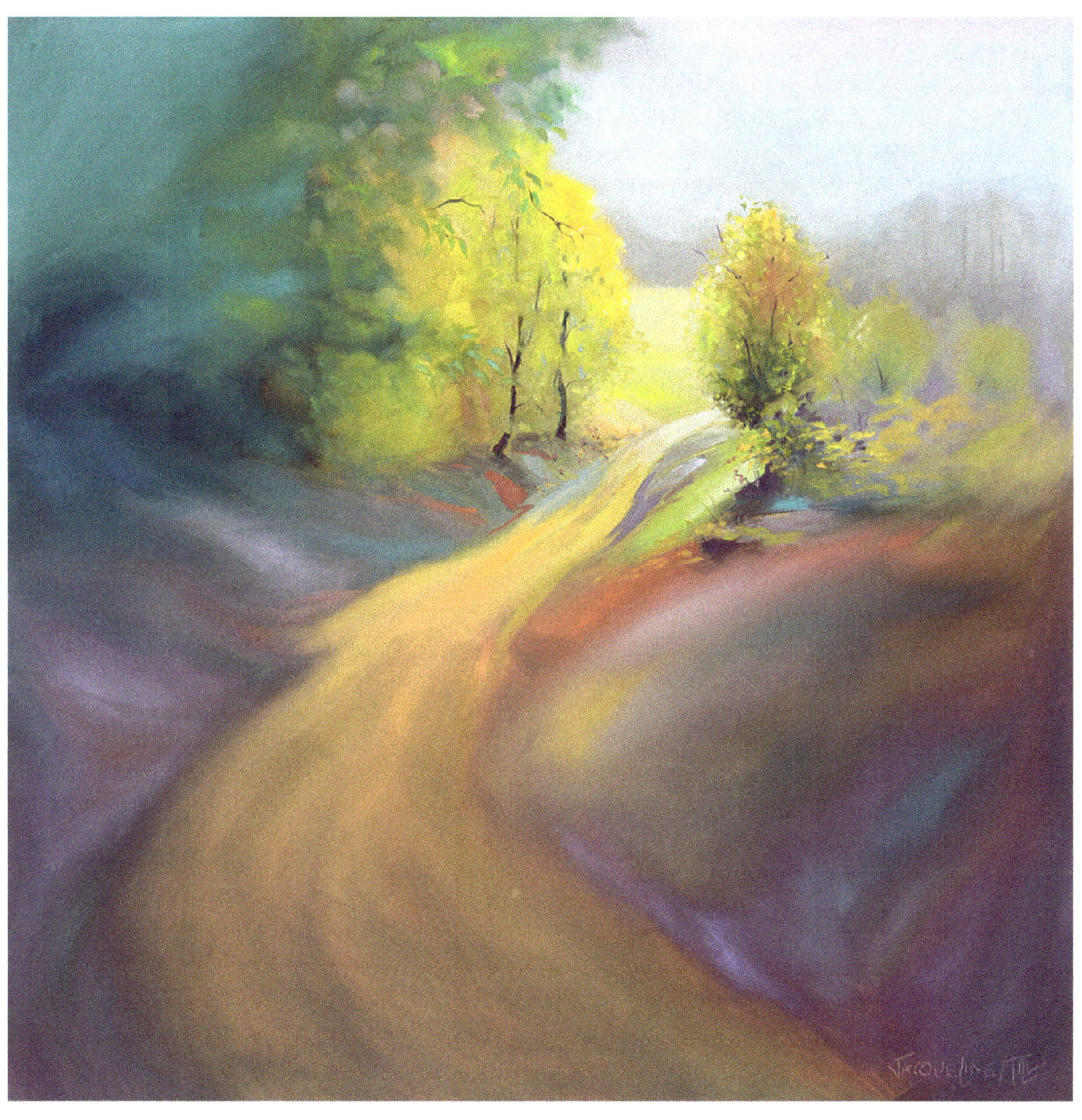

12-1 'Serenity Road' (Tasmania) Oil on Canvas 81 x 81cm (32 x 32")
Zen Landscape Series

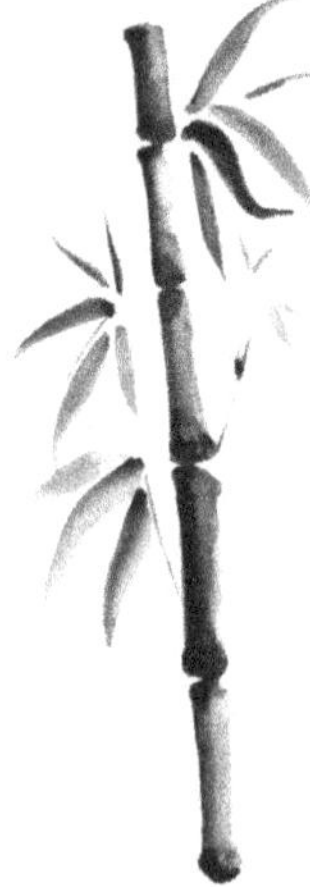

'Sensei, I've been practising that colour mixing you showed me,' said Jojo. 'I love it! It's amazing to be able to control colour and deliberately make it either as pure and clean as I want, or as muddy and muted as I want.

'I'm still having trouble remembering the complementary colours off the top of my head, but I keep my colour chart handy so I don't have to remember.'

'You will remember them with time,' said The Master. 'Practice is the only way, as you are seeing. It is not enough to have the knowledge. The mastery is in the doing.'

'It's opened my eyes wide,' said Jojo. 'I am not so afraid to start my paintings now. It's so good to have the power to mix any colour I want.'

'You have learned about shape, tone and colour mixing mastery,' said The Master. 'It is no wonder you are feeling more confident.

'And now you are ready to learn some more advanced colour knowledge,' he said.

How to Mix Any Colour You Can Imagine

So now you know how to mix any colour you want — from only six tubes of paint.

You can mix pure, clean secondary colours and you can knock back colours so that they are muted, dusty or browny.

Any colour you imagine can be at your fingertips.

Isn't that a wonderful thought?

Mixing with Confidence

All you need to know off by heart to make the process easy is the colour wheel. You need to remember which colour is opposite which.

Keep a colour wheel that you have painted close by while you are getting used to all of this.

After a while you will remember the pairs of the main complements: blue–orange, green–red and purple–yellow.

Then you can automatically knock back any colour you pick up.

Have fun!

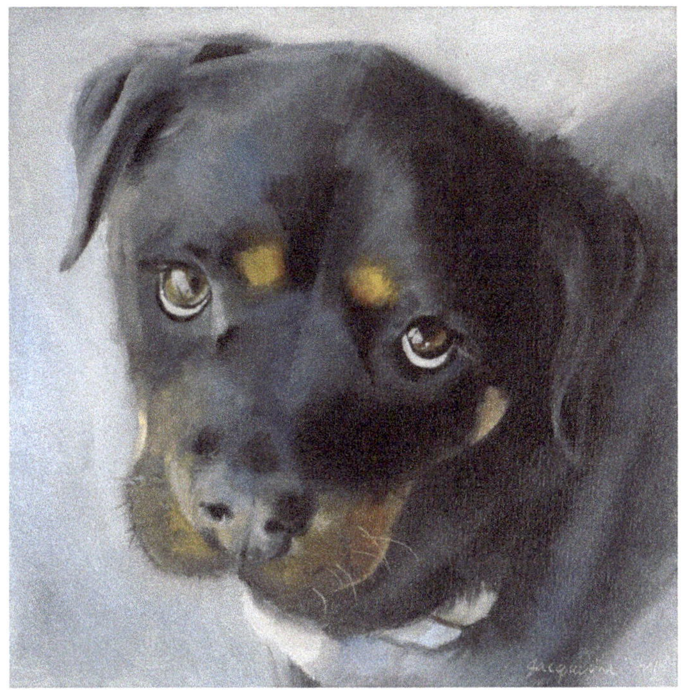

12-2 'Mae' Oil on Canvas 30 x 30cm (12 x 12")
Memory portrait commission. Private collection, Australia

More Useful Colours

Once you are confident with the basic set of three or six primaries, you can consider adding individual tubes of colour to your collection.

Here are a couple of useful colours to have in your set.

Using Premixed Browns

These are my two favourite browns that I keep in my sets of paints:

- Burnt Sienna (BS) — a *warm* brown

- Burnt Umber (BU) — a *cool* brown

Burnt Sienna (BS) is a beautiful golden orange brown that is transparent in most brands of professional paints. It's a great colour to use as a base skin colour when mixed with white.

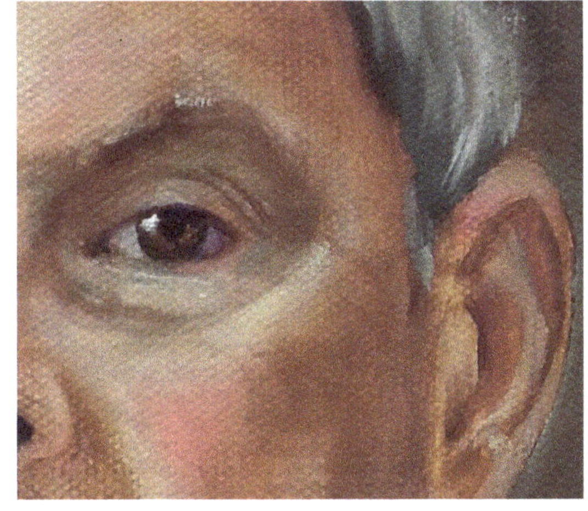

12-3 'Portrait of Surgeon Dr Bob Edwards' (Detail) Oil on Linen 60 x 70cm (24 x 28")
Commission. Public collection, Australia

Here is a really warm painting, using the same base colour for skin:

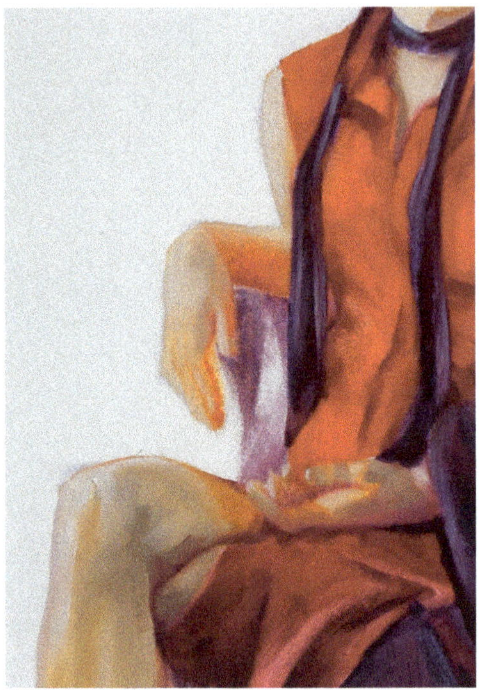

12-4 'Patience' (Detail) Oil on Canvas 61 x 71cm (24 x 28")

Burnt Umber (BU) is a lovely colour to mix with white to get that beautiful pale grey-brown that you see on the smooth bark of eucalyptus tree trunks.

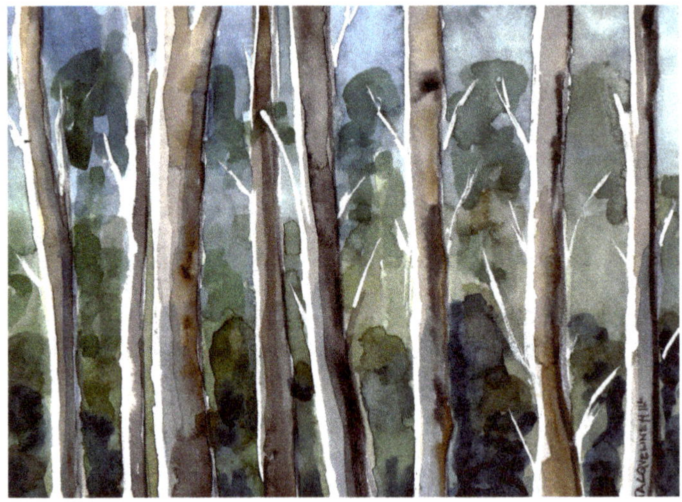

12-5 'Gumtrees' Watercolour on Paper. Small sketch for mural commission.

Both of these colours mix with French Ultramarine Blue (FUB) to make beautiful mouse colours of black, grey and brown.

Mixing Greens

I very rarely buy a tube of green paint. None of them looks anything like the greens I see in nature. The closest colour I've found is Sap Green (SG), but even this one needs to be knocked back.

These days I mix up my own greens.

Nature has a lot of greens on display. Varying your green colours across your painting makes it look so much better. So if you are mixing your own greens, vary the amount of each colour when you mix to get the variations.

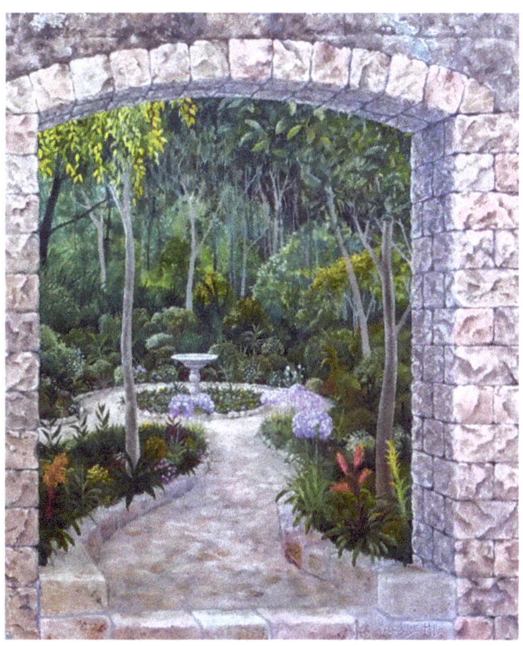

12-6 'Trompe Secret Garden' (Detail) trompe l'oeil mural commission, 10 x 3m (33 x 10')
This entire mural is painted on a completely flat wall. Private Commission, Inner Brisbane, Australia

My Favourite Way to Mix Natural Greens

In Australia we don't have as many wintery green colours (cool greens) as other countries. Our eucalyptus trees and native shrubs often have a golden tinge to them.

So here's how I mix my favourite greens.

I start off with French Ultramarine Blue (FUB) and Cadmium Yellow (CaY).

You might notice that French Ultramarine Blue (FUB) is a warm blue — it has a hint of red in it and is a bit purply.

And Cadmium Yellow (CaY) is a warm yellow — it has a hint of red in it and is a bit goldy-orange.

So already we are using what I call the 'wrong blue' and the 'wrong yellow' if we wanted to get a pure green. There is a hint of red in both colours I started with, so the green will be a bit muted.

This is like taking a shortcut. We deliberately use the two 'wrong' colours so that we mix a muted, more natural green right from the start.

The blue I chose is a strong dark. This lets me change the tone to quite a dark green if I need, which is great for shadows and getting a good wide tonal range.

We start by mixing the muted green.

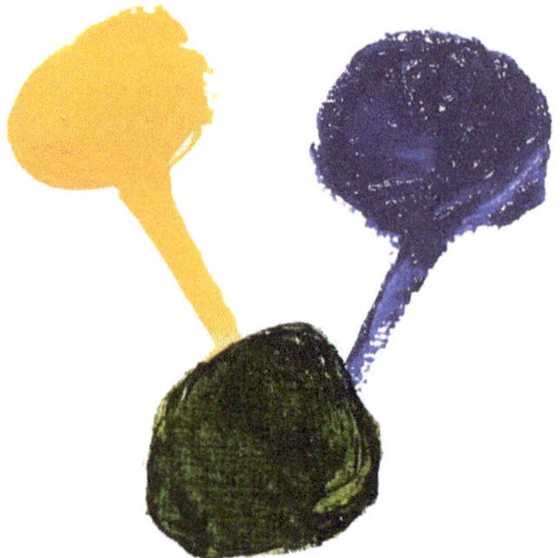

To get a nice golden green for painting trees and fields, I may want to make it even more muted.

To knock back the green, I would normally choose the complement of green — its opposite on the colour wheel. That's red.

But to create a more golden green, I would shift a little towards yellow to find the best colour to adjust my green.

Orange is a good choice. Cadmium Orange (CaO) or Transparent Orange (TO) would work. Just watch out, cadmium is a bully (don't forget it's toxic) and Transparent Orange is weak and wimpy. More information about this concept later. So you would need to add either a tiny little bit of Cadmium Orange or a bit more of Transparent Orange.

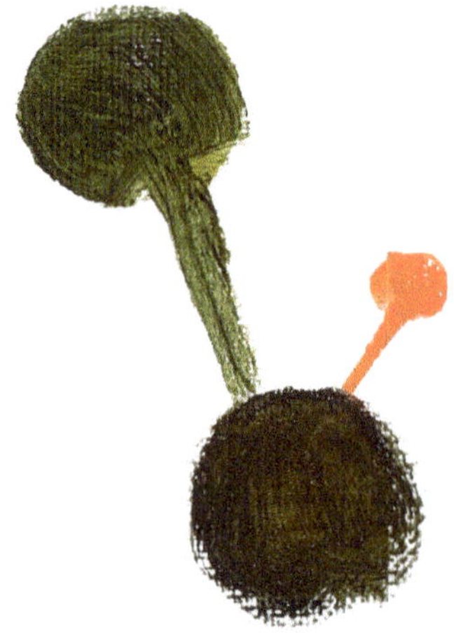

Another colour that I like using to knock back green is a deeper version of orange, Burnt Sienna (BS). It's a lovely transparent orangey brown and one of my favourite colours to keep handy.

If I mix Burnt Sienna (BS) into my green, I get a lovely muted green colour.

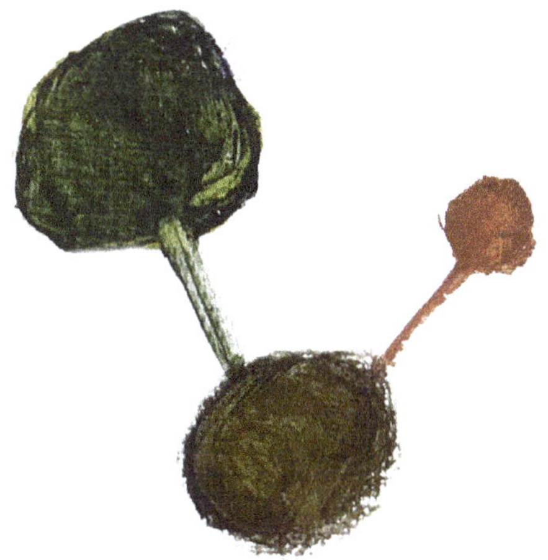

The good thing about using Burnt Sienna (BS) to knock back green is that Burnt Sienna is a darker colour compared to orange. This gives us a strong dark green to start with that we can lighten any time with yellow where the sun hits the leaves.

We can also darken our green to nearly black by adding more of our strong dark, French Ultramarine Blue (FUB).

It's great to use the full tonal range.

If we started out with weak, pale colours, we would have a weak, pale green and it would be difficult to get the strong darks.

Colour Personalities

Let's look at some more advanced colour techniques in the chemistry lab.

You have a lot more power when you know the personalities (properties) of your paints.

The companies who manufacture the professional artists' paints put only some of this information on their colour charts.

You will find this information out yourself just by using the pigments, but it takes time and lots of trial and error. If you understand these basics now, it will help you to select the right colour in future.

The more you paint, the more and more important these properties will become.

Transparent v Opaque Colours

Transparent[13] colours are lovely to use for soft layers of colour that you can see through. They're also a great way to add colour over tonal underpaintings.

Some brands mark a colour's transparency on the tube. This mark is a small circle or square that may be an empty shape to mean transparent or filled in for opaque.

On some colours the shape is half filled in, meaning it is semi-transparent (or semi-opaque). On the tubes shown, the symbols mean (from top to bottom):

- Semi-opaque

- Transparent

- Opaque

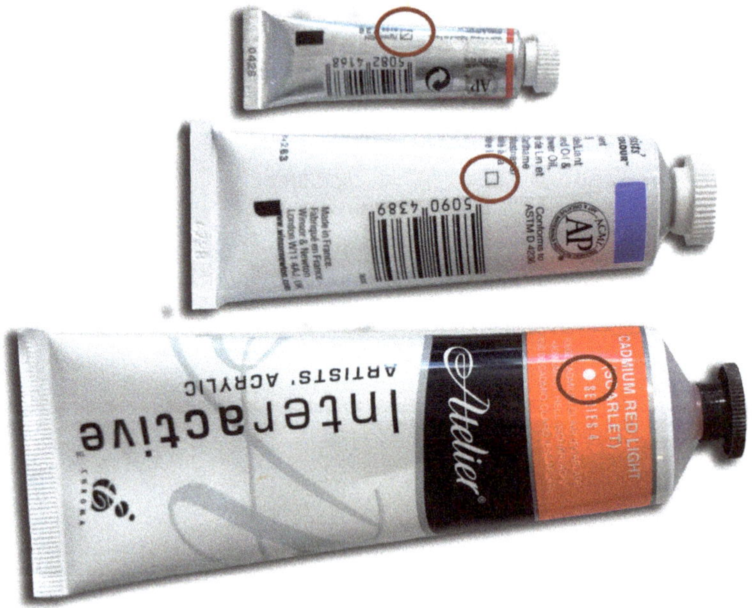

If the symbol is not on the tube, it should be on the colour chart. If you don't have a copy of the colour chart, Uncle Google will most certainly help you free of charge. We have already started the hunt for you and assembled a list of colour charts for common brands[26].

I always add the transparency symbol to my painted colour chart, as it really helps me when I am choosing colours.

Bullies & Wimps

The cadmium colours are strong and tend to overpower other colours. They are opaque as well. When you mix them with other colours, you need to be very careful to add these 'bully' colours in small amounts.

You will come across what I call 'wimpy' colours as well. The transparent yellows and rose are often weak when mixed with other colours. You'll need to use a lot more of them in the mix.

Lights & Darks

As we've seen before, some colours are naturally light, like most of the yellows. And some are naturally dark, like French Ultramarine Blue (FUB), Diox Purple (DP), Alizarin Crimson (AC) and all the phthalo colours.

It's important to be aware of this property, especially now you know how important tone is!

Knowing the light and dark colours helps you select a colour to suit the tone you want. It also helps when you mix colours together to know in advance if the tone is going to shift.

For example, when I am mixing a touch of yellow into my lovely dark Diox Purple (DP) to knock it back, I would not choose Cadmium Yellow (CaY), since it is a bully and opaque. If I mixed in that yellow, I would lighten the colour and change my transparent dark purple into an opaque browny purple.

Instead I would choose a transparent yellow, like Indian Yellow (IY) or Aureolin Yellow (AY). Because they are transparent, they will knock back the purple without lightening it or turning it opaque. It means I won't accidentally knock back my pretty purple too much as these yellows are not bullies.

Lightfastness

Have you ever seen really old framed art prints that have faded down to just pink and pale blue? No green or red remains in the image. That is because all the yellow and red colours have faded out with the effects of light on them over the years.

Some colours are not as lightfast as others. In the professional artists' ranges of paints, they mostly are. In the student ranges, they often are not.

You can tell which pigments are lightfast by looking at the colour chart[26] published by the company. There is an ASTM rating (see Glossary) to tell you how lightfast the pigments are. Choose colours with rating I or II to get the most long-lasting colours.

If you paint with cheaper colours that are not lightfast, in a few years your painting will start to fade away just in those colours.

Strong sunlight on a painting day after day will speed up this process even more.

Paints that fade really quickly are called 'fugitive' colours (the pigments run away from the light).

Always try to find paints that are as lightfast as possible.

I used the most lightfast quality paints to create this mural. After two years of full Australian summer sun on it, the yellows, hot pinks and reds are still strong and bright.

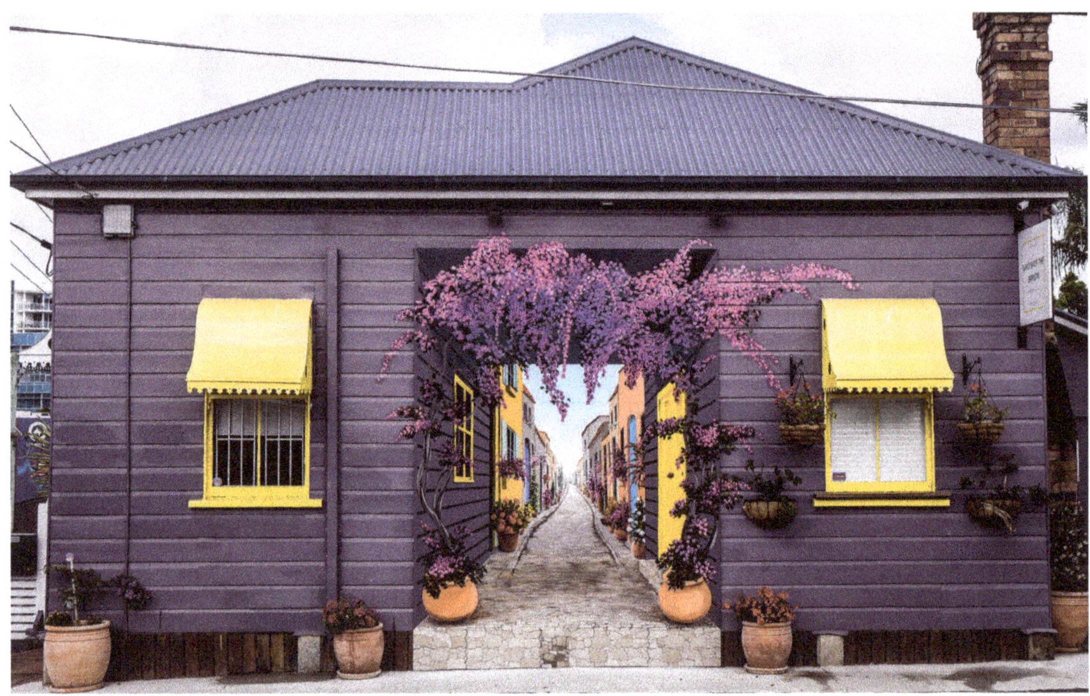

12-7 'Trompe Tuscany' trompe l'oeil mural commission 2 x 3m (6.5 x 10')
The central panel is a flat wall. Mural commission for coffee shop. West End, Brisbane, Australia

Staining Colours

Phthalo colours and Prussian Blue (PrB) are examples of strong stainers.

Staining colours leave a stain in the paper or the canvas even after you have used the usual ways to remove that paint. They often leave your fingertips stained for a day or so too. Watch out for your clothes!

The staining level is listed alongside each colour in a good colour chart[26] from a professional colour range.

The most important thing to remember about staining colours is that *they are difficult to lift off*.

For example, you may want to use the wipeout (rubout) method with an oil underpainting, where you paint solid colour over first and then use a rag to rub out the paler tones. In this case, don't use a staining colour like Prussian Blue (PrB) — it just won't rub off back to white canvas.

Or if you want to lift colour off in your watercolour painting, don't use a staining colour like Phthalo Turquoise (PhT) — it will always leave a ghostly stain behind. You won't be able to get it back to white paper.

Play Time

Discovering the Personalities

Good colour charts will show each colour's properties in detail. For example, they will not only show whether the colour is transparent or opaque, but also whether it is a staining colour or not and what level of lightfastness it is.

Go through and label each colour chip on your own painted colour chart with a letter or symbol to show how much of a staining colour it is. You can also jot down the lightfastness rating number.

As you get to know each colour by using it in paintings, you can also label each chip to show whether the colour is a bully or a wimp. When you invent a symbol or letter, write a key to your symbols on the back of the chart.

Take a look at the colour charts[26] online to see if this information is available. Then label your charts.

Tree Trunks

Find a photo of a gum tree with a pale grey tree trunk.

Do a simple small painting of it, using the Burnt Umber (BU) trick described in this chapter.

Simplify everything you can in the image.

Skin Tones

1. Try mixing up some skin tones and tint the colour to cooler, warmer or tinted with colours that the skin might be reflecting. Don't worry too much about details. Make sure to add some lighter and darker tones.

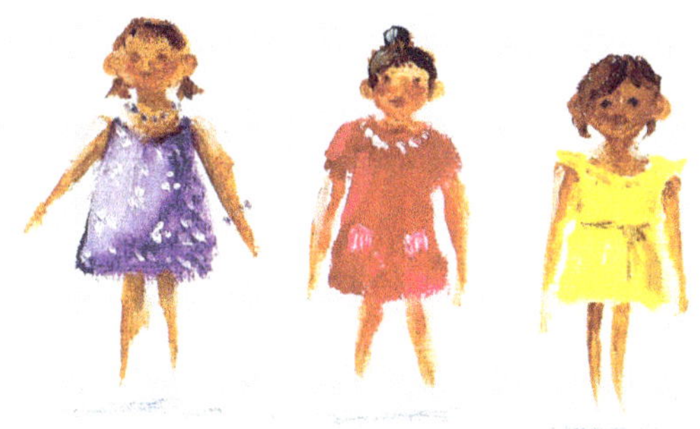

Take another look at the painting 'Patience' shown in this chapter. Can you see how the colour of the clothing reflects up onto the skin to warm it up?

JOURNEYING ON

Keep on painting and drawing. Don't let anything stop you. It's all about the miles in the brush.

Challenge yourself to paint or draw something every day, however small. Or weekly at the least.

Make it easy to do by getting a small journal or a pile of small canvases and all the supplies you need. You don't need much! Set them up in a place where you see them every day.

Choose what time of day you are going to draw or paint then commit to it.

Get up a little earlier each day and paint before everyone else gets up, if necessary. Do whatever you can.

Read this book again after a little while — you never know what gems you will pick up the second time around. When learning something new it usually takes me three revisions before new information sinks in properly.

Keep practising.

Nurture your Zen Mind. It's there, waiting for you.

Enjoy your art.

Enjoy the challenge.

Enjoy the joy. You deserve it!

Love,

Jacqui

GRATITUDE

The creation of this book was a team effort.

Our little office in the leafy outskirts of Brisbane is a tiny powerhouse of productivity and creativity. This book wouldn't have been possible without the wisdom, skill, hard work and cheerfulness of my personal assistant Kyla Bagnall, who launched into the project with intelligence, thoughtfulness and enthusiasm. Kyla, you are such a joy to work with! Thanks also to Leisha who cheerfully manages all the accounts and bookkeeping so I can keep creating.

Thank you also goes to our Launch Team who helped to get the word out to all and sundry to spread the joy of Zen learning and creativity in Zen and the Art of Art.

Yvonne Hill, my mother, is a lovely person with amazing energy levels who keeps achieving incredible things, and inspiring me year after year.

I am indebted to all the proofreaders, including Yvonne, and especially Norm and Rae who each spent days on the job and gave so much useful and detailed feedback.

Thank you to all of you for investing your time in this project.

Thanks to all of the hundreds of people who have attended my Learn to Draw and Learn to Paint classes in our Art at Heart Studio Gallery in Western Brisbane, Australia. Thank you for trusting me to teach you what you need to know for understanding how to paint.

I am blessed to have you as students, since it is through teaching that I learn so much. Working with all of you, I am sure my own skills improve while I am aiming to verbalise information and demonstrate more clearly for complete beginners. I learn so much through teaching you, and you are a constant source of inspiration for me to remember why art is such good medicine for us all.

Thank you to all the lovely collectors of my art, many of whom have become lifelong friends. Your enjoyment of my art is one of the great delights in my process of painting and creating.

Love,

Jacqueline

Jacqueline Hill B.Sc Hons.
Artist, Author, Teacher, Speaker.

Jacqueline Hill Prestige Art Collection & Trompe L'Oeil Murals
www.jacquelinehill.com

Art at Heart Gallery & Studio
www.artatheart.com.au

Author of the Zen and the Art of Art book series
www.zenartart.com

International Art Retreats
www.baliartretreat.com

RESOURCES

Please enjoy delving into these sources. I hope you find them really helpful.

In this section, you'll also find free bonuses for you, to say thank you for purchasing this book.

Must Have Books for Artists

These are ones that I believe every artist should own:

1. *The War of Art* by Stephen Pressfield

2. *Making Color Sing* by Jeanne Dobie

3. *Ish* by Peter H. Reynolds

4. *The Artist's Way* by Julia Cameron

5. *The Artist's Complete Health and Safety Guide* by Monona Rossol

Here are some others I have really enjoyed:

· *Art Escapes* by Dory Kanter

· *Being an Artist* by Lewis Lehrman

· *Life, Paint & Passion* by Michell Cassou & Stewart Cuble

This list is updated every now and then. To see the latest, please visit: *www.zenartart.com/must-have-books.*

Artists I Admire

People are sometimes curious about which artists I admire or those who inspire me.

I think it's important to visit galleries — especially those ones in real buildings where you can see the actual brushstrokes on the paintings — and be inspired by other artists.

It does *not* mean copying what they do. An artist's creative spirit is uplifted by seeing other artists' creative outputs.

I get inspired by many wonderful artists. To see some of my favourites, visit: *www.zenartart.com/favourite-artists.*

Thank you

I'd like to also say thank you to the following artists who have inspired me with their wise words in masterclasses I attended with them:

- Tony Smibert *www.smibert.com* — one of my favourite watercolour artists who has a similar leaning to the Eastern wisdom as I do. The East influences both of our painting styles. He taught me to use a chart to experiment making marks with my brush. And to always use the biggest brush possible. And a hundred other things.

- Don Waters *www.djwaters.com.au* — a wonderful acrylics semi-abstract painter who taught me that no painting is a failure — it's just not finished yet. He also taught me to only look at the one, loudest thing in a painting that needs attention and sort that out first.

- Max Wilks *www.maxwellwilks.com* — who, through his kindness in an oil masterclass, healed me from the wounding a previous teacher had done to my artist's spirit. And who taught me to turn around while *en plein air* painting and look at a scene through my knees to judge colour and tone.

Useful Apps

Here are some great apps and software tools for artists.

See more at *www.zenartart.com/apps*

All of these apps are free in their basic versions. As soon as you want to store a lot of data, or you want extended features, you may need to pay a monthly plan.

These apps run on nearly every device you own:

- your desktop computer (Windows or Mac)

- a browser, such as Google Chrome or Apple Safari

- your phone (Android or iPhone)

- your Android tablet or Apple iPad

Since they are cloud tools, you only have to add something once on one device and it will immediately be available on all your other devices.

Evernote

This is a little app that I love to use as a memory notepad. If I need to remember anything, I take a photo or write a note and put it into Evernote. You can also easily save websites you are researching, or clippings off web pages, or handwrite notes if you have a phone or tablet with a pen.

Evernote is a great place to put photos along with a written note. Having the ability to write a note alongside the photo is much easier than just having a photo sitting in your Camera folder, and when you look back on it you can't remember why you took it.

The best part about Evernote is that you can search on anything and quickly find a note. If you have taken a photo of a written page, then the Evernote search will find a word on that page, even if it is just a photo of the handwriting or typing.

It's much harder than trying to locate a photo I took in my Camera folder a while ago. I would need to scroll back through months of photos and look at every photo to find something. It's much easier to search for a specific thing in Evernote, which finds it for me much faster.

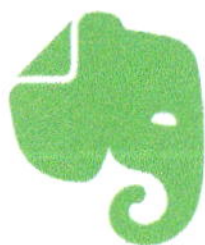

www.evernote.com

EVERNOTE, the Evernote Elephant logo and REMEMBER EVERYTHING are trademarks of Evernote Corporation and used under a license.

Google

Uncle Google is our friend whenever we want to know something, like which famous artist painted the *Mona Lisa,* and what does the famous painting *Girl with a Pearl Earring* look like.

Ok it's not really an app. But Google Images is a great resource for finding photos to paint from, when you search in the right way to avoid breaching copyright.

For more info on how to use Google to find photos you can safely paint from, without breaching copyright, look at *www.zenartart.com/copyright-free-images*

Of course an even better tool is your camera (or phone), which you can use to take your very own photos.

www.google.com

Zen and the Art of Art *is not affiliated with or otherwise sponsored by Google, Inc.*

Dropbox

This is a must for storing photos and files and making sure they are backed up all the time. I keep all my files in Dropbox, so I can use them on the computer on my desk and then access the same files from my phone or iPad when I am on the road. I never have to worry about them not being backed up, as they are stored safely in multiple places.

Apple iCloud has a similar way of storing photos and files and keeping them safe and shared between devices, but it doesn't like talking to devices that are not Apple. So I prefer Dropbox, which talks very nicely to every device, regardless of who makes it.

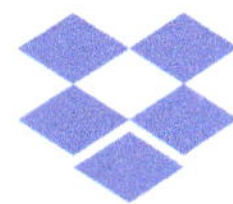

www.dropbox.com

Zen and the Art of Art *is not affiliated with or otherwise sponsored by Dropbox, Inc.*

Asana

If you are running around trying to keep a million things in your head for all the stuff you gotta do, it will send you crazy. The best way to release this stress is to write it all down. Get it all out of your head and you will feel a lot better.

The problem with writing things down on a To Do pad of paper or notebook, is that you have to take it with you everywhere. When you cross things off it turns into a mess and you need to rewrite tasks out again.

Asana is a To Do list that works beautifully in any browser, and there are phone and tablet apps available as well.

You can organise your tasks into projects, so that you focus on like tasks at the same time, which increases your efficiency.

For example, you might have projects called:

- Art to Paint
- Galleries to Visit for Inspiration
- Art Supplies to Buy
- Home Stuff to Do
- Business Stuff to Do

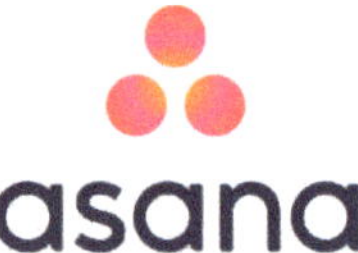

www.asana.com

Asana is a trademark and service mark of Asana, Inc., registered in the U.S. and in other countries.

LastPass

In this day and age of having dozens of passwords and PINs to remember, it is getting impossible to remember them all.

You can store all these passwords in LastPass, and then unlock them with a single master password. It is the Last Password you'll ever have to remember. Nobody else can get into your Lastpass if you keep your Master Password safe, so all your other passwords are kept safely locked away inside the vault there.

LastPass is available as an app or it will also work on your desktop in any browser, and it will feed your login details into the screen without you having to type them in.

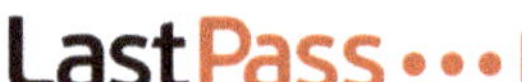

www.lastpass.com

Zen and the Art of Art *is not affiliated with or otherwise sponsored by LastPass or LogMeIn, Inc.*

Want to Learn More?

Thank you for purchasing this book. I want to help you in your art journey. Please enjoy these bonus gifts on me!

Free Downloads

Visit *www.zenartart.com/foundations* to access free step-by-step tutorials, PDF downloads and more.

Free Video Tutorials

Visit *www.zenartart.com/foundations*

Here you'll find an introductory membership to get access to free painting and drawing video tutorials. Your password as a reader of this book is 3emperors

Art Classes in Our Studio

Visit *www.artatheart.com.au/classes*

I would love to meet and teach you in person!

If you're local, come join one of my art classes for all levels on all sorts of mediums and topics at my studio, located in the leafy western suburbs of Brisbane, Australia.

Art Retreats — Travel and Paint with Me!

Visit *www.artatheart.com.au/retreats*

I also run one or two travel art retreats each year — in a beautiful art-inspiring location in Australia or Bali or other country. They run for a week and will lift your creativity and take your art to another level, while exploring local culture and unique places.

GLOSSARY

ASTM — see *lightfastness.*

binder is the liquid substance that is mixed in with the *pigment* powder to make the paint. The binder used is oil for oil paint, a clear painting medium for acrylics, and gum arabic for watercolour tubes, pans and pastel sticks.

crosshatching is a shading technique of overlaying lines using a pencil, pen or thin brush.

dojo is a hall for meditation and immersive learning. The literal meaning in Japanese is 'place of the way'.

en plein air (pronounced 'on plan air') is a French term meaning outdoors. Painting outdoors is also known as painting 'on location'.

ferrule (pronounced the same as 'feral') is the metal part of the brush that grips the bristles.

focal point is the part of the painting that is the most important area that you want your viewer's eye to rest on.

gesso (pronounced 'jesso') is a primer paint for canvas that you use underneath acrylic and oil paintings.

glazes — see *transparency.*

gouache (pronounced 'gwarsh') is a painting medium similar to watercolour, except it's opaque instead of transparent.

lightfastness is a measure of how lightfast the pigment is. A very lightfast paint doesn't fade over time, but a pigment with poor lightfastness fades quickly. Poor lightfast pigments are called fugitive pigments. Lightfastness is usually measured in ASTM (American Standard Test Measure). ASTM ratings of I or II are the most lightfast, down to V which is very poor. I always try to choose ASTM I colours for my painting.

medium (for diluting paint) The word medium is used in two ways. You pick up a bottle of medium to dilute your paints, and make them more transparent, or make them dry more slowly or quickly, and so on. The medium is mixed in with the original paint and then used.

medium (what you use to paint with) When a painting is labelled as 'The Mona Lisa – oil', then we say that the medium used for the Mona Lisa was oil. Someone might be admiring your painting and then ask, 'What medium did you use?' and you would answer, for example, 'Watercolour'.

phthalo (pronounced 'thay-low' — just ignore the first 'ph') colours are transparent, staining colours in the range of turquoise, blues and greens. They are often strong darks.

pigment is the original mineral that is used to mix in with the clear *binder* to make paint. The pigments are very finely ground up mineral powders that make the pure colour of the paint. Pigments have varying degrees of lightfastness.

sensei (pronounced 'sen-say') is the name for teacher or master in Japanese. The literal meaning is 'the one who has come before'.

spirits, white spirits — see *turps*.

thinner — see *turps*.

torchon, tortillon, blending stick, paper stump — all the same thing, compressed paper in a stick that you can use for blending dry media such as pastel, graphite or charcoal.

transparent colours are ones that you can see through. You can dilute the paint with a clear medium and make layers of washes. These transparent layers are called *glazes*.

turps, turpentine — a solvent used as a thinning medium for oil paint, as well as cleaning up oil brushes. In the USA it's known as *spirits* or *white spirit*.

vignette (pronounced 'vin-yet') is a technique that softly darkens (or lightens) all around the edges of a photograph.

Yupo paper is a synthetic paper that has a feel like plastic but it accepts watercolour and alcohol inks. The paint doesn't soak in but instead sits on the surface, so it performs very differently from normal watercolour paper.

END NOTES

For more information, downloadables, free videos and tutorials on the How To notes below, visit *www.zenartart.com/foundations*

1   See Glossary — *dojo* .

2   For the entire *Zen and the Art of Art* series and the recommended reading order, see *www.zenartart.com/reading-order*. This list will be updated as each new book is released.

3   You'll see some downloadable charts for Studio Etiquette and Artists' Safety, as well as a book on Artist Safety in the book reading list at *www.zenartart.com/foundations*

4   See Glossary — *turps* or *turpentine.*

5   'The Little Engine That Could' is an American fairytale popularised when Platt & Munk published an illustrated children's book version in 1930.

6   In portraiture, this comes down to millimetre accuracy of measurement and proportions. For this reason, portraiture is one of the most challenging subjects to attempt.

7   See Glossary — *en plein air.*

8   Learn how to create a Tonal Ruler at *www.zenartart.com/foundations*

9   Richard Rogers *www.richardrogers.com.au*

10   Once you've finished the Play Time at the end of Chapter 1 Three Emperors, see finished examples on the Zen and the Art of Art website at *www.zenartart.com/foundations*

11   Use your grey pencil and a shading or cross-hatching technique (see Glossary — *crosshatching*). For more tips on how to do this, see *www.zenartart.com/foundations*

12   See Glossary — *gouache.*

13   Transparent colours (see Glossary) can be diluted and layered in *glazes*. Multiple layers of transparent colour glazes create beautiful rich, shimmering effects in paintings and can give them delicious depth and jewel-like colours.

14   More on learning to draw in the in the *Zen and the Art of Art* series book *Learn to Draw* at *www.zenartart.com/learn-to-draw*

I also created a short video for you. It will help you understand the method of drawing by measuring with a pencil. It really helps to knock out the Modern Mind. Watch the video at *www.zenartart.com/foundations*

15   Tricks about using erasers at *www.zenartart.com/foundations*

16   See Glossary — *torchon, tortillon, blending stick, paper stump.*

17   See Glossary — *ferrule.*

18 *Making Color Sing* by Jeanne Dobie. This book really resonated with my philosophy of using complementary colours. Even though this book is for watercolour painting, the colour theory works for any medium. This book is on my list of Must Have Books for Artists.

19 See Glossary — *phthalo*.

20 See Glossary — *gesso*.

21 See Glossary — *Yupo*.

22 Evernote is a free app that you can use to store photos with text notes. I use it for all sorts of things. See the list of Useful Apps in the Resources section of this book.

23 Colour Mixing formulae from the Secret Lab at *www.zenartart.com/foundations*

24 *Bee's* or *Ant's bum* — also *butt*. Technical term on the insect: *abdomen*!

25 See a finished example of the Complements Chart at *www.zenartart.com/foundations*

26 See *www.zenartart.com/foundations* for a list of colour charts online from some of the most well-known brands of colours.

ABOUT THE AUTHOR

Jacqueline Hill gave up her childhood dream of being an astronaut when the NASA manned space program was closed. Since walking away from a lucrative twenty year IT career, she has been a full time professional artist and won many awards and broken records with art sales. She has had huge success inspiring and teaching complete beginners how to draw and paint beautiful paintings that they never thought possible.

Jacqueline lives on the country property alongside her studio, with her sculptor husband and their crazy Burmese cat. She runs her own professional art gallery, art school and studio practice in the leafy outskirts of Brisbane, Australia.

See more of Jacqueline's art:

www.jacquelinehill.com

www.artatheart.com.au